MW00463365

The Battle of Hastings 1066

It is puzzling given the enormous interest in Hastings that, despite the digging of foundations for the abbey, for the old primary school, for all the houses along the main road, all the digging in gardens, the road making, not a single trace of the battle has been found. Have people simply been looking in the wrong place?

Jim Bradbury, *The Battle of Hastings*

The Battle of Hastings 1066:

The Uncomfortable Truth

Revealing the true location of England's most famous battle

John Grehan and Martin Mace

Pen & Sword
MILITARY

First published in Great Britain in 2012 by
Pen & Sword Military
an Imprint of
Pen & Sword Books Ltd
47 Church Street
Barnsley
South Yorkshire
S70 2AS

ISBN: 978 1 84884 827 6

A CIP catalogue record for this book is available from the British Library.

Typeset in 11pt Ehrhardt by
Mac Style, Beverley, E. Yorkshire

Printed and bound in the UK by CPI Group (UK) Ltd, Croydon, CRO 4YY

Pen & Sword Books Ltd incorporates the Imprints of Pen & Sword Aviation,
Pen & Sword Family History, Pen & Sword Maritime, Pen & Sword Military,
Pen & Sword Discovery, Wharncliffe Local History, Wharncliffe True Crime,
Wharncliffe Transport, Pen & Sword Select, Pen & Sword Military Classics,
Leo Cooper, The Praetorian Press, Remember When, Seaforth Publishing
and Frontline Publishing.

For a complete list of Pen & Sword titles please contact
PEN & SWORD BOOKS LIMITED
47 Church Street, Barnsley, South Yorkshire, S70 2AS, England
E-mail: enquiries@pen-and-sword.co.uk
Website: www.pen-and-sword.co.uk

Contents

Acknowledgements

If we had not read Jim Bradbury's 1998 publication, *The Battle of Hastings*, we might have doubted our capacity to find documentary evidence to support our hypothesis, and this book would never have been written. He was, as far as we know, the first person in modern times to have suggested that the battle may not have been fought at the traditionally accepted site – where the ruins of Battle Abbey now stand. That he welcomed our development of his idea is highly gratifying and it gave us the heart to see this venture through.

Yet, if Jim Bradbury was the inspiration, the team around us provided the perspiration. Stephen Hocking trudged every mile from Pevensey to Hastings and back, providing logistical support and an unending stream of healthy scepticism. Kelvin Nelson piloted the aircraft which enabled us to take the aerial photographs of the battlefield. Dave Cassan compiled the diagrams, adding much of his own interpretation. Dennis Mace's diligent proof reading was as meticulous as usual. Sarah Mitchell, with her knowledge of local medieval matters, cast her careful eye over the final manuscript.

Finally, we could never have found the time to complete our investigations had we not had the patient support of Leanne and Hannah.

John Grehan and Martin Mace
Storrington, 2012

Introduction

"In the case of Hastings we know the basic facts ... The rest is a matter of possibility, probability and reasoned surmise."

Brigadier C.N. Barclay, *Battle 1066*

The warriors stood defiantly on the front of the low hill, their untamed hair and drab clothing contrasting sharply with the glistening, polished steel of their swords and battleaxes. Below them at the foot of the rising ground were the mounted knights resplendent in chain mail and domed helmets.

With a single uttered command, the Normans urged their horses up the slope to engage the English. It was the start of the Battle of Hastings. The date was 14 October 2006.

It was a re-enactment of the most famous battle in English history and it was as realistic as the 2,000 or so participants could make it. Yet for all the banging of shields and defiant cries, and the thrust of lance and swing of sword, something was obviously wrong.

* * *

We had joined the many spectators for the annual re-playing of the Battle of Hastings which takes place every autumn in the grounds of Battle Abbey. We mingled with the crowds and meandered round the stalls selling chain mail for the purists and plastic swords for the kids.

We had read a good deal about the battle before we came. We knew that the English had stood upon a dominating ridge and that the Normans had struggled up the steep slope to hack and thrust at the defenders on the hill. What we saw on that pleasant October afternoon, however, was something quite different.

The English re-enactors had indeed placed themselves and their formidable shield wall as close to the top of the hill as the Abbey's buildings would permit. Against this position the heavily armoured Norman infantry and mounted knights flung themselves with authentic ardour. Yet this was not a difficult climb for the would-be Norman foot soldiers – it was an easy walk up a very gentle slope. For the Norman knights the terrain was perfect for them to urge their steeds into a fully fledged gallop. This was not how it was supposed to be. The battle, we had been told, was fought on a steep and difficult hill which severely hampered the efforts of the attackers. Had we turned up at the wrong venue?

The day wore on and the clash of arms and the grunts of the happy participants continued repetitiously as must surely have happened almost nine and a half centuries ago. When we had seen enough of this bloodless battle we withdrew and decided to follow the route of the retreating English in 1066.

This took us over Caldbec Hill down to Oakwood Gill, the site of the famous English rearguard action at the *Malfosse*. As soon as we left the car park to walk across the lower slopes of Caldbec Hill we were immediately struck by the rugged terrain and the severity of the incline. We reached the top, not exactly breathless, but certainly conscious that we had climbed a not-inconsiderable hill.

From the summit we gazed southwards. Opposite we could see the heights of Telham Hill and then, below, a long way below, was Battle Abbey. It stood, from our lofty perspective, on a low, almost insignificant little ridge. Behind us, and to either side, the ground fell steeply away, just as steeply as in the front. We were standing on an excellent defensive position with commanding views all around. If Caldbec Hill was where Harold concentrated his army on the eve of the battle, as most believe, why would he abandon such a dominant spot to occupy an entirely inferior one?

It was a question for which we could find no answer. The more we looked, the more puzzled we became. We turned to each other and both voiced our thoughts. Has everyone got it wrong? Was the most significant battle in English history fought on Battle Hill, or somewhere else altogether?

Chapter 1

The Contradictory Evidence

"Few subjects in English history have been studied more and for longer than the Norman Conquest, and few have been more bent in the process by biased interpretations based upon unhistorical prejudices."
R. Allen Brown, *The Normans and the Norman Conquest*

In 1070 four Monks from the Benedictine abbey of Marmoutier on the Loire arrived at a place close to the Andresweald some eight miles or so to the north of Hastings. They were there on the orders of King William I of England. Following a visit to London by the representatives of Pope Alexander II, William agreed to pay a penance for the terrible slaughter he had caused when he invaded England. That penance was the building of a great monastery on the site of the battle where he had won the English crown. This part of Sussex was thinly populated and William wanted to ensure that no invader would be able to land as easily as he had and march upon London, so this monastery was granted special privileges to help it attract settlers to its extensive lands.

These four monks duly built a fine monastery on the site where the ruins of Battle Abbey now stand. Though these men had not been present at the battle four years earlier they were apparently able to positively identify the battlefield amongst the rolling hills of the Weald with astonishing precision, laying the stone of the high altar on the very spot where King Harold had been killed.

From that time onwards the site of the battlefield has been set and few have dared to suggest otherwise. Yet many historians have conceded that our knowledge of the Battle of Hastings is far from perfect. "Few things are more difficult to describe than the events of a battlefield," wrote Mark Anthony Lower in a paper read at Battle Abbey in 1852, "… it must be a matter of great difficulty to frame an intelligible history of the sanguinary conflicts of ancient times from the materials furnished us by partial and often incompetent chroniclers, and written from oral traditions at periods considerably subsequent to the transactions themselves."[1]

The main problem for historians is that there is no eyewitness testimony to be found. Indeed, as Brigadier C.N. Barclay was quick to point out, the slaughter amongst the leading English characters was so great that most of them were killed in the battle. We therefore have, with few exceptions, evidence from only one side of the conflict and that is drawn from individuals who were not present at the battle.[2]

Edwin Tetlow, after half a century of research on the subject, realised that "the picture built up upon scanty original evidence by nine centuries of historians, novelists and romantics is a distorted one, often influenced by prejudice and propaganda."[3] David Howarth made a similar observation: "Strictly speaking, every sentence in a story nine centuries old should include the word *perhaps*: nothing is perfectly certain." He also accepts that whilst the Battle of Hastings "has been fought on paper innumerable times" strictly military accounts of it "have always had to leave some mysteries unsolved."[4] Two decades later, R. Allen Brown also conceded that the only really undisputed fact about Hastings was that the Normans won![5] Harriet Wood acknowledged that the story of the Battle of Hastings is compounded by "its insoluble puzzles and ambiguities."[6]

Matthew Bennett agreed. In the Preface to an investigation into the sources of the Battle of Hastings, he wrote that "enshrined as it is in historiography as a pivotal event in English history … described in numerous contemporary accounts, and remarkably celebrated pictorially in the Bayeux Tapestry, unique by its survival, can still only at this great distance of time, be dimly perceived." In the same book, Doctor Stephen Morillo concedes that, whilst the main sequence of events, leading up to and including the battle itself is generally agreed upon, "it is the details and the speculation about possibilities and probabilities that continues to generate heat." He concludes that "much speculation must go into even a basic reconstruction of the battle."[7]

What information is available from the twelfth and early thirteenth centuries, amounting to seventeen documents, provides us with considerable evidence of some aspects of the battle and the events leading up to the Norman invasion, whilst other elements are neglected. These documents are, generally speaking, one-sided – like so much of history the early story of the Battle of Hastings was written by the victors. Even so, one of these early chroniclers, William of Poitiers, accepts that it is impossible to describe all the exploits of even the most prominent protagonists during the battle.[8]

Equally, despite this comparative wealth of source material there are few genuinely established facts. In the introduction to her translation of one of those early sources, *The History of the English People* by the twelfth-century historian Henry of Huntingdon, Diana Greenway warns us about taking the medieval writers too literally: "Henry was not a collector of facts for their own sake. The idea of objective study of history would have been quite alien to him and his contemporaries. In his world, history was a literary genre, and the writing of history required imagination and rhetorical skills. He did not seek to be a realistic reporter, but rather to represent selected events in an overarching interpretation and in appropriate style."[9]

This was something noted by Brigadier Barclay, who observed that "no writer could hope to complete a book of this sort [on the Battle of Hastings] based solely on established facts. If he tried he would not get much beyond a short magazine article and it would make very dull reading." As possibly the most senior military figure to have written in depth about the battle, the brigadier was scathing in his condemnation of modern writers who were "scholars rather than men of military experience". In his opinion, "modern historians have placed too much reliance on the old records, and assumed to be facts many incidents which are, in my view, clearly in doubt."[10]

To a great degree he is correct and this dearth of hard facts has led to much "interpretation" by historians of the events leading up to and including the battle itself. Because of the scarcity of impartial or even particularly solid facts, people have had to fill in the gaps using what details are available. This has driven historians to make the few known facts about the battle fit the ground and has led to a number of quite remarkable conclusions. The most extraordinary of these is the supposed identification of the hillock depicted on the Bayeux Tapestry. The scene in question shows Norman knights coming to grief at the foot of a steep-sided hill. Historians have scrutinised the battlefield in an effort to find such a prominent feature. All that they have been able to find is a low mound which could not have held more than one or two hundred men. Despite this, and the fact that there is no certainty at all that this hillock is the image shown on the Bayeux Tapestry, writer after writer has declared it to be so without qualification.

Others, of course, are more wary. Benton Rain Patterson was troubled with the lack of real evidence when he wrote his *Harold & William*: "In parts of the story there was not much in the historical record to go on. Authentic scenes would be hard to reproduce without actual details ... How much licence could I take to fill the gap?" He answers this question by deciding that "writing history requires at least some speculation, and so I began to feel justified in employing it in the story of *Harold and William*". To further justify the literary license he was about to employ he quotes historian Will Durant: "all history should be taken as hypothesis ... of yesterday there is no certainty."[11]

David Howarth, writing about the Battle of Hastings in 1977, explained how he dealt with this problem: "Any modern historian has to use his judgement pretty freely. When he finds contradictory stories he has to decide which is most probable, which writer had the best reason to know the truth – or which, on the other hand, had reason to distort it."[12]

Despite such words of caution by wise historians, few have ever thought to question the site of the Battle of Hastings, or, as the pre-eminent early historian Edward Freeman remarked, even to examine the battlefield: "Most of the accounts of the battle show little understanding of the site," he remarked. "The modern accounts seem to have been written with little or no attention to the ground. If we learn from them that Harold's position was on a hill, it is as much as we do."[13]

This has led to the almost universally accepted assumption that the battle must have taken place where the ruins of Battle Abbey now sit. Yet some of the historians who have studied the battlefield have clearly been troubled by the obvious flaws in the choice of that particular site as the place where Harold fought in defence of his crown. There are many question marks against placing the site on Battle Hill, and historian Jim Bradbury warns us that "we should keep a more open mind on the matter than has been the case to date."

M.K. Lawson wisely commented that "the very natural desire to know, and of the informer to inform, has often led to descriptions of the conflict wearing an appearance of certainty which the nature of the primary sources actually does little to warrant ... In fact, there is not a single eye-witness to be had, and the primary sources that do exist, relatively plentiful as they are, all suffer from significant limitations which need to be clearly understood before use can be made of them. What emerges from this process ... is not that there is nothing that can be known about the battle of Hastings, but that there are many important things that cannot, and never will be known. Thus seekers after easy hard facts – how many men there were on each side, for example, and where they were positioned at different points during the day – will not find them."[14]

Richard Huscroft, in his book *The Norman Conquest*, recently wrote that "the scope for differing views and interpretations is enormous, as is the amount of space within which a lively historical imagination can wander and speculate." Such speculation is borne out of the unreliability of the sources, "and it is the problems with the sources and the uncertainty they generate which make the Conquest such a fertile field for ongoing and probably endless scholarly cultivation."[15]

Frank Stenton, in considering the battle and in particular King Harold's position, makes no pretence at knowing more than the original sources reveal: "The only certainty that can be reached about its [the English army's] disposition is that Harold and his best men were grouped around a standard set near the summit of the hill." Any statements beyond this can only be, at best, considered guesses.[16]

Even the very name of the traditionally accepted site of the battle has been the subject of much debate. For a long time, following the writings of Orderic Vitalis in the early twelfth century, what today is called Battle Hill was known as Senlac Hill. The notable Victorian historian Edward Freeman declared that Orderic cannot have invented the word, implying that it was of Anglo-Saxon origin. Others disputed this. Sir George Duckett said that the word was a purely Norman compound of the words "Sang", i.e. blood, and "lac" or lake. Thus, he claimed, the word was used by Vitalis figuratively and therefore, because of the blood that was shed at the battle, the hill had become the lake of blood. Remarkable though it may seem, this topic has never been satisfactorily settled.[17] This may seem like a trivial point to argue over but, as the medieval historian Jim Bradbury explains, the name of the hill may have a bearing on exactly where the Battle of Hastings was really fought. "Orderic knew a name for the place," Bradbury recently wrote, but which place? "Senlac means literally 'sand-lake', and there is no lake close by Battle Hill ... The hill itself would certainly not be called 'sand-lake' and there is no reason to think that Senlac means Battle Hill." However, there was a lake, or at least a pool, close by Caldbec Hill, near Oakwood Gill, this latter place, as we will see, playing a significant part in the final stages of the battle.[18]

Though it seems but an insignificant fact, even the date of the battle is misleading. Whilst it is true that the battle was fought on 14 October 1066, this was the date on the old Julian calendar, which was abandoned in 1582. By our present-day calendar, the Gregorian, the battle was fought eleven days later on 25 October.[19]

The contradictory aspect of even the smallest of matters relating to the battle can be gauged by the subject of King Harold's death. Apart from the uncertain nature and time of his death, which will be investigated at length later, there is a problem with where he died. As we have already learned it is said with great conviction that the altar stone of the original church that was built on Battle Hill was laid at the precise place where Harold was killed. This is the summit of the hill where allegedly Harold had proudly raised his standards for all to see. We are also told, with equal assurance, that after the battle Harold's body could not be found and that his common–law wife/mistress, Edith Swan Neck, had to be brought to the scene to help identify the fallen king. How, four years later, the monks from Marmoutier were supposed to have known where Harold fell has never been explained.

Yet all such doubt could easily be erased if there was a firm archaeological basis to support the generally accepted view of the battle. "Much of the confusion and contradiction which swirls around the whole story [of the Battle of Hastings] would have been dissipated, if even the battlefield and the rest of the campaigning area of Sussex and Kent had yielded some tangible evidence," explained Edwin Tetlow. "Unhappily, not one relic or fragment, not a vestige of bone or even a rusted piece of steel or other metal has emerged from the field of combat. This singular void has led to all manner of theorising, from an extreme suggestion that the battle never happened to theories that it was fought elsewhere."[20]

This latter theory was considered by Jim Bradbury, who, in declaring that "in ninety-nine cases out of a hundred, the precise location of a battle is guesswork", confessed to "a wry grin" at the thought that the traditional site just might be wrong, "and that all those people who have so carefully measured Battle Hill to calculate how many men stood on it if each had three feet of ground, the little signs all over the place to mark who stood where, the confident guides in the abbey, or whatever ..."[21]

We conclude this opening statement with the words of William Seymour, who has reminded us that "walking the actual site of conflict is to decide for ourselves, with what information is available, just how it happened, and in some cases exactly where." That is exactly what we have done and it has led us to draw some startling conclusions.[22]

* * *

In order that the reader can understand where the Battle of Hastings was really fought, it is necessary to explain the circumstances both leading up to and during the famous battle as well as the weapons and tactics of the combatants and the nature of the terrain upon which they gave battle. As Steve Morillo appreciated, "Understanding the logistical limits within which armies operated and generals made their decisions, is crucial to understanding the strategies used by both sides in 1066."[23]

We will also study the prime medieval sources upon which our understanding of the battle is based and the interpretations which some of the many historians have given to those early documents. The literature that this most famous of battles has generated is, understandably, vast and it is not possible to analyse all of this body of work in a single volume. What is presented here is therefore subjective, but it covers a wide range of publications from the academic to the simplistic.

We have also, through the limitations of space and the desire not to repeat the same information too often, extracted that information which best suits our hypothesis. As M.K. Lawson wrote in his book *The Battle of Hastings 1066*, "the impression one gets of the battle depends very much upon which elements of the evidence one chooses to stress."[24] J.J. Bagley also understood that "every history book is the author's own interpretation of his own selection of facts."[25] Or as Jim Bradbury put it, "what each historian chooses to use or disregard makes his own individual view."[26]

What we will demonstrate is that much of what has been written about the Battle of Hastings is little more than well-considered conjecture and that some is even factually incorrect. Furthermore, the only seemingly, and quite literally solid fact, that Battle Abbey was built on the site of the battle, is almost certainly wrong. "Historians have to rely on narrative sources," Emma Mason observed, "all of which have some inbuilt bias, whether of omission, of exaggeration or of wilful misrepresentation." Where, therefore, lays the truth?[27]

Chapter 2

A Family Affair

"The Norman Conquest of 1066 was not a matter of opportunism, but the product of a long history of cross-channel involvement and careful calculation."
David Crouch, *The Normans*

The histories of England and Normandy had been very closely linked long before the momentous events of 1066. The Scandinavian warriors that had sailed up the Seine to occupy the Frankish city of Rouen at the start of the tenth century in what we now know as Normandy were little different from those that had raided and invaded Britain since the end of the eigth century.

The Vikings had attacked the decrepit Frankish kingdom a number of times before they finally established themselves at Rouen under their leader Hrólfr and came to terms with the neighbouring Frankish nobles. Soon Hrólfr (whose Latinised name was Rollo) and his sons were calling themselves "counts of Rouen" and, having been converted to Christianity, they were able to claim equality with the Frankish aristocracy. However, it took a direct attack upon Paris by Rollo's forces before the French king Charles the Simple officially conceded to Rollo the city of Rouen and the provinces as far west as Brittany. The Franks, for their part, did not fully accept these intruders and they referred to them as the Northmen – the *Northmanni*.[1]

Rollo's son, William Longsword, expanded his inherited territory, incorporating a previously isolated Viking colony to the west of Bayeux and securing control of the whole of the Cotentin peninsula. Though the Northmen's lands contracted for a period of time, they stabilised under Richard I in whose fifty-one-year reign this territory became accepted as the "land of the Normans".

As the Northmen on one side of the Channel became established in their new realm, across the Channel the fortunes of their Norse brethren waxed and waned. Invasions of the former Roman province of Britain had led to the formation of a number of Anglo-Saxon kingdoms, the smaller ones of which had by the ninth century been incorporated into the four largest – East Anglia, Northumbria, Mercia and Wessex.[2] Throughout the eigth and ninth centuries these kingdoms had come under repeated attack by the Northmen, the Vikings of Denmark and Norway. In the face of these attacks only the West Saxon (Wessex) kingdom survived thanks to the victories of Alfred the Great. The strength of Wessex grew under Alfred's successors at the expense of the Danish-held north until, in 927, the country was unified and the kingdom of England came into being. It has been said that it was because of the difficulty that the Vikings experienced in attacking England they sought easier pickings on the Continent. There is a strong argument, says David Crouch, that the founding of Normandy was a direct consequence of the strength of the Anglo-Saxon dynasty it would eventually replace in 1066.[3]

A new wave of Norwegian Vikings appeared in England in 947 when Erik Bloodaxe captured York. Viking raids continued against Saxon England throughout the rest of the century. At first, they made small raids along the coast, but as the years passed their boldness grew. Their raids became bigger, more brutal, and struck deeper into the heart of England. Much of their plunder was taken across the Channel and sold to the Normans. Such disreputable dealings were not discouraged by Richard, who was happy that it was not his villages that were being ravished. Eventually Æthelred, the English king, negotiated a treaty with Richard, the latter agreeing no longer to harbour the Viking raiders.

Nevertheless, the raids continued and Æthelred could organise no effective military resistance to the invaders. So instead, Æthelred took to paying them to go away – "better for you to buy off an attack with treasure," Æthelred was told, "rather than face men as fierce as us in battle", and he agreed. These payments were given the polite word of Danegeld, but in reality were nothing more or less than extortion. In 991 the English handed over £10,000. Three years later the Danes returned and demanded £16,000. Again and again they came back and each time they wanted an increased payment.[4]

In 996, Richard I of Normandy died and was succeeded by his son Richard. The first years of his reign saw a worsening of the situation in England. A huge force of Danish Vikings swept across the southern counties. Despite the treaty signed by his father, Richard II allowed many of the Vikings to retire to Normandy. Æthelred continued to try to deter the raids by increasing the amount of Danegeld he paid, but, predictably, such a policy only encouraged more raids. Æthelred needed to deny the Vikings a winter refuge and a market for their plunder so he sent ambassadors to Normandy to try and secure a more permanent agreement between the two realms – by marriage.

Thus it was that, in the late spring of 1002, Æthelred married Duke Richard's sister Emma, giving her the city of Exeter as a dowry. Believing that he was now in a strong position Æthelred attacked and massacred the Danes that had settled in the south-east of England (the St Brice's Day Massacre) many of whom had lived in the area for generations. This proved a disastrous mistake as it was rumoured that Gunhilde, sister of Sweyn Forkbeard, King of Denmark, was among the victims.

Whether Gunhide was amongst those murdered or not, the massacre gave justification for further attacks from Denmark. Soon Sweyn brought a huge fleet to England. By 1013, the Danes had overrun much of England and Æthelred's influence counted for so little that Sweyn travelled to Rouen to conclude his own alliance with Richard – one that completely revoked Richard's agreement with Æthelred. The new arrangement ensured that the Normans would offer aid and shelter to Danish crews seeking a safe harbour, and secondly that the Danes would be permitted to sell their plunder in Normandy.

By the end of 1013, English resistance had collapsed and Sweyn had conquered the country. Sweyn had in fact been well-received in many of the northern parts of the country, indicating how unpopular Æthelred had become.[5] Æthelred fled with his family to Normandy where he was received (probably with some reluctance) into the court of his brother-in-law, Duke Richard II.

* * *

Sweyn had conquered England but he did not enjoy his success for long, as he died on 3 February 1014. His son Canute (Cnut) succeeded him, but this was not universally accepted by the English nobles and a deputation was sent to Normandy with an invitation to Æthelred. If he returned to England they would give him their support.

Consequently, in April of that year, Æthelred raised a fleet, to a large degree manned by Viking and Norman mercenaries, and mounted an operation against Canute to regain his realm. The Danish leader was not prepared for a war and he withdrew from England. Æthelred sat once more upon the English throne. Of course, as with everything at that time, it was not as simple as that. Before Æthelred could re-establish his authority in England his second son, Edmund Ironside, had revolted against his father and established himself in the Danish-controlled areas of England.

The country was therefore divided and remained so until Canute returned with a large army late in 1015/early 1016, the Dane quickly overrunning large parts of the country. This external threat drove Edmund to join forces with his father. During this conflict Æthelred's unhappy reign ended when he died on 23 April 1016.

Edmund and Canute finally met at the Battle of Ashingdon on 18 October 1016. The result was a decisive victory for the Danes. Yet Edmund's reputation as a warrior was such that Canute agreed to divide England, Edmund taking Wessex and Canute the whole of the country beyond the Thames.

Unfortunately, Edmund died on 30 November (reputedly assasinated, though he may simply have died from wounds received during the battle) and his son Eadwig (Edwy) was driven out by Canute, who became king of the whole country. However, Edmund had an infant son, Edward Atheling (Atheling meant prince of the royal line), and he was smuggled out of the country to a safe home in Hungary and for many years his existence was forgotten as Canute firmly established his control over England. In an effort to maintain stability and legitimise his rule, Canute married Æthelred's widow, Queen Emma of Norway.

During this period of Scandinavian rule in England, Duke Richard II looked after Æthelred's family in Normandy. Æthelred and Emma's children, the young princes Edward and Alfred, spent many of their formative years at the Norman court, and French became their principal language. Their cousin William, who was to become the Conquer of England in 1066, was born in 1028.

With the death of Richard II, another Richard (III) succeeded to the Norman ducal title. He died after only a year and was in turn succeeded by William's father, Robert. Duke Robert I, rather mysteriously, undertook a pilgrimage to the Holy Land in 1035 and never returned. This meant that the young William became William II, Duke of Normandy, at the tender age of seven.

The exiled princes Edward and Alfred, meanwhile, had made an attempt to wrestle the English throne back from the Danes with the help of their Norman friends, but the expedition got no further than Jersey, which at that time was part of the Norman dukedom.[6] In 1035 Canute died and was succeeded by his son Harthacnut. At the time Harthacnut was in Scandinavia and so Canute's half-brother, Harold Harefoot, sat on the English throne theoretically as regent until Harthacnut returned from Denmark.

In the first year of Harold Harefoot's reign, in 1036, the young Prince Alfred journeyed from Normandy to England, supposedly to visit his mother, Emma, after she had asked to see him. He took only a few men with him. When he landed he was captured by Godwin, Earl of Wessex (more of whom later), who handed him over to Harefoot. Alfred's men were murdered or mutilated and Alfred himself was savagely blinded, dying of his wounds at Ely. Emma retreated into exile in Normandy.

Four years later Harefoot himself died and Harthacnut returned to England. During his brief reign Harthacnut adopted an entirely different approach to his predecessors, inviting his half-brother Edward to return from Normandy to England and, it is assumed, inviting him to succeed him. The bitter struggle between the Vikings and the English appeared to be over. Yet when Harthacnut collapsed and died in 1042, Magnus, King of Norway, laid claim to the English and Danish thrones under an agreement made between him and Harthacnut. However, he in turn died in 1047 and was succeeded by Harald Hardrada, who had his hands full in a protracted struggle against the Danes and had no interest in the English throne. The happy result of this was that Edward's accession was unchallenged.[7]

* * *

With the dynastic disputes resolved peace reigned throughout the land. The only real problem for Edward (who became known as "the Confessor" because of his supposed piety) was in his dealings with the Earl of Wessex, who was undoubtedly the most powerful of Edward's subjects. Here this family affair took on an even more complicated twist.

Edward was actually a descendent of the Wessex kings and in recognition of this he held his coronation at Winchester, the royal seat of the West-Saxons. Though only a distant relative by marriage, Earl Godwin of Wessex was, nevertheless, of the same royal house. From comparatively obscure origins (he may have been the son of the Wulfnoth Cild, a Sussex thegn) Godwin married into a branch of the Danish royal family and in time became one of Canute's most trusted subordinates. When Edward became king, Godwin established himself as the power behind the throne.[8]

The connection between Godwin and Edward was further strengthened when the King married Godwin's daughter Edith in 1045. When one recalls that Godwin was the man who had seized Edward's brother Alfred and handed him over to Harold Harefoot to be murdered, this cannot have been easy for Edward. No doubt he did it to keep peace in his realm and the marriage should have brought the two families closer together.[9] But Edward had grown up in Normandy and quite naturally he wanted to have some of his Norman friends around him in England. Godwin and many of the English nobles were unhappy with Edward's pro-Norman sentiments, and the growing influence of Normans invited from across the Channel at the Confessor's court.

This came to a head in 1050 when the archbishopric of Canterbury fell vacant on the death of Archbishop Eadsige. Godwin wanted one of his family to get the post but Edward chose a Norman, Robert of Jumièges. The final break in relation between the country's two leading figures came the following year.

One of Edward's Norman friends, his sister's husband, Eustace Count of Boulogne, was returning to France from a visit to Gloucester, where the king was holding court, when he entered Dover fully armed and demanded accommodation for himself and his entourage. One of the townsfolk refused to admit an armed foreigner into his house and a fight broke out. Others became involved and at the end of the dispute nineteen Normans and twenty English lay dead and many others were wounded.[10]

Eustace hurried straight back to Gloucester demanding that the people of Dover should be punished. As Dover fell within Earl Godwin's domains, Edward ordered Godwin to carry out the deed. Godwin refused charging

Eustace and his knights with unprovoked murder. A violent row ensued in which Godwin accused Edward of protecting his Norman favourites. In response Edward accused Godwin of killing his brother Alfred.

The earl stormed from the royal presence and he raised an army against the king and marched on Gloucester, hoping that the northern earls would join him. But Leofric of Mercia and Siward of Northumbria remained loyal to Edward and, together with the king's household troops, they outnumbered those of Wessex. Instead of the disagreement degenerating into civil war, Godwin agreed to leave England peacefully.[11] He and most of his family went into exile in Flanders (two of his sons, Harold – the future king – and Leofwine, went instead to Ireland), which had become linked to the Godwins when the earl's third son, Tostig, married Judith, the daughter of Count Baldwin IV, half-sister of Baldwin V of Flanders. The remarkable intertwining of the leading English and Norman families was to continue as Judith was the aunt of Matilda – the woman who married Duke William of Normandy, the man who would become the Conqueror. The breach with the Godwins was certainly total, as Edward also sent Edith, his own wife and Queen, into a nunnery.[12]

Godwin's exile lasted less than a year. It seems possible that it was during the absence of the leading Saxon family, and the family that epitomised English opposition to the Normans, that Edward hinted he would offer the throne to Duke William. This caused great resentment amongst the English and many of them crossed the Channel to offer Godwin their support. This enabled him to return to England with a strong force and he advanced with his son Harold (who had arrived with another body of men from Ireland) upon London.[13]

Edward drew up his forces and the opposing armies faced each other across the Thames. Edward, faced with such opposition, sought negotiation rather than confrontation and a deal was struck in which Godwin was restored to his former lands and many of the highly placed Normans were expelled (or in fact fled when they saw the strength of feeling amongst the English).[14] It was not quite the one-sided deal that this may imply, however, as Edward demanded hostages from Godwin to ensure his future good conduct. Godwin complied and he handed over Harold's brother Wulfnoth and his nephew, who were sent by Edward to Normandy into William's custody.

At Easter 1053, Earl Godwin suffered a stroke, whilst at dinner with the king. He died a few days later.[15] His son Harold Godwinson became the Earl of Wessex.

Harold, it seems, may have been less confrontational than his father and he handled his relationship with Edward skilfully. The influence of the Godwin family also increased. When Siward of Northumbria died in 1055, Harold's brother Tostig took that earldom. With Gyrth Godwinson holding East Anglia, Middlesex and Hertfordshire being held by Leofwine, and Harold himself extending his own West-Saxon lands to include Herefordshire and

Gloucestershire, it meant that only one of the great English earldoms, that of Mercia, was not held by the Godwins. Collectively, the Godwins held lands which exceeded the value of those held by the king himself.[16]

This then was the state of affairs in England towards the end of the 1050s. Edward's reign is seen to have been a relatively settled and successful one by the standards of the day. There was, however, a problem in the offing.

Edward was getting older and he had no children. The question of his succession was certain to be a troubling one. Though the English monarchy was a strongly established institution, it could not be said for certain that the rules of succession were clearly defined. It was something Edward had considered and it appears that he promised his throne to a number of the likely candidates. This may have been to keep them happy and quiet during his lifetime but it resulted in much bloodshed after he died.[17]

In pure hereditary terms his nephew was the most legitimate successor. This was Edgar the Exile (or Atheling), who was the son of Edward Atheling, who, it may be recalled, had become exiled as a child in Hungary. In 1054 Edward sought to settle the succession issue by recalling Edward Atheling but warfare in central Europe made communications with the Hungarian court difficult. Bishop Ealdred of Worcester was sent to visit the Holy Roman Emperor (Henry III of Germany) in Cologne to ask for his help in contacting the King of Hungary to arrange for the repatriation of Edward.[18]

It took three years of diplomatic dealings and perilous journeys across war-torn Europe before Edgar and his family arrived back in England in 1057 as Edward's heir apparent. That August he dropped dead but he had two children, one of whom was the boy Edgar, who had been born in 1050. Edgar was the only true male descendant of the Anglo–Saxon royal house. But he was still a child and, whereas that was not in itself a problem (as many other juvenile princes had turned into successful rulers), the other contenders were strong and powerful men.[19]

Of those contenders, Harold Godwinson was certainly the one who expected to be crowned King of England after Edward's death, his interest in the throne possibly being aroused after the death of Edward Atheling when it became clear that there was no longer an obvious successor.[20] Apart from his family connections – Edward was, after all, his brother-in-law and his father had married Ulf, who was Canute's brother-in-law – he had become increasingly important to Edward. In fact Harold had become Edward's *subregulus*, or under-king, and, as Edward grew older, less well and less interested in affairs of state, Harold had for all practical purposes been running the country.[21] He also proved himself a fine warrior in defeating the Welsh and extending Edward's sovereignty into south Wales. Harold, along with his brother Tostig, conducted a series of campaigns (1062–63) against Gruffydd ap Llywelyn of Gwynedd, the conflict ending with Gruffydd's defeat and his death at the hands of his own troops.[22] The Welsh swore fealty and obedience jointly to Edward and Harold, further reinforcing the latter's position as Edward's natural successor.[23] This highly successful campaign also earned Earl Harold a reputation for speed and surprise.[24]

If Harold had a claim on the English throne through his family line, tenuous though it may have been, then his brother Tostig also qualified. He was, though, the younger of the two brothers and his claim was far weaker than his elder sibling. Tostig had risen on the coat-tails of firstly his father's growing influence in England and then that of his brother Harold after his father's death. In 1055 he was made Earl of Northumbria following the death of Siward.

Tostig ruled Northumbria for ten years but there was growing unrest in his earldom over his harsh rule which came to a head after he had increased taxes by 100 per cent and killed three young Northumbrian nobles. This was more than the Northumbrians could take and on 3 October, whilst Tostig was at court with King Edward, they rose up in rebellion. The rebels marched upon Tostig's capital, York, broke into the treasury and armoury and took everything. The leading Northumbrian earls met and by their own authority stripped Tostig of his title.[25]

The Northumbrians called on Morcar, brother of Edwin the Earl of Mercia, to be their earl and, with the support of the Mercians, they advanced southwards. Edward sent Harold to resolve the dispute. Harold failed to pacify the rebels and with the whole of Mercia and Northumbria in arms Edward was forced to accede to their demands. Morcar was appointed to the earldom and Tostig was exiled.[26]

The significance in these events as they relate to the Battle of Hastings is that Tostig accused Harold of not supporting him wholeheartedly in his dispute and the two brothers became bitter enemies and, consequently, rivals for the throne. Tositg sought exile in Flanders, where he was well-received by his brother-in-law Count Baldwin, and planned his revenge, and he was the first man to challenge Harold's right to the throne after Edward's death.[27]

In April 1066 Tostig, supported by Flemish forces, assembled a fleet and raided the south coast from Hampshire through to Kent. Harold moved against him and Tostig sailed off northwards to Lindsey on the Lincolnshire coast but was met by the forces of Morcar and Edwin and he was severely beaten. Most of those men that survived deserted Tostig, who escaped to Scotland with just twelve ships, where he was sheltered by his "sworn" brother, King Malcolm. Tostig, however, was not finished and more will be heard of him later.[28]

To add to the inter-family complexities there was yet another relative of Edward's who might have staked a claim for the English throne. This was Sweyn Estrithsson of Denmark. Sweyn was Canute's nephew and the grandson of Sweyn Forkbeard, both of whom had been kings of England. Sweyn, however, had a more pressing matter, being involved in a protracted war with Norway.[29]

By the same token, Harald Hardrada of Norway, the man who Sweyn was fighting, had a long-standing claim to the English crown.

Another of the contenders for the throne was William II of Normandy. As his great-aunt was Edward's mother's sister, he and Edward were cousins – technically, first cousins once removed. He was therefore a blood relative, and, though admittedly not in the direct line of descent, he was the closest living adult male.

Whoever might emerge from this group as the leading figure, he would have to be accepted by the *Witan Gemoot*, the Council of Wise Men. As can be seen from earlier events hereditary factors did not always guarantee the crown. In theory the king would be selected by the *Witan*, who would choose the *capax imperii*, i.e. the best man to govern. In its decision-making the *Witan* would consider the royal bloodline, the wishes of the late king and the claimant's ability to defend the kingdom. In practice, the last factor was the most important and this usually meant the most powerful man around, whatever his antecedents may be.

On the night of 4 January 1066, Edward the Confessor died. The following morning he was buried at the new abbey of West Minster. Edward had personally planned and supervised the construction of the great building and he was the first man to be interred within its walls. That same afternoon the *Witan* approved the succession of Harold as King of England. Harold had proven himself more than capable of defending the country, as demonstrated by his successes over the Welsh. According to the *Anglo-Saxon Chronicle* (C and D versions) Edward had nominated Harold to the *Witan* as his successor: "And the wise king entrusted that kingdom to the high-ranking men, Harold himself, the noble earl, who at all times faithfully obeyed his lord in word and deed, neglecting nothing of which the king had need; and here Harold was hallowed as king." The *Waltham Chronicle* confirms that Harold's appointment was unanimous "for there was no one in the land more knowledgeable, more vigorous in arms, wiser in the laws of the land or more highly regarded for his prowess of every kind."[30]

Regardless of all this hyperbole, there can be little doubt that on his deathbed Edward would have indicated to the *Witan* that he wished Harold to succeed him, and he must have genuinely seemed to be the logical choice at the time, especially with regards to his family's known antipathy towards the Normans, whom no one wanted to see regain their influence in England.[31]

Though the northern earls Morcar and Edwin were not happy with Harold's succession, their allegiance was won by the marriage of their sister to the new king – yet another twist in the tangled threads of the family affair.[32]

Chapter 3

Swords Around the Throne

"As so often in medieval history, the surviving evidence is teasingly incomplete."
Andrew Bridgeford, *1066, The Hidden*
History of the Bayeux Tapestry

It is presumed that it was Normans living in England that first brought the news of Edward's death to William – and of Harold's accession to the throne.[1] It is said that William was hunting in the Quévilly forest near Rouen when he was told of Harold's coronation – and he was far from pleased.[2]

He claimed that his cousin Edward had promised the throne to him not just once but on two occasions. The first time was when Edward was still living in Normandy and had told the young William that if he became the King of England William could succeed him. There is no evidence of this but equally there is nothing to say that such a promise was not made between cousins. It must also be recalled that there was no certainty at that time that Edward would ever become king, or even that William would live that long in those dangerous times. So such an offer could be made without much expectation that it would ever be fulfilled.

Nevertheless it was William's contention that such a promise was made and when Edward did succeed to the English throne, that promise was confirmed. The date given for this is 1051. The (D) version of the *Anglo-Saxon Chronicle* says that in that year William visited England, though no reference to William's visit is made in any of the other versions of the *Chronicle*. Significantly, none of the Norman sources mention the visit.[3]

William of Poitiers states that, during William's visit to England, Edward renewed his offer of the throne to his cousin in front of the most important men in the country – the three earls, Godwin of Wessex, Siward of Northumbria and Leofric of Mercia, along with Stigand the Archbishop of Canterbury. There are very obvious flaws in this, as Wood points out.[4] The first of these is that 1051 was the year when Edward had banished the Godwins and they could not have been present; the second is that Stigand was not the Archbishop of Canterbury at that time!

The date of 1051 is also significant in that the situation in Normandy was unstable and it seems highly improbable that William would leave his troubled domain at such a time. William had succeeded his father in 1035 at the age of just seven and as Duke Robert's bastard son (he was frequently called William the Bastard) there was considerable resentment in Normandy at his succession. He had a troubled minority which manifested itself in 1046 in a rebellion led by his cousin, Guy of Brionne, who was supported by many Norman nobles. William was driven out of Normandy, taking refuge with his overlord, King Henry of France.

Henry helped William regain his dukedom, defeating the rebels at the Battle of Val-ès-Dune in 1047. Guy sought refuge in his castle at Brionne and it took William about three years to force his surrender. At the same time King Henry asked for William's assistance against Geoffrey Martel, Count of Anjou, who had challenged Henry's authority. William duly obliged but Henry now saw the young duke as a greater threat than Martel, and the king joined forces with the count. As a result William was occupied in defending his own lands in 1051 and could never have risked leaving Normandy.[5]

William must also have known that there were other rebellions in the offing. In 1052 his uncle the Count of Arques, supported by Henry and Martel, mounted a challenge to William's rule. William defeated his uncle and sent him off into exile but the King of France and the Count of Anjou continued to threaten Normandy until 1060 when they both died. Harriet Woods' view of all this is that the idea that in the midst of these threats to his rule, actual or threatened, William would have contemplated leaving his duchy undefended for long enough to pay a visit to his cousin in England, even with the possibility that he might receive the promise of a throne in the course of it, "is quite simply incredible."[6]

The only thing that does lend credibility to the timing of William's visit in 1051 is that this was the year when the Godwins had been exiled and Norman influence at the English court would have been at its highest. If there was ever a time when Edward was likely to offer the throne to Duke William then it was in 1051.[7]

William of Jumièges does offer a different explanation. He does not claim that Duke William left Normandy at all. Instead he has the promise of the English throne being presented to the duke through a third party. He states that Robert of Jumièges, who succeeded Eadsige as Archbishop of Canterbury in 1051, went off to Rome to receive his pallium from the Pope[8] and on this trip Robert travelled down to Normandy and delivered Edward's promise to Duke William.[9]

Such a promise, even if it had been given, brought with it no certainty that William would be offered the throne by the *Witan*. Whatever Edward may have wished, once he was dead, his influence counted for little. Though his views would be taken into consideration by the *Witan* its members alone would choose the man they thought would best be able to govern and protect the kingdom. The repeated references to Edward's offer of the throne to William by Norman chroniclers were merely attempts to legitimise William's actions.

Another incident may have occurred in the summer of 1064 relating to William's claim to the English throne which is as difficult to substantiate as the earlier references. According to the Norman sources in that year Harold crossed the Channel. The reason for this trip, according to William of Poitiers, was that he was sent by King Edward to confirm his earlier promise of the throne to William.[10] Why Harold would have agreed to this when, as events would soon show, he had his own sights set on the throne, is a mystery. His power matched that of Edward's and the king was becoming old and frail. Edward would never have dared risk a breach with Harold if the earl had refused to go to Normandy.

Nevertheless, if indeed such a journey was undertaken, it went seriously wrong. Harold is shown on the Bayeux Tapestry bidding farewell to Edward at one of his palaces and taking a ship from his own family's port of Bosham with his hunting dogs and birds. Whether by storm or poor navigation Harold was cast up on the coast of Ponthieu (in modern-day Picardy). His ship foundered and he and his companions were taken prisoner. The locals were reputed to be wreckers, displaying misleading lights to lure unsuspecting ships onto dangerous parts of the coastline. The crews would be captured and ransomed for large sums of money. Harold might have ensured his release with the payment of a ransom had not his captors recognised that one of their prisoners was the Earl of Wessex.

The Count of Ponthieu soon learnt of the valuable prize which had landed in his lands and Harold and his men were taken by the count and incarcerated in a dungeon. It has been inferred from the Bayeux Tapestry, where a moustached man, i.e. an Englishman, is shown addressing William, that one of Harold's men managed to escape to Normandy to ask for Duke William's help.

William, who was Guy of Ponthieu's overlord and not a man to mess with, demanded that Harold should be released into his custody. The count handed over the Earl of Wessex in return for an amount of money and a little land.

William, it seems, treated Harold with great respect and the earl remained in Normandy for some time. They even went on campaign together against Count Conan in Brittany where, it is said, Harold displayed great bravery in rescuing two of William's soldiers from quicksands with his great strength. This event is represented in the Bayeux Tapestry, which shows Harold carrying men and shields across the River Couesnon.[11] As a result, it is said, William knighted Harold, in other words Harold became William's "man". Though, as Peter Poyntz Wright points out, it is questionable whether the duke of a small continental state outranked an English earl who was subservient only to a king.[12]

Certainly Emma Mason considered Harold's status as *subregulus* of England was greater than William's. Moreover, both men were sometimes styled *dux*, a title that denoted that the holder was the military leader of his nation.[13]

The key point in all this is that before Harold returned to England he supposedly swore an oath on some kind of casket which, unbeknown to Harold, contained a number of holy relics. In his oath Harold swore that he would back William's claim to the throne when Edward died. In return for this William told Harold he would retain his existing lands and he also promised "everything which you ask of me which can reasonably be granted". Whatever was said, or offered, Harold, stranded in Normandy with just a few followers, was in no position to refuse.[14]

Eadmer expands upon this and states that William sought to tie Harold closer to him by proposing that Harold's sister should marry one of the great Norman nobles and that Harold himself should marry William's daughter Agatha. As N.J. Higham explains, *King Harald's Saga* emphasises the proposed marriage alliance and does not mention Harold's oath at all, which may indicate that this was the more important part of the entire procedure which had the potential to bind together the policies of two powerful figures whose interests were not entirely compatible.[15] The swearing of the oath would be in relation to his promise of marriage.

There is, however, evidence which points to an entirely different reason for Harold's trip to the Continent. This evidence again comes from Eadmer, who states that Harold went of his own volition (and indeed against the advice of Edward, who told him that William was not to be trusted), to try and recover his brother and nephew who had been given to William as hostages. As it transpired Harold was able to take his nephew Hakon back to England but not his brother Wulfnoth. The latter would be released when William succeeded to the throne.[16]

According to Henry of Huntingdon, in his *Historia Anglorum*, Harold was actually on a journey to Flanders, not to Normandy, and was blown southwards to Ponthieu by a storm. We know that the Godwins and the Baldwins of Flanders were close allies and related by marriage so this is quite plausible.[17] Another version of events declares that Harold had simply gone off on a leisurely voyage with no intention of going to anywhere on the Continent and had been caught in a storm and blown onto the foreign shore. The fact that in the Tapestry Harold is seen travelling off to the coast with his hunting hawk and his dogs may support this view.[18]

As with everything related to the Battle of Hastings and the Norman invasion extracting the truth from the disparate sources is not easy. Peter Poyntz Wright declared, "Unless he had some secret purpose, of which we have no evidence, everything suggests that he was forced ashore by bad weather." This he believes is evident because if Harold was travelling as an emissary of Edward he would have been covered by diplomatic immunity and consequently William would not have paid any ransom to Count Guy for Harold's release.[19]

Harriet Wood follows Eadmer but bases her version of events upon an interpretation of the Bayeux Tapestry. This is that the first panel or frame shows Kind Edward sitting in his chair of state, holding his sceptre and apparently conversing affably with two men standing beside him. The taller and more impressive of these is not named but is assumed to be Harold. This is the image that has been interpreted by Norman historians as Edward instructing Harold to travel to Normandy to confirm his promise to William. There is absolutely nothing in the picture or the text to confirm this. Harold might be asking permission to go on a fishing or hunting trip or to Flanders or to go to redeem the hostages from Normandy. The tapestry then follows the usual, or Norman, account. It shows, in particular, Harold swearing the oath to William on the bones of saints. Wood then moves onto the panel which shows Harold returning to England and debriefing with Edward, whose appearance has considerably changed: "He is drawn and haggard, the finger extended towards Harold is no longer indicating merely conversation but rather admonition or accusation. Harold for his part is apologetic and contrite, his head bowed, his hands extended in an exculpatory gesture." Another interpretation of Edward's demeanour is that Edward was reaching the end of his life – which is why he is portrayed as looking so frail – and was concerned about his succession. Oddly, Harold certainly appears contrite. "It is impossible to misread this scene," continues Wood, "the king has heard something that worries and distresses him greatly, Harold is apologizing and excusing himself. If Harold had gone in the first place to confirm promises and make vows on the king's behalf, why should he be apologizing? The only obvious answer is that he did not go to do this, but he has, for whatever reason, sworn a vow and in doing so has landed himself in bad trouble with his king."[20]

The only explanation that makes sense of everything is, according to Wood, the one provided by Eadmer above, which is that Harold wanted to redeem the family hostages in Normandy and had asked King Edward's permission to do so. Wood continues, quoting Eadmer: "The king apparently gave [his permission] reluctantly, but warned him that he would only bring misfortune on the whole kingdom and discredit upon himself, for 'I know that the Duke is not so simple as to be inclined to give them up to you unless he foresees that in doing so he will secure some great advantage to himself' .... No wonder that on his return the king is reported by Eadmer as saying reproachfully, 'Did I not tell you that I knew William and that your going might bring untold calamity upon this kingdom?'" The flaw in Harriet Wood's reasoning is that those who commissioned the Tapestry would be unlikely to have allowed such an interpretation, which does not portray William in a very favourable light, to have been recorded in hard copy.[21]

Andrew Bridgeford agrees with Wood, which his controversial interpretation of the Tapestry reveals. That Harold's journey was to beg for the release of his brother and nephew is demonstrated in the scene which depicts the Earl of Wessex's meeting with William at his court (presumably Rouen).

There is no inscription to guide us with this scene, only the woven images: "William, as we would expect, is seated authoritatively on his throne, with its dragon-headed arms, fine cushion and attendant blue footstool; for he is Duke of Normandy and this is his palace. Harold stands ... Observe, now, how Harold, while busy talking to William, points at the armed and bearded man standing to his left, and how this man reciprocates the gesture. Evidently this man is the subject of Harold's conversation with William." Bridgeford points out that the man in question is quite different in appearance to the other Normans in the scene. In particular he is shown with long black hair and a black beard. It is known that the Normans shaved the back of their heads but not the English, and throughout the Tapestry the English are portrayed with long hair. Bridgeford believes that this long-haired, bearded man is none other than Harold's brother Wulfnoth. The Tapestry, if this is then the correct interpretation of the scene, tells us quite clearly that Harold had journeyed to Normandy to try and persuade William to allow his brother and nephew to return home.

The entire episode is most strange and there is no certainty that the visit took place at all. None of the Norman sources place a date on the trip and the early English chroniclers made no mention of the event despite recording the journeys of other diplomats who crossed the Channel during Edward's reign.[22] Another contemporary record, the *Vita Ædwardi Regis*, refers in some detail to an expedition to the Continent by Harold in 1056 or 1058 but is silent regarding any subsequent visit. In this trip Harold went on a pilgrimage to Rome via Saxony and spent some time in France studying "Frankish customs".[23] There is also no agreement on where the meeting with William took place. The Tapestry places the event at Bayeux, William of Poitiers has it at Bonneville and Orderic Vitalis says it was at Rouen.[24] It is also utterly inconceivable that Harold, who was de facto ruler England, would have knowingly or willingly travelled to the land of a man who had declared that Edward had promised him the English throne. It certainly shows that Harold did not consider William to be a rival for the crown or he would never had put himself in such a compromising position.[25] Yet there can be little doubt that William projected himself as Edward's nominated successor and that he believed he had secured Harold's acceptance of that fact. These two opposing views would only be reconciled on the battlefield.

If Harold was in Normandy in 1064, for whatever the reason, the fact that he swore an oath on holy relics, even though he was deceived or coerced into doing so, enabled William to seize the moral high ground. When Edward died he was quick to exploit this by claiming that Harold had broken a holy vow, thus enabling him to appeal to Pope Alexander for his support. According to Stephen Morillo, papal sanction was "the key pretext" for William's expedition. David Howarth makes this one of the central themes of his book, *1066: The Year of the Conquest*, claiming that Harold's seemingly inept performance at Hastings was because he believed that God was not on his side.[26] As we will see, there is much evidence to oppose this traditional view.

* * *

Regardless of the rights or wrongs of his claim to the English throne, when William learned of Harold's coronation he consulted his half-brothers Odo, Bishop of Bayeux, and Robert of Mortain and his step-father, Herluin Vicome de Conteville, and, according to William of Poitiers, they resolved to win the English crown by force of arms.[27] Of course these nobles and the other Norman barons were obliged by terms of their feudal tenures to provide him with knights, men, arms and equipment in pre-determined quantities in times of national emergency. But an overseas expedition was something entirely different.

If William of Poitiers is to be believed, the duke then sent an emissary to England to demand that Harold relinquish his crown. When this was rejected by Harold, William knew that he would have to fight to win the throne of England.[28] To accomplish this William would need all the help he could get and this included spiritual as well as physical support. For the former he sent a delegation to the Vatican.

The Pope, it was said, needed little persuasion to support William's bid to seize the English throne because of an ongoing dispute over the appointment of Stigand as Archbishop of Canterbury in 1052 without papal approval. This caused a breach in relations between England and Rome which, by 1066, had still not been healed. With God now officially on his side, William was able to attract knights to join him from across Europe and further delegations were despatched as far afield as Germany and Denmark.

Like everything connected with the Norman invasion even this claim of papal support, which most writers on the subject accept without comment, is open to question. The basis of this comes from the words of the heavily biased William of Poitiers and William of Malmesbury, who states that Pope Alexander gave William a "standard".[29] Yet nowhere in the Bayeux Tapestry is there any reference to the pope, nor has the papal banner been identified with certainty amongst the many flags embroidered on this great treasure.[30]

David Bates also refers to a letter of 24 April 1080 written by Pope Gregory VIII, who, as Archdeacon Hildebrand had been prominent in papal counsels in 1066, suggested that he had been one of William's supporters but that the mission had not been favourably received in Rome. One Christian country conquering another was not unusual in those times but to do so in the name of the pope was something altogether different.[31] Furthermore, Stigand retained his position as head of the English church after the Conquest. If the Pope had indeed sanctioned William's invasion then Stigand would surely have been removed from his archbishopric with little delay. It was only in 1070, when papal legates were sent to England, that Stigand was deposed. As Ian Walker concludes, the most likely scenario is that what William of Poitiers and others describe in their accounts is "a later retrospective sanction by the Papal court for the *fait accompli* represented by William's conquest."[32] This would explain why when the papal delegates reached England they imposed a penance upon the Norman knights who had fought at Hastings. This would be a very strange course of action to take against men who had fought under the papal banner.[33]

This is of considerable consequence in terms of the building of Battle Abbey; as Wood writes this explanation of a retrospective sanction would explain the events of 1070 very convincingly; not only the penance imposed on the Norman troops by the papal legates, but also the second coronation of William during their visit, surely unnecessary after his coronation by Ealdred in Westminster Abbey in 1066 except as a papal endorsement of a *fait accompli*. It is tempting also to see this legatine council as the cause of William's foundation of Battle Abbey on the site of the English defence, as his own personal part of the Norman penance.

It is known, however, that William did attract men from across France and other countries. It was the promise of land and riches should they succeed in conquering the English that encouraged men to join the expedition. Plunder rather than piety was likely to have been the principal determining factor and the result of this was that Harold was left without any Continental allies.[34]

It was in the early spring when William called all the barons of Normandy together for a meeting, given by some as a council of war, at his castle at Lillebonne. This gathering included Robert de Mortain, Robert Count of Eu, Richard Count of Evreux, Roger de Montgomerie, William fitzOsbern and Hugh the Vicomte. He told them of his great enterprise – to transport a medieval army, complete with fully armoured knights and their warhorses, across the Channel.

According to Wace the idea was not well-received and the meeting broke up in disharmony. William was not going to be deterred by this, though, and he resorted to individual interviews to persuade his knights to follow him, no doubt with the offer of lands as much as the threat of incurring his disfavour.[35] A second council was held at Bonneville-sur-Touques, where the provisioning of the ships for the invasion was discussed and a third council took place at Caen in June, by which time most of the key nobles had given William their backing.

Soon William began to gather together his invasion army and build the hundreds of ships that would be needed to carry his great army over the

Channel. The men that were to form William's army came from across France, especially Brittany, which was full of impoverished knights. The news that William was offering land in England to his leaders and booty for everyone had spread far and wide. It is also possible that William encouraged the belief that he had papal support, or at least that he had right on his side. As David Howarth put it, the expedition offered "a fortune if they succeeded or heaven if they failed: this call has attracted armies all through history."[36] So from Flanders and Artois, Picardy, Maine, Champagne, Poitou and Apulia they came. Emperor Henry IV promised German help and Sweyn of Demark promised to stay neutral and not interfere with William's plans.[37]

Whilst William was preparing for the invasion, Harold was assembling his forces in the south of England to counter the invasion he knew would come from Normandy. Tostig's raid in April had convinced Harold that his brother was in league with William and he expected another attack to be delivered at any time. By early summer he had, according to the *Anglo Saxon Chronicle*, "gathered such a great naval force, and a land force also, as no other king in the land had gathered before."[38]

For Harold, the raising of a large army was a straightforward business. The backbone of his land forces were the *housecarls*, who were full-time, professional soldiers. Kings and earls all had their own *housecarls* and as Harold was still the Earl of Wessex he had a substantial force at his disposal. These, though, may have amounted to no more than 2,000 men and the bulk of the English force was made up of locally raised part-time soldiers of the *fyrd*.

This local force was composed of noblemen and lesser landowners, who in return for their land were obliged to provide their lords with up two months' military service a year, and from each local district or "hundred" a number of fighting men were drawn. Even more locally, men would also take to arms to protect their own villages. The two armies will be discussed in more detail in Chapter 5.

With a fleet drawn from the Cinque Ports and the other harbours along the south coast Harold took up a position on the Isle of Wight with the bulk of his army. The remainder of his forces were spread along the coast. The object of this arrangement was that in the event of a landing the lookouts on the coast would signal the arrival of the enemy (probably by lighting a beacon) and Harold would then sail from the Isle of Wight with his army to fall upon the invaders.

Any invaders sailing from France, and particularly from Normandy, would almost certainly make landfall at some point along the Sussex or Kent coast. It may seem strange, therefore, that Harold had positioned his forces on the Isle of Wight but the reason for this is that the prevailing wind, particularly during the summer months, is from the south-west. By positioning his fleet on the Isle of Wight Harold would be able to sail with the wind as soon as news of the sighting of the enemy ships reached him. Indeed, it was more than likely that the wind that would carry the invading fleet would be the same upon which Harold would sail, to land behind the invaders or on an adjacent beach.

Their armies assembled, the two great men waited on their respective sides of the Channel for the wind that would carry them both to the shingle beaches of Sussex. The Norman ships, clearly defined in the Bayeux Tapestry, had long, shallow keels and single masts bearing a square sail. Such vessels would have limited ability to sail to windward and their shallow keels would have little effect in preventing leeway. William therefore had no choice but to wait for the wind to blow from the south or the south-west, or, as the wind normally blows from this direction in the Channel, to wait until Harold's forces had dispersed.

Harold waited as spring turned into summer with no reappearance of Tostig or of William. On one hand this was, of course, wonderful. But on the other hand Harold could not keep a large part of the male population of the south of the country sitting around waiting for action. Most people worked on the land in eleventh-century England and fields and animals needed tending. Furthermore, the men were only obliged to serve under arms for two months and if the invasion did not come soon these men would be agitating for a return to their demesnes.

Harold managed to keep his forces together until early September – never before, it is said, had any of Harold's *fyrd* been away from their homes for so long.[39] But the men's supplies had run out and they could not be kept away from their homes any longer. The sailing season was also drawing to a close for the year and there was much for the men to do before the winter set in. Ships would need to be safely berthed and prepared for the winter. On land the harvest could be delayed no longer and the men would also need to build up their stocks of food and wood before the bad weather was upon them.

These factors affected the Normans as much as the English. If William had attempted to assemble an invading army, as was thought to be the case, then he too would be struggling to keep his forces together. There was now little chance of an invasion.

Around the first week in September the *fyrd* went home. Harold himself left his home of Bosham at some time between 13 and 16 September and rode to London with his *housecarls*.

Yet, on the other side of the Channel, William had not the slightest intention of abandoning his invasion plans. He probably knew that if he failed to attack England in 1066 his credibility would be severely damaged and he would never be able to gather together such a large army again. So, on 12 September the great invasion fleet at last set sail from Dives-sur-Mer.

The Norman fleet encountered strong westerly winds which blew the ships along the Norman coast. Some ships were lost and a number of men were drowned. The invasion fleet found shelter at St Valéry in the Somme estuary, more than 250 kilometres to the east of Dives.[40] Whether this move down the coast was intentional or not is open to debate. William must have been aware that Harold had amassed a huge fleet and, if the Norman ships were spotted at sea, the English fleet would be able to bear down upon them as they reached land, with the potential for utter disaster. The crossing from St Valéry to the south coast of England is considerably shorter than from Dives–sur–Mer, which would enable William to make the crossing in the course of a single night so such a move would have made great sense.[41] It has also been said that William's original plan was to sail from Dives to the Isle of Wight and then on to the Hampshire coast. From there he would be in marching distance of Winchester, the capital of Wessex, which would form his operating base from where he could strike against London. It was only when spies informed him that Harold had disbanded the *fyrd* that William changed his plans and moved down to St Valéry sur Somme for the shorter crossing to the open, and now undefended, beaches of Sussex.[42]

William buried his dead in secret, so as not to dishearten the rest of the troops, and waited again for a favourable wind. But the north wind continued to blow (this time, being September, it may well have been genuine) keeping William land-bound. There were some desertions from the disgruntled troops in response to which William increased the daily ration of food and the daily prayers. But it was that very north wind which kept William anchored in the Somme that blew Tostig back to England and with him was the most feared warrior of the age, Harald Hardrada, King of the Vikings.

Tostig had spent little time in Scotland before seeking an ally in his bitter conflict with his brother Harold. Tostig probably wasn't too bothered who ruled England as long as he got back his earldom and it is said that he had travelled back to Flanders and then Demark in a bid to find someone who would support him. Whilst the Count of Flanders and the King of Denmark had offered him refuge, neither was prepared to contemplate attacking England. With few remaining options he sailed to Oslofjord in Norway to meet Harald III, who had been fighting since at least the age of fifteen and had barely stopped fighting since. A huge man, Harald had earned a formidable reputation as a warrior (William of Poitiers described him as "the greatest warrior under heaven"[43]) and had become known as Hardrada, which roughly translated as "hard ruler".[44] Yet when Tostig arrived in Norway, Harald, for almost the first time since he was a boy, had no one to fight. Tostig could not have visited Harald at a more opportune time.

Harald, who was the grandson of Canute and so could claim some link to the English throne, needed little persuasion to invade England and, even though Tostig did not reach Norway until June, Harald was soon able to assemble his forces for an invasion.[45] The Vikings, above all of the medieval peoples, were accustomed to amphibious operations and had attacked England many times before. It is said that he called for men to join him from across Norway and demanded a levy on half his people. Whilst the terms of this levy are unclear he was quickly able to raise a formidable fleet manned by fierce Norse warriors. By early August Harald was ready and on or about 12 August, with the wind in their favour, the Viking long boats rendezvoused off the island of Solund and headed out across the North Sea with a force said to have numbered over 7,000 men. He collected support from the Shetland Islands, joined Tostig and his remaining Flemish mercenaries, either in Scotland or at the mouth of the River Tyne, and sailed down the east coast of Northumbria.[46]

Harald and Tostig entered the Humber and the Ouse, disembarked on about 16 September at Ricall and advanced towards York, the great capital of the north. York closed its gates to the invaders and waited to be relieved. A combined force raised by the northern English earls marched from York to meet the invaders and the opposing armies clashed just two miles outside York on 20 September at Gate Fulford, which is now a suburb of the city. Here the English were soundly beaten after a prolonged struggle and the two earls, Edwin of Mercia and Morcar of Northumbria, made peace with Hardrada.[47]

York opened its gates to the Scandinavians and the Yorkshire men agreed to provision Hardrada's men and to accept his sovereignty. The Vikings withdrew to Stamford Bridge over the River Derwent on the borders of the North and East Ridings, to await hostages with part of their forces, the remainder returning to their ships at Ricall.

King Harold, as soon as he learnt of Hardrada's arrival, sent a summons for the men of the *fyrd* to reassemble, just days after they had been released from their long summer vigil. Having gathered as many of his men as he could muster he started for the north at some point between the 18th and the 20th of September. The English army marched 190 miles from London to York in just four days. This was a considerable achievement but it must not be assumed, as many have, that the journey was made on foot. The Anglo-Saxons, from Alfred the Great to the Duke of Wellington, have excelled as infantry and Harold's army was no different. But the men that accompanied Harold were the *housecarls* and men of rank.[48]

These were elite troops, not foot sloggers, and they would have ridden not walked to York. Traditionally the Anglo-Saxons fought on foot with the horse being seen merely as a means of transportation and it was therefore on horseback that Harold and many of his men travelled from London to York.[49] This implies that those lesser members of the *fyrd* who did not possess horses would have remained at their homes, though it may well be the case that they were following Harold as fast as their legs could carry them.

Harold reached Tadcaster, less than ten miles from York, on 24 September. There he rested overnight and early the following morning – believed to be around 0600 hours – he marched through York to Stamford Bridge (a distance of sixteen miles) and fell upon the unsuspecting Vikings.[50]

Considering the distance which the English had to travel, they cannot have reached Stamford Bridge until late morning at the earliest. Their advance would not have been visible to the Vikings in the valley of the Derwent until they crested the ridge a mile to the west of Stamford Bridge at the village of Gate Heemsley. Apparently Hardrada summoned Tostig and asked him who all these people could be, never suspecting that King Harold could possibly have marched all the way from London so quickly. Tostig replied that it might be a hostile force, although it was also possible that they were Northumbrians coming to pay homage to the victor of the Battle of Gate Fulford. From this we can see that Hardrada was so confident in his military prowess and so certain that he had crushed the northerners that he did not bother posting any guards or lookouts. So it was, as Snorri Sturluson later wrote, "the closer the army came, the greater it grew, and their glittering weapons sparkled like a field of broken ice." It was only then that Hardrada realised that he was looking at the English army bearing down upon him. Tostig said that they should retreat back to Ricall. Hardrada rejected this as being unworthy of a Viking warrior. They would stand and fight.[51]

When the English first appeared at Gate Helmsley the Norwegians were scattered along both banks of the Derwent. The invaders had been taken completely by surprise and many of the Norsemen had been caught without their shields and armour. Nevertheless, those on the west bank were told to hold the bridge and delay the English advance whilst the main army on the east bank formed up to give battle.

Facing overwhelming numbers the Vikings held the bridge. The English attacked and overcame the defenders of the bridge. It is said that one particular giant of a man held the bridge single-handed, felling all his attackers with swings from his battleaxe. He was only defeated when he was stabbed from below by a man who was floated down the river under the bridge with a spear.

The English were now able to cross the bridge and it seems they were allowed to form up without interference from the Norwegians, who had sent messengers back to Ricall to call up the rest of the invading force. Hardrada's and Tostig's men formed their shield wall on rising ground in a succession of hedged pastures, known today as Battle Flats, some 300 yards from the river. It is said the Norwegians pinned one of their flanks on the river and stretched their line so that their weaker flank rested on a dyke and could not be "rounded".[52]

Just after 1500 hours the battle began. Saxons and Vikings stood toe to toe and swung their battle axes and swords in mortal conflict. Outnumbered, lacking armour and weapons, the Norwegian shield wall was pierced. Tostig was killed and Hardrada himself was shot through his windpipe by an arrow.

Just as victory was assured the rest of the Viking army, fully armed and armoured, appeared on the scene from Ricall. The Norwegians immediately delivered a ferocious charge which almost broke the English. The fighting continued until nightfall and both sides lost many men, but finally the invaders were pushed back to their longboats after suffering terrible losses. It is said that the Norsemen sailed to England in 300 ships yet they needed only twenty-five of those ships to take the survivors back to Norway.[53]

Harold had earned a remarkable victory against an enemy force probably larger than the one that William had assembled in Normandy. It was not often that an English army defeated a Norwegian horde but the invaders were so decisively beaten that never again would the Vikings threaten the shores of England. If its memory had not been overshadowed by the events that followed, the Battle of Stamford Bridge would have been regarded as the greatest victory ever achieved by the English Saxons.

The booty that the Vikings had stolen was considerable and this was seized by the victorious English army. It would be expected that this plunder would be shared out amongst the victors but on this occasion Harold did not distribute the booty. This, it is said, was because Harold knew that he might still have to face William, if not immediately then at some point in the future. The treasure might prove vital in helping to maintain his army in the field over an extended period, or for paying mercenaries.[54]

Harold marched back to York. After the battle the English would have had to bury the dead and remove everything of value from the battlefield. How long this took and exactly when Harold returned to York is not known. Some time must have been spent recuperating and celebrating the astonishing victory. Time would also be needed to take care of the wounded and to repair broken equipment. It was whilst Harold was at York, or shortly after he had set off back on the road to London, he learnt the terrible news that he had feared all summer – William of Normandy had landed in Sussex.[55]

Chapter 4

The Opening Moves

"The reconstruction of medieval battles is largely a matter of reasoned conjecture. Or one can say, 'It's anyone's guess.'"

Lieutenant Colonel Alfred Bourne, Foreword to
Charles Lemmon, *The Field of Hastings*

Two days after the defeat of Hardrada and Tostig, on Wednesday 27 September, the wind in the Channel changed. William ordered embarkation to begin immediately, which was completed by the late evening. At nightfall the ships left St Valéry harbour (which was in the territory of Count Guy of Ponthieu) and assembled outside the estuary of the Somme before setting off for the coast of England.[1]

William's ship, the *Mora*, led the way, with a lantern slung from its mast head for the others to follow. But in the darkness the heavily laden ships of the invasion fleet fell far behind, and when dawn broke William found himself all alone in mid-Channel. This was the most dangerous moment of the expedition for William and he had to wait anxiously for the rest of the fleet to join him.[2]

Fortunately for the duke the English ships were now laid up for the winter and the rest of his fleet soon joined him, the principal part of which made landfall at around 09:00 that morning in what is now called Norman's Bay, Pevensey. They then had to wait a further two hours for the tide before they could start to disembark.[3] In reality the Norman ships, given as 696 but certainly many hundreds, could never had arrived at Pevensey at one go and one account states that the disembarkation took place at intervals along the shore.[4] We know that some ships grounded at Romney, far to the east, so that such a large fleet must inevitably have been scattered along the coast. Nevertheless, to have transported such a large force of cavalry across the Channel was a magnificent, in fact unprecedented, achievement and just two vessels were lost on the voyage – one of which carried William's soothsayer who failed to foresee his own demise.[5] The soothsayer would probably have soon been unemployed anyway as he had told William that he would take the English throne without a fight![6]

No medieval commander had previously dared attempt such an operation. But the mounted troops were the flower of the Norman army and William had to take them with him if he was to have any chance of success. In the end, it would be these men that would tip the scales of victory in favour of the invaders.

In the eleventh century Pevensey was on the coast, a narrow peninsula jutting out into the sea, with to the east a large inland lagoon (which is now the Pevensey Levels) which extended from the South Downs on the west to Hastings in the east. Here the Norman fleet was able to anchor safely until the tide fell and the flat-bottomed boats dried out. It is believed that there was also a network of docks there used by the Saxon fleet and William was able to land 3,000 battle-ready troops in a single day. Eventually all the Norman ships concentrated there.[7]

William must have expected his landing to be opposed by at least some of the locals and his disembarkation was conducted in true military fashion, as Robert Wace explained just 100 years later: "The archers were the first to land, each with his bow bent and his quiver full of arrows slung at his side. All were shaven and shorn, and all clad in short garments, ready to attack, to shoot, to wheel about and skirmish. All stood well equipped, and of good courage for the fight; and they scoured the whole shore, but found not an armed man there. The knights landed next, "all armed, with their hauberks on, their shields slung at their necks and their helmets laced."[8]

Yet it is said that there was no opposition to the Norman landing as all the available English warriors had marched north with their king. William's timing could not have been better.[9]

If Harold's forces had still been gathered in the south William might never have been able to establish a beach head on the Sussex coast. But William's arrival at Pevensey whilst the coast was undefended might have owed more to cunning than coincidence. Apart from the fact that he had probably been informed of the disbanding of the *fyrd*, is also possible that William had colluded with Tostig and Harald for both invading forces to attack England at the same time. Thierry Leprévost and Georges Bernage believe that since the spring of 1066 William and Hardrada had an agreement that while the Vikings created a diversion in northern England the Normans would land in the south. They would divide the spoils in the same way – the north for Norway, the south for Normandy.[10]

The idea that William used Tostig and Hardrada to his advantage is an interesting one. Most authorities accept William of Poitiers' statement that William was delayed for four weeks at Dives due to "contrary" winds and another two weeks at St Valéry. Contrary means opposite in nature which therefore indicates northerly or easterly winds. As we have already noted the prevailing winds in the Channel are from the south-west, which would have suited William admirably. Continuous northerly winds in the Channel throughout the summer are positively unknown. William must have been waiting for the right moment to launch his invasion and possibly that moment was when he heard that the Vikings had landed in Yorkshire.[11]

Whilst his men erected a wooden castle within the walls of Pevensey Roman fort, the duke rode out with an escort of just twenty-five men, including William fitzOsbern, one of his key military advisors, and undertook a reconnaissance of the area. He would have found that the country around Pevensey was one of uninhabited salt marshes cut up with tidal inlets. A Roman road which travelled westwards to Lewes and London provided the sole communication inland.[12] This made it ideal for defence, which is why the place had been chosen by the Romans, but it was entirely unsuitable as a base from which to launch an offensive. Not only would his army have experienced considerable problems crossing such difficult terrain, it also offered little in the way of sustenance for his troops.

William therefore had no choice but to move. Nearby was Hastings, which suited William's requirements far better. It was a significant port in those days and here he could live off the land, or more accurately the people. Furthermore, a main road ran north to London which could carry his army into the heart of Harold's kingdom.

It seems that William transferred his army, or at least the mounted element, by land to Hastings rather than endure the difficulty and danger of re-embarking and disembarking the horses again. The ships were sailed (or rowed) round to join William at Hastings.

The route to Hastings, today forming part of the 1066 Country Walk, was through Boreham Street, Brownbread Street, Catsfield and what is now Battle, turning south at the foot of Caldbec Hill and down to the coast to the western side of Hastings. It is assumed that it was at Hastings that William was made aware of the result of the Battle of Stamford Bridge and that he knew that it would be Harold not Harald he would have to fight if he were to gain the throne.[13]

William then established his new operational base at Hastings, once again erecting a wooden castle, possibly within the embankments of the old ninth-century *burh*. It is believed that the Normans brought three prefabricated castles with them. They were made from oak and chestnut with prepared fitting parts and could be quickly assembled as required, being held together by wooden pegs that had been taken across the Channel in barrels.[14] It is said that they could be assembled in various ways to make best use of the configuration of a site for defence.[15] Though such a structure would not have great value in defending an army of many thousands, it might prove invaluable for covering an enforced embarkation in the event of a defeat at the hands of the English.[16]

With his castle or castles built, it seems that William was then content to wait for Harold to march against him. William had thrown down the gauntlet by landing in England and it was up to Harold to pick it up and accept the challenge. In purely practical terms this had the advantage of keeping his lines of communication with his fleet as short as possible and of permitting an easy retreat to his ships if circumstances made this a necessity.[17]

The Hastings peninsula, fifty miles square, made an excellent short-term base where William could find provisions for his army and to where reinforcements from Normandy could be received. It was also a difficult place for Harold's army to attack, as to the west was the Bulverhythe lagoon and to the east the marshy valleys of the Brede and the Rother curved round northwards towards the great Andresweald forest which was cut by boggy streams.[18] According to J.A. Williamson there was no better place along the whole southern coastline for William's purpose.[19]

Whilst William was establishing his army in Sussex, the English king had rushed back to London. According to Master Wace, Harold was informed about William's arrival by a Sussex "chevalier" who had watched the landing and had ridden up to York to warn the king.[20] Exactly when this occurred is not known. General Fuller suggests that Harold received the news on Sunday, 1 October and from that has deduced that he set off from York the following day.[21] Professor Douglas considers that Harold may already have been on his way back to London when he was informed of the Norman landing.[22]

Histories always remark upon the speed of Harold's march from York to London but, if he was already on the move by the time he received the news of William's arrival on 1 October, the fact that he reached London on 6 October is not so surprising. Along with his *housecarls* he would have ridden day and night with relays of horses which would have enabled him to cover forty miles a day. This, though, does mean that Harold spent no more than a couple of days recuperating from the fighting at Stamford Bridge before setting off for his capital.

As Harold hastened back to London with his younger brother Leofwyne he most likely sent messengers ahead to his other brother Gyrth to muster as many men as possible, though the news of the appearance of the Normans would have spread rapidly and the *fyrdsmen* of Wessex would already be sharpening their swords. Those members of the *fyrd* from the southern counties would not have been told to march upon London to join Harold, they would have been instructed to gather at the pre-arranged assembly point, which was at the Hoar Apple Tree. This is commonly agreed was on Caldbec Hill some eight or nine miles north of Hastings.

Harold had a desperate need to make up for the losses he had incurred at Stamford Bridge and we can imagine his men making stops all the way through Mercia and the south central shires to spread the astonishing news of Harold's great victory and impressing upon thegns and peasants alike the need for fighting men to preserve the kingdom from yet another invader. The likely picture, then, wrote Edwin Tetlow, "is of Harold and his bodyguard riding pell mell for London along unkept Roman roads, by forest tracks, and through clusters of farms and homesteads. Other *housecarls* ride more slowly after them, stopping to propagandize and recruit. The foot soldiers, recruits, camp followers and others follow at whatever speed they can manage."[23] Harold also sent for help directly to Earls Edwin and Morcar but it does not seem that any of these men reached Harold in time to be part of his army that marched to meet the Normans in Sussex.[24]

Instead of going directly to London, Harold stopped off at Waltham Abbey to contemplate and to consider his next move. We can only guess at his state of mind at this time. After his overwhelming victory against the Vikings did he consider himself invincible or, after two weeks of marching and fighting, was the news of the Franco-Norman invasion a crushing blow to Harold's belief in his right to the throne?

We have no idea how many of the infantry that had followed Harold up to York were able to reach London in time to join him in his advance into Sussex. It has been estimated that the foot soldiers would have been capable of marching twenty miles a day, which means that the English infantry may have arrived at York too late to take part in the battle at Stamford Bridge and, upon reaching York, were informed that they would have to turn round immediately and march back the way they had come! It is far from impossible that considerable numbers of Englishmen spent the two most crucial weeks in the history of the Anglo-Saxon nation marching up and down the country without striking a blow in its defence.

But if they had marched consistently at twenty miles a day, having left York on 1 October, they would have reached London on 10 October.[25] Later armies, for which we have more definite proof, travelled at a much slower pace over such long distances, and it is unlikely that the footsloggers could have achieved such a feat. According to Stephen Morillo it was "hopelessly beyond the capacity of any eleventh-century infantry". It seems then that a large part of Harold's army might well have still been tramping into London long after he had left the capital to confront the Normans.[26]

Whilst Harold attended to administrative affairs and waited impatiently for his troops to file into London, he sent a monk to William (whose real purpose was no doubt to spy out the Norman camp) emphasising Edward's death-bed wish that Harold should succeed him. "King Harold commands you," the emissary supposedly told the duke. "The Kingdom is mine by right, granted by my Lord, the King, by a deathbed grant. Withdraw from this land with your forces, otherwise I shall break friendship and all agreements made with you in Normandy and place all responsibility for that on you!" William responded in a similar fashion, sending back one of his own monks (Hugh Margot from Fécamp) and inviting Harold to settle the matter through litigation. If Harold was unwilling to have the case examined in law, William offered to meet Harold in single combat.[27]

Some have doubted whether or not such an exchange of messages would have been possible. For most of the fortnight between William setting up his base at Hastings and his violent meeting with Harold on Caldbec Hill, the antagonists were hundreds of miles apart. In Harold's case he was almost constantly on the move during this time.[28]

The narrator of the *Carmen de Hastingae Proelio* tells us that the English hoped to take the Normans by surprise as they had the Vikings a few days earlier.[29] If indeed there had been an exchange of emissaries (which Harriet Wood states was a perfectly normal proceeding in such a situation) then any suggestion that William might be surprised by Harold is utterly implausible. Both sides would be on high alert. William would be ready and waiting, and Harold, who knew Sussex well and who had been expecting the Normans to appear all summer, would have his strategy well thought out. His knowledge of the area to the north of Hastings was also considerable, as the parishes of Crowhurst and Whatlington formed part of his personal estates before he had become Earl of Wessex.

As soon as practically possible, Harold set off for Sussex with whatever force he had at his disposal, having ordered his fleet out to sea to block the invaders' line of retreat back across the Channel. Historians have queried Harold's seemingly hasty rush to confront William when a number of other strategies offered themselves. He could have simply waited for William to come to him.

William could not remain at Hastings indefinitely. At some point he would have to take the gamble and move upon London. The usual reason given for Harold's rapid march into Sussex is that his ancestral homeland was being ravished by the invaders. This is clearly portrayed in the Tapestry, which shows a house being set on fire by the invaders from which a woman and child flee in panic. William of Poitiers also notes that Harold "was hastening his march all the more because he had heard that the lands near the Norman camp were being laid to waste." William could be certain that Harold would respond quickly to the news that his land and his people were being brutally treated, for contemporary notions of honour demanded immediate retaliation, understood McLynn, "or the entire notion of lordship would fail".[30]

Tetlow contemptuously dismisses this view. Harold moved rapidly into Sussex with the aim of blocking the invaders' route to London until William was forced to abandon his expedition in the fogs and damps of an English winter or until Harold had amassed the strength to overwhelm the invaders from the land whilst their rear was assailed by an English fleet. "One looks vainly for an alternative explanation of Harold's moves and tactics," Tetlow insists. "It simply will not suffice to argue that he careered down the length of England and hurled himself against William simply because his heart was bleeding for the sufferings of the comparatively few people overrun by William in the [Hastings] peninsula."[31]

Huon Mallalieu also points out that, along with such places as Ashburnham, Bexhill, Crowhurst and Wilting, at least two of the villages the Normans destroyed, Guestling and Icklesham, were in the manor belonging to the Norman Abbey of Fécamp.[32]

Harold may also have been worried that the longer he waited the more chance there was of William receiving reinforcements from across the Channel.[33] It has also been said that Harold moved quickly because he wanted to keep the Normans penned in the Hastings peninsula. The area had had to support the *fyrd* all summer and had also suffered from Tostig's raid earlier in the year. Food stocks must have been low and the Normans would soon need to move, and this would mean even more villages being devastated. If Harold did travel to Normandy in 1064 as is thought, he would have seen at first hand William's way of conducting warfare. The duke would lay waste to the land until his enemy acceded to his demands. Clearly, then, there were a number of compelling reasons why Harold chose to move quickly down to Sussex.[34]

In addition Freeman thought that William's challenge of trial by combat "insulted and mocked" Harold as it was "the most stinging that had ever been spoken to a crowned king upon his throne." William had got under Harold's skin.[35]

Though Harold had sound strategic, and possibly emotional, reasons for his rapid advance towards the south coast, the most prudent policy open to Harold was for him to find a defensive position near to London and allow his troops a few more days to recuperate. When the Normans finally marched upon London they would find the entire English army rested and ready for battle, supported by the population of the nation's capital.

It is said that his brother Gyrth offered to lead the army against William, leaving Harold in London. Gyrth supposedly gave three good reasons for this. Firstly, Harold was exhausted after Stamford Bridge and his rapid march down from York. Secondly, if Harold lost and was killed in battle, the kingdom was lost, but if Gyrth was killed Harold could still raise another army and fight on. The third reason is one of a sound strategic nature, as David Howarth explains – whilst Gyrth faced William at Hastings, Harold should empty the whole of the countryside behind him, block the roads, burn the villages and destroy the food. So, even if Gyrth was beaten, William's army would starve in the wasted countryside as winter closed in and would be forced either to move upon London, where the rest of the English forces would be waiting, or return to their ships.[36]

There was also the doubtful circumstance of the oath sworn by Harold when he was with William in Normandy in 1064. Gyrth had not made any kind of promise to William and so he could confront the invaders with a clear conscience.

There is no question that from a military viewpoint Harold made the wrong decision when he rejected Gyrth's advice and insisted in going south himself and going without delay. Even Florence of Worcester wrote that if Harold had waited for all his forces to join him he could have mustered three times as many fighting men. This may have included his corps of archers as there were few English bowmen at the Battle of Hastings.[37] Whether or not the northern earls were also marching south is not known. Realistically it is hard to imagine that Harold expected Edwin and Morcar to fight on the south coast. They had, after all, spent the whole of 1066 from Easter onwards guarding the shores of the Midlands and the north while Harold watched the south. They had also suffered terribly at Gate Fulford. It has also been said by Frank Stenton that the loyalty of Mercia and Northumbria was at best doubtful and delay on Harold's part might have enabled Edwin and Morcar to "come over effectively to William's side." Emma Mason agrees that Harold's haste to confront William was to prevent him "from doing a secret deal" with the two northern earls.[38]

Yet the Normans had invaded Harold's land, they had trespassed upon his territory. This was an insult that had to be avenged. Possibly even more significant was that Harold's right to be king of England was being challenged. In reality this left him with no choice but to face William in person as soon as he could.[39]

It is universally accepted that Harold confronted William with less troops than might have been expected, but his hasty march to Caldbec Hill may not have been the reason. R. Allen Brown, after having taken into consideration the words of William of Malmesbury, believes that many men deserted Harold's cause after he failed to distribute the loot taken from the Vikings. (Harold clearly intended to keep the money for official purposes, since he placed it in the care of Archbishop Ealdred.)[40] He says that Harold took with him to Sussex mainly stipendiary troops and a few from the provinces. In William of Malmesbury's opinion the reason why Harold was defeated at the Battle of Hastings was not because of the prowess of the Normans but because the English "were few in number".[41]

Whilst it may be the case that Harold refused to distribute the spoils from Stamford Bridge, there are other reasons why Harold's force was not as large as it might have been. Even if the preparation for the summonses to the *fyrd* had been taken in hand at York as soon as Harold received news of the Norman landing late on 1 October, it would have taken at least a day to complete and despatch them. This left little more than a week for the riders to reach their destinations all around the kingdom and, once contacted, for the *fyrdsmen* to make their way to join Harold in London before he set off for Sussex. It would have been simply impossible for the ordinary thegns from the furthest regions to reach Harold in time.[42]

It is believed that Harold left London on Wednesday, 11 October, though Howarth states that it was not until the morning of the 12th, to march the fifty-eight miles to the designated place on Caldbec Hill where his army would concentrate.[43] With just the troops that had gathered in the capital and men of the London *fyrd* – possibly as few as 5,000 men – Harold crossed the Thames and rode down through the Weald. The English army could have travelled along one of two routes. The first of these was via the Lewes Way, turning off at Maresfield and marching through Netherfield – a distance of sixty-one miles from London. Alternatively, and this seems to have been the one Harold selected, it could have followed Watling Street as far as Rochester, from where an old Roman road ran south, via Cripps Corner, to Sedlescombe. Here it was necessary to cross the River Brede, so called because of its breadth. At this point the river was some 200 yards wide in 1066 and travellers had to take a ferry to reach the other side.

Harold, it would seem, decided that a ferry crossing was impractical for his army and he turned towards the south-west along a narrow, ancient trackway that ran along a wooded ridge to a point where the Brede could be forded. From there the track would have carried the marching men to the assembly point on the High Weald.[44] That this was the most likely route is supported by the fact that in 1876 over 1,000 coins of Edward the Confessor, in the remains of a box, were found close to the Roman road, just behind the site of the old village hall at Sedlescombe. It has always been supposed that this was part of Harold's army pay chest.[45]

The Sussex and Kent *fyrd* were told to join Harold's force at a well-known point on the Wealden Hills where the districts, or Hundreds, of Baldslow, Ninfield and Hailesaltede met – the place of the Hoar (grey) Apple Tree on Caldbec Hill. The use of the word hoar or hoary probably indicated that the tree was covered with lichen, signifying that it grew in the open and was old and gnarled. Peter Marren thinks that it was likely to have been a large crab-apple tree.[46]

This place had been thoughtfully selected by Harold as it stood on the intersection of the two above routes to London. William could not march upon the capital without crossing Caldbec Hill and to this place most of the fighting men of Wessex and beyond must have made their way to do battle for their king.[47]

Arriving at the concentration point late on the 13th, Harold placed his banner on the summit of Caldbec Hill to mark the position of his command post. Harold appears to have had two banners, the Wessex dragon banner (also called the Wyvern) which is shown on the Bayeux Tapestry and his own personal banner, that of the Fighting Man.[48]

It was said by Wace that the English had erected some kind of defensive wall and this is normally interpreted as being the famous Saxon shield-wall. This view has been challenged, particularly by Freeman, who considered that it might have been a palisade. If the English met on Caldbec Hill they would not have all arrived there at exactly the same time.

The *fyrd,* composed of men from all around the southern shires, must inevitably have reached Caldbec Hill over the course of a day or two. With the enemy only a march away, the erection of a defensive palisade whilst they waited for Harold and the rest of the men to appear would be an entirely sensible thing to do and, as Emma Mason points out, this would require minimal technology and the raw materials were readily at hand.[49]

Peter Rex agrees; the English, he states, knowing that they were about to face cavalry, might well have positioned hurdles and branches in their front and possibly even planted spears in the ground angled forwards.[50] It must also be remembered that in Anglo–Saxon times the usual method of building ordinary houses was by driving large stakes into the ground and then filling up the gaps with wattle and daub, so this would be a quite natural thing for them to do.[51] The Normans themselves had done almost exactly the same as soon as they had landed by erecting their castles at Pevensey and Hastings. So the concept of a palisade should not be dismissed too readily.

With few exceptions, historians state that at some moment in time, usually given as on the morning of the 14th, the English army left Caldbec Hill to take up a defensive position on Battle Hill. We consider this to be entirely implausible and amongst the many reasons why such a move can be discounted (all of which will be explored in due course) is that if the English had built a palisade around their high, commanding position, to abandon it in the presence of the enemy to take up an altogether inferior position is utterly illogical.

Part of this particular discussion is the question raised by Jim Bradbury: why did Harold need an assembly point? As Bradbury explains, the usual assumption is that this was necessary to allow Harold to "sort out" his army. In other words this was to organise his troops into some kind of battle order. The collection of men that formed Harold's army ranged from heavily armed *housecarls* to locals carrying little more than farm implements. Whether it was Harold's intention to stand and fight or to deliver a stunning attack, he would need time to organise his force. To quote Bradbury, "In the [i.e. this] situation, it again is possible but seems unlikely that he then advanced further towards William [to Battle Hill] and was halted again. If we are right and this was a broader assembly point, it would be a place where Harold would be forced to delay; troops which are assembling do not arrive and place themselves neatly within minutes. We know that William was informed of Harold's movements, the likelihood is that he caught him at the assembly place."[52]

This, to some extent, is supported by the *Anglo-Saxon Chronicle*, which states that the battle commenced before all the English troops had arrived at the assembly point, and by Florence of Worcester, who said that half Harold's army had not arrived by 0900 hours on the morning of the 14th, the day of the great battle. The traditional view that Harold left his assembly point to march with his men down to Battle Hill makes even less sense if he was still waiting for a large part of his army to join him.

This may, in fact, be the reason we have been looking for to explain Harold's rapid move down to Sussex. He may not have expected to fight William quite so soon. The duke had landed more than two weeks ago but he had not left the coast indeed Harold may have been told about the castles that William had built, which further indicated that the duke had no desire to move inland from his fortified base. This could only mean that either William wanted Harold to come to him at Hastings or that he was frightened of moving far from his ships.[53]

In considering this Peter Poyntz Wright suggests that William, upon hearing of the English army's concentration on Caldbec Hill late on Friday night, realised that he had a chance of catching Harold by surprise, if he could march upon the king before the concentration of his army was complete.[54] To accomplish this it would require preparations and briefings late into the night. First light would have been at 0523 hours, an hour before sunrise, depending on the cloud cover, and William could have been on the road by 0600 hours.

If the Normans were on the move at dawn then we can be certain that at least part of the English army would also have been awake by that time. In medieval times daily life began with the sunrise and those that were not too tired would have risen with the sun. If it was Harold's intention to attack the Normans, the English would have been up and in a battle-ready state early, but we know that he was not ready for action when the Normans appeared on the skyline to the south. The distance between Caldbec Hill and Battle Hill is barely a mile. Hastings is seven miles. If Harold planned to fight his battle on Battle Hill, how could he possibly be taken by surprise when he only had to move one mile when the Normans had to march seven times that distance? Equally, if Harold was planning on attacking the Normans at Hastings, how come he had only marched one mile by the time the leading units of the enemy's forces had travelled all the way from the coast?

We know that Harold had set off from Tadcaster at first light to surprise the Vikings. If he intended to attack the Normans and drive them into the sea Harold would have been halfway to Hastings when he encountered the invaders. As Bradbury observes, if the English had been on the march southwards or had taken up a new position in advance of their overnight assembly point they would have been in no more disarray than the Normans, who were also advancing from their assembly point. If the English were expecting to meet the invaders they would have been in battle array and fully prepared for fighting. The repeated references to Harold having been taken by surprise can only mean that he was caught unprepared by the Normans at his assembly point.[55]

It is quite clear that the English, having marched all the way from London, would have been drifting into the camp on Caldbec Hill throughout the course of the night. They would be in no condition to fight a battle until they had had a good few hours' sleep.[56] Harold cannot possibly have planned on attacking William with his army in such an exhausted state. According to Brigadier Barclay, the purpose of strategy, as applied to medieval warfare, "was to bring the largest possible force to the appropriate battle field in the best fighting condition."[57]

Harold, an experienced commander, would have endeavoured to do this and clearly was not expecting to fight on the morning of the 14th with the tired and incomplete force gathered on Caldbec Hill. This explains why it was said that Harold was taken by surprise, because indeed he was as he had no intention of committing them to battle until his men had rested and the remainder of his troops had arrived. It is quite possible that some of the more recent arrivals were still sound asleep when the Normans came into view on the crest of Telham Hill.[58]

As it happens Harold had chosen a wonderful assembly point for his army because this was without doubt the best place to concentrate his forces. It was the most easily defended position in the area and it was one that blocked William's route from the coast. If William came to attack him before his army was fully formed, fine, he had a perfect spot to fight a defensive battle. If William remained at Hastings then when Harold had amassed all his forces he would march upon the invaders and throw them back into the sea. Equally, his position effectively blockaded William within the confines of the Hastings area and he could happily wait there until William was forced to come to him and fight Harold on the ground of his own choosing.[59]

There are conflicting views on the situation of Harold's army on the eve of the battle. The traditional view presented by the Norman writers is that the English spent the night in drunken revelry: "... the English as we have heard passed the night without sleep, in drinking and singing," claimed Wace. "All the night they ate and drank, and never lay down on their beds. They might be seen carousing, gambolling and dancing and singing."[60] Whilst this is not untypical of the English/British army throughout history, and may well have been the case on the evening of Friday, 13 October 1066, this description was written simply to portray the English as being unholy by comparison with the Normans, who spent their evening in prayer. God, the chroniclers wanted to show, was on William's side. In all probability most of the English would have been too exhausted from their long march to do anything other than fall to the ground and sleep. But, as Freeman wrote, "if our men sang some of the old battle-songs, we shall not think the worse of them."[61]

The true significance of these words, however, is that at least some part of the English army had arrived at the rendezvous point during, or throughout, the day and were already in possession of Caldbec Hill. The Normans were now little more than eight miles away and would be certain to have seen the English arriving.

It is to be expected that the English and the Normans would have maintained the sharpest lookout. Whilst it is usually stated that the opposing armies first spied each other as the Normans reached Telham Hill on the morning of the 14th, this is obviously nonsense. Firstly, and most obviously, why would the entire Norman army be marching up the London road if it was unaware of the English presence? Secondly, William of Jumièges tells us that William in "taking precautions in case of night attack, ordered his army to stand to arms from dusk to dawn." We can be absolutely certain that William knew of the English army gathering upon Caldbec Hill during the daytime on the 13th.[62]

In the case of the English, they were fighting on home turf. The Normans had been pillaging the area for almost two weeks and would have made few friends. Harold, therefore, would have been very well informed by the locals of exactly, and every, move the invaders made. How then are we to interpret Harold's well-documented lack of preparedness on the morning of the 14th?

David Howarth completely dismisses this: "Harold himself was encamped that night in the middle of his mass of men, alone with his doubt. It seems to me perfectly clear that he was not surprised by William's attack ... and he expected to fight the next day."[63]

Rupert Furneaux uses Wace to further reinforce this view, "the English, fearing night attack, kept guard all night, and that at break of day Harold and his brother Gyrth stole out of the camp, mounted their horses, and went, unaccompanied by any guard, to reconnoitre the Norman camp. They examined the ground between the two armies and looked down from a hill upon the Norman host. They saw a great many huts, made of branches of trees, tents, well-equipped pavilions and banners. They heard horses neighing and beheld the glitter of armour."[64] Harold, Wace asserts, was shocked at seeing such a large army, and especially the obviously great number of horses which indicated William had been able to transport a large force of cavalry across the Channel. Harold had not expected this. Infantry he could deal with, as he had many times before. But heavily armed knights were an entirely different proposition. Mace then claims that having seen the size and composition of the Norman army Harold considered withdrawing back to London. It is certainly possible that Harold did undertake a reconnaissance of the Norman encampment and that he realised he might have been a little too hasty in rushing off to confront William.

Edwin Tetlow holds a different view: "The circumstances proclaim the certainty that neither they [the English] nor Harold had any thought of launching themselves against William within a matter of hours. They were really in no condition to do so. They had just arrived in the area. They were expecting more men to join them during the next two or three days, not in a few hours. Their enemy was nowhere near them; he was several miles away and dispersed about the peninsula [or so they thought]. They needed time to establish themselves firmly along the ridge and perhaps to build some obstacles and fortifications to protect them from a sudden attack. They were manning the ridge, then, as a blocking force. A prudent and seasoned general, Harold was placing them there as soon as possible because he wished to make sure that William's troops did not sneak out of the peninsula while the only exit was still open ... Why on earth should he provoke battle before he was ready?"[65]

To conclude this discussion, let us examine what we now know. It is generally accepted that the English army concentrated on Caldbec Hill throughout the course of Friday, 13 October, with many men still arriving at the English camp the following morning. William had shown no sign of leaving his fortified position at Hastings, and Harold did not expect the Normans to attack him. Yet, as he waited for the rest of his troops to reach him, William seized the initiative and marched upon the English whilst they were still unprepared. Harold had indeed been taken by surprise.[66]

* * *

We know that the Normans set off from Hastings at first light on the 14th to face the English army. "Without losing a moment," says Poitiers, "the duke ordered all those in camp to arm themselves, although that day a large section of his troops had gone off foraging." This statement contradicts itself. It implies that the Normans were unaware of the English presence until that morning yet we know that could not be the case. It also suggests that the foragers went off on their search for food whilst it was still dark, which makes little sense.[67]

What is probably meant by this is that the Normans were spread all around the Hastings peninsula searching for food. The area around Hastings itself would have soon been stripped of all supplies and the Normans would have had to travel ever farther afield to find food. Many might well have been some considerable distance from Hastings on the 13th when riders galloped up to tell them that the English were massing on Caldbec Hill and that they should prepare themselves for battle and join the rest of the army at first light the next day.

"They would all converge from their billets upon the London-Hastings track, forming an eventual crocodile procession two to three miles long," wrote Tetlow, "archers and other infantrymen trudging along stolidly; high-born knights walking alongside their horses, across whose backs lay the chain mail the warriors would don later; small wooden carts with crudely-made wheels rasping and creaking as they rolled along with their burden of arms and stores; sergeants and other outriders rallying laggards and enforcing some kind of order in the procession."[68] According to Poitiers, William organised his troops for the march. "In the first line William put infantry, armed with bows and crossbows, in the second line he placed more infantry, better armed and in hauberks, finally came squadrons of cavalry, with William in the centre with the stronger force."

The *Chronicle of Battle Abbey* states that the Normans halted their march at Hedgland (or Hechelande) to put on their armour. This is entirely understandable. They would not have wished to march all the way from Hastings in their heavy chain mail. Hedgland, which means heathland, has been identified as Telham Hill, the summit of which is Blackhorse Hill. This is the highest point along the road from Hastings and once they had climbed to the top the most arduous part of the march would have been over. Here also William took the reins of his charger, apparently a stallion given to him by King Alfonso of Spain. It was said that when William first put on his hauberk it was back-to-front. The superstitious men around him saw this as a bad omen, but William shrugged the incident off with a joke saying that it was a sign that as he had changed round his armour so he would soon change his dukedom for a kingdom![69]

The English, no doubt still sleeping off the effects of the previous night's drinking or recovering from their long march might well have had a terrible shock when the Normans appeared on the hill opposite. It was now evident to Harold that he could not catch the Normans unprepared as he had the Vikings, but at least he was in possession of an excellent defensive position, one which would negate the advantages the Norman cavalry would otherwise have had against the English infantry. His men formed up on Caldbec Hill, "and all packed densely together on foot," wrote John of Worcester.

The opposing forces, it is thought, were evenly matched, with the number of troops on each side numbering something in the region of between 7,000 and 10,000 men. Such estimates are based on the number of men that could have stood on top of Battle Hill. Standing shoulder to shoulder, one thousand men would have stretched from end to end across the ridge. The same applies to Caldbec Hill. The width of Caldbec Hill along the 300–foot contour is similar to the 225–foot summit of Battle Hill, thus we can accept the generally agreed numbers without argument. "Many military experts have worked it out," commented David Howarth, "and they do not differ much."[70] The average of their findings is that William had around three thousand horsemen, one thousand archers and three or four thousand infantry. This is discussed in detail in a later chapter.

Harold it is thought had slightly more and in which case they would have been stood eight men deep. No consensus has emerged regarding the distribution of Harold's *housecarls*. Some have it that they were distributed along the length of the front rank, others that they were concentrated in the centre leaving the weaker *fyrd* on the wings, and there are those who believe they were interspersed amongst the *fyrdmen*.[71]

According to the *Carmen de Hastingae Proelio*, Harold "strengthened both his wings with noble men."[72] The *fyrd* would be gathered in their shire groupings under their sheriffs and within each group the men from their separate hundreds stood together commanded by their Hundredman. Finally, there were the Danes who had volunteered to fight with Harold. We are led to believe that there were considerable numbers of these and it seems that they were given a flank to defend, possibly the left-hand flank of the English position.[73]

There is also the often-stated view that the men of Kent occupied their customary position in the front line. Traditionally the Kentish warriors held the position of honour and were always the first onto the battlefield and the last to leave. According to Peter Rex, behind them were the men of Wiltshire, Devon and Cornwall whilst the Londoners formed round the Wyvern standard in the centre. The Church also provided a number of units of the army amongst which were the men of Peterborough Abbey and the fighting monks of New Minster, Winchester.[74]

William drew his army up at the foot of the hill entirely unmolested by the English. This seems quite extraordinary as this was the time when the Normans were at their most vulnerable. It has been suggested that this was due to some kind of noble protocol whereby nobody attacked until the battle had been formally opened with fanfares and flourishes. But all's fair in love and war and if Harold could have gained an advantage by attacking the enemy as he formed up he would have done so, just as he seemingly did at Stamford Bridge. So we should look for a more pragmatic reason and this must surely be because of the nature of the ground. Not only did Caldbec Hill present very great advantages for the defenders, which they would be reluctant to leave, but the distance from their positions on the hill down to the lower levels where the Normans would have been forming up would have been too great. Whilst the English, running down the long slopes, would have been able to wreak havoc amongst the lightly armed Norman archers and the Norman infantry as they filed onto the open ground at the foot of Caldbec Hill, the Norman knights would have soon been upon the English with devastating consequences.[75]

So the English stood their ground and waited for the Normans to form up in battle array. Then to the "awesome baying" of trumpets the most momentous event in English history began.

Chapter 5

Men at Arms

"The tactics of a battle are conditioned, broadly speaking, by the ground where it is fought."

Young and Adair, *From Hastings to Culloden*

In order to fully appreciate how and why the battle was fought on Caldbec Hill, it is helpful to have a basic understanding of the nature of medieval warfare and the weapons both sides were able to employ. Tactics of every era are to a large extent moulded by the weaponry available and tactics in turn considerably influence strategic decisions.[1]

Since the second decade of the eleventh century the English kings, as well as the powerful earls, had possessed a body of paid, armed retainers. These were the household troops, some of whom may have lived in or around the king's or earl's palace, though by the time of Edward it is said that many lived on their own estates. Originally instituted by King Canute, these household troops, the *housecarls*, were men of high standing and who formed a disciplined military brotherhood. Totally dedicated to their lord, they would fight and if necessary die for him. They were well-trained and well-armed professional soldiers and, as Frank Stenton wrote, wherever they lived the *housecarls* were always ready for war.[2]

Such household soldiers cannot have been very great in number. It is known that Canute retained just forty ships of warriors who it is thought by some formed his *housecarls*.[3] In the comparatively peaceful reign of Edward this number declined to fourteen in 1050 and five in 1051. The *Anglo-Saxon Chronicle* allows us to calculate how many men there were in each ship from the amount they were paid and this works out at around sixty. Thus Canute commanded around 2,500 *housecarls* and Edward only a few hundred.[4] This is confirmed by the events of 1051 when Earl Godwin was able to compel Edward to restore his lands with a show of force. If Edward had a large body of troops at hand this could never have happened.

It is usually stated that at the Battle of Hastings Harold commanded a large body of *housecarls* (inevitably figures vary). These soldiers would have included the household troops of Harold's brothers Leofwin and Gyrth as well as his own personal bodyguard, but numbers of such elite troops cannot have increased greatly in the intervening years.

The bulk of the Anglo-Saxon army was composed of the *fyrd*. The *fyrd* is often portrayed as being composed of poorly armed peasants but this is highly inaccurate. The majority of the *fyrd* were men who were obliged to undertake military service (*fyrdfaereld*) in return for the land that they held. These men were thanes or thegns (*ðegns*).

In the early days of the Anglo-Saxon settlement of England, a thegn was a companion of a warlord and therefore a member of the warrior class. The word thegn simply meaning "one who serves". It is possible that originally thegns and *housecarls* were in fact one and the same and the apparent decrease in *housecarls* was occasioned by the increase in those who had settled on their own lands and were now considered to be thegns. This is the view of Nicholas Hooper who, in "debunking" the *housecarls*, states that "the *housecarls* did not form a distinctive element in Old English military organisation ... Those who held land must have been indistinguishable from their neighbours."[5]

The probable reason why the *housecarls* are usually considered to be different from the thegns is that by the mid-eleventh century the term thegn was used to denote anyone of the landed class. Many thegns were "king's thegns" whose lord was the king himself, as opposed to one of the richer thegns or earls. The former held their lands from the king and could lose them (and sometimes their lives) if they did not answer the king's summons. Often they held land in many parts of the country. Their service to the king was performed on a rota basis and they would accompany him everywhere, both as bodyguards and lesser officials. They were still primarily warriors but they also had other, local, duties to carry out; these were the "common burdens" of service in the *fyrd*, overseeing fortress maintenance (*burhbot*) and bridge repairs (*brycegeweorc*).

In reading many of the twentieth-century publications on the Battle of Hastings one could be forgiven for believing that the composition of the *fyrd* was reasonably well-understood. Yet, as with most aspects of the Battle of Hastings, there is little common agreement amongst academics about the nature of the military obligation required of the thegns. It has been stated that at this period of time someone who held five hides of land or more was considered a thegn, though by the time of the Conquest this general rule no longer applied. This is because the title had become hereditary, resulting in the splitting of land between descendents. A man could be called a thegn even if his land holding only amounted to a couple of hides. (A hide meant a household and may originally have defined the area of land needed to support a family.)

There is some agreement, nevertheless, that from every five hides a thegn, or thegns, had to supply one armed soldier. Often, therefore, not only would the thegn present himself for military service but he would also be accompanied by one or more of his tenants, suitably armed, depending on the size of his holding. This five-hide rule seems to have been confirmed by J.H. Round's examination of the Domesday Book, which reveals that the hides in virtually every hidated shire [one organised into Hundreds] were organised in fives or multiples of five.[6]

The smaller landholders, who did not rank as thegns, were expected to provide a proportion of a man-at-arms relevant to the number of hides held. These landowners were called *ceorls* (also referred to as villeins). These were freemen who were farmers and independent landed householders who formed the mainstay of the Anglo-Saxon kingdom, based as it was on a rural economy. They were expected to bear arms and be considered "*fyrd* worthy". The thegns and the *ceorls* were likely to be well-armed and armoured.

This, however, seems to be a slight oversimplification. In reality an individual's obligation to take up arms could be, as Richard Abels explains, territorial, tenural or personal. "The obligation to serve the king in arms rested in the eleventh century upon a dual foundation of land-tenure and lordship," Abels wrote in 1996. "On the one hand, those who possessed land either in book-right or as a royal loan were obliged to render the military service due from their holdings, just as they owed the payment of geld [money]. On the other hand, those thegns who were personally commended to the king were expected to attend him on campaign if so ordered."[7]

To help us understand how the pre-Conquest system worked, Richard Abels has investigated a number of documents. One of these is the Domesday survey of Worcestershire. The compilers of the Domesday Book were primarily concerned with the wealth and resources of William's new kingdom and their interest in military affairs is purely fiscally driven. "When a king goes against the enemy, should anyone summoned by his edict remain, if he is a man so free that he has soke and sake [i.e. has jurisdiction over his own estates and those persons living within them] and can go with his land to whomever he wishes, he is in the king's mercy for all of his land. But if the free man of some other lord leads another man to the host in his place, he pays 40s to his lord who received the summons. But if nobody goes at all in his place, he shall pay his lord 40s; but his lord shall pay the entire amount to the king."[8]

Abels' investigation confirms that there were two distinct types of *fyrdmen*. The first were the great landholders, all of whom held privileged tenures and rights over other freemen. These were the men to whom the king addressed his summons if military service was required. Below these were the lesser *fyrdmen* drawn from the lower rungs of free society. The right of every freeman to bear arms was a Germanic tradition which was continued by the Anglo-Saxons, as was the tradition that it was dishonourable to leave the battlefield on which your lord had been slain. This would have a considerable bearing on events at the battle on Saturday, 14 October.[9]

All the above formed what was known as the "Select" *fyrd*. Beyond that was the "Great" *fyrd* which effectively means every able-bodied freeman. In the case of national emergency the king could call on every freeman to fight with him to defend his homeland.[10]

The hierarchy of the English army was therefore as follows: the king with his great earls as his divisional commanders, the elite professional *housecarls* and thegns, and then the *fyrd* composed of well-armed lesser thegns and wealthier *ceorls* and with them the poorly armed and equipped lesser *ceorls*. Then, if the country was threatened with invasion, the Great *fyrd* would be summoned and every man in the area would turn out, armed with whatever weapons he could lay his hands on.

Gravett states that if the king ordered every freeman to take up arms beyond the normal five-hides-per-man stipulation (i.e. he called out the Great *fyrd*) this was limited to a single day's service (from sunrise to sunset) at their own expense. If asked to serve for longer than this (and if they served so far afield that they could not return to their homes by sunset) they had the right to payment by the king. These men, not being of the warrior classes, were likely to be protected with little more than leather jerkins and armed with agricultural implements. Wace tells us that at the Battle of Hastings, "The villeins were also called together from the villages, bearing such arms as they found; clubs and great picks, iron forks and stakes."[11]

During times of war the Select *fyrd* could be called out for a period of two months. Each *fyrdman* (one from each five hides, remember) was given four shillings from each hide for his two months' service. In emergencies this could be repeated as many times as necessary. The members of the Select *fyrd* were also expected to serve beyond their shire boundaries if required. It has been estimated that in total the *fyrd* of 1066 had a potential strength of 48,000 men, but that it was unlikely that more than 12,000 could have been assembled at any one time.[12]

Another calculation of the manpower available to the English king in 1066 has been made by Professor Barlow. He estimated that the rate of conscription was about one soldier for every seventy to 100 inhabitants. As the population of England was about a million and a half (a figure derived from the Domesday Survey) we can work out that Harold would have been able to call up an army of between 15,000 and 20,000 men. This, though, is from the whole country and it is self-evident that many of those fighting men from the farthest reaches of the land could not have reached Caldbec Hill by 14 October.[13]

It is usually said that when the *fyrd* was demobilised on 8 September 1066 it was because they had been out all summer and that the men needed to return to their homes to bring in the harvest. Lieutenant Colonel Lemmon demolishes this reasoning by pointing out that by this date most of the harvest would already have been gathered in (bearing in mind that the true date was eleven days later, i.e.19 September). He says that the reason for the *fyrd*'s disbandment was because the men had performed their two-monthly service, presumably from as early as May when Tostig had raided the south coast, others had replaced them for their two-months in turn, and that by September he had run out of men. There was no national emergency at the time which would have enabled Harold to keep the men under arms as, despite the persistent rumours, the Normans had not appeared.[14]

Professor Frank McLynn dismisses the romantic view that Harold's army was composed of patriotic freemen defending liberal Anglo–Saxon England from the oppression of Norman feudalism. The English were fighting for Harold because the men were so inextricably bound by covenants to their lords they simply could not refuse.[15]

Terry Wise believes that the members of the *fyrd* that fought at the Battle of Hastings were drawn entirely from the Select *fyrd*.[16] Yet the references to some of the English bearing little more than agricultural implements (see below) clearly indicate that elements of the Great *fyrd* must also have been present.[17] These men, no doubt, included those locals who had already suffered at the hands of the marauding Normans over the past couple of weeks.

It is worth, at this point, mentioning the English naval forces for, as we shall see, they formed part of the Select *fyrd*. The English navy of this period comprised three elements. The first of these were the "lithsmen" and their ships. These were mercenaries who were hired to form a small semi-permanent navy. Secondly, there were the ships and men provided as a special obligation by certain coastal towns, and, finally, there was a general territorial obligation to perform sea duty and subscribe to the building of ships. This also stemmed from the days of Scandinavian rule, as the Viking warriors were also the men who pulled the oars of their longboats.

This maritime obligation was not confined to coastal regions. Inland regions paid a tax to the king, known as ship-scot, in place of the coastal regions who supplied the ships and men, this being called the ship-soke. For the latter it seems the five-hide rule again applied, as the five-hide units were combined into larger districts of 300 hides to create a ship-soke. Such a unit would be capable of building a ship, aided by money raised by the ship-scot, and providing the sixty warrior-seamen needed to man a typical ship of the period.

"It would appear, therefore, that the Select *fyrd* and the ship-*fyrd* were one and the same," explained Terry Wise, "expected to serve on land or sea depending on need, and led by the same commander, who was thus both general and admiral." However, there were regional variations. Wise cites Warwick as an example of this. If the Select *fyrd* was called out Warwick was expected to supply ten armed men, but if the *fyrd* was to serve at sea the town sent four boatswains or £4 in lieu.[18]

* * *

There does not seem to be quite the same precise arrangement for the supply of men-at-arms to the ruler of Normandy as existed in England. The major landholders, often members of the ducal family, provided knights from their hereditary estates. This also applied to some of the religious houses. There is no evidence of specific quotas being levied. Christopher Gravett states that the length of service was probably forty days a year. The expedition to England was therefore of an entirely different nature to the usual obligations. In theory, therefore, all the troops taken by William to England were volunteers, but whether or not in practice any individual, great or small, could have refused is another matter. According to Wace, William was able to extract promises from his barons of twice the normal number of men. As with the *housecarls*, some of the Norman knights would have resided at their lord's castle whilst others may have lived on their own estates.[19]

Though the knights were considered the flower of the Norman army, the bulk of William's force consisted of heavily armed infantry and archers. Many of these would simply have been the vassals of the knights, others though were likely to have been mercenaries, tempted to join William by the prospect of winning their fortunes on the field of battle should William prove victorious.

It is said that the Normans knights were the most effective in the whole of "Christendom". The knights performed well in southern Italy in a number of battles during the eleventh century, and at Civitate in 1053 they confronted German knights in the service of Pope Leo IX and routed them. The reason given for this is that the German knights only employed swords whereas the Normans had become proficient in the lance, which gave them a considerable reach advantage. According to Leprévost and Bernage, the Normans also understood how to manoeuvre in formation and how to charge in a compact group.[20]

Tactically, the Norman knights were organised into small units called "*conrois*". These units were built up in multiples of five to arrive at groups of say twenty-five, thirty, thirty-five, and so on. Once formed into a *conrois*, the group would then operate as a single body. This is significant in terms of the Battle of Hastings with regard to the controversial "feigned" retreats, as it shows that if such actions occurred they were most likely to have been done by individual *conrois* or a number of *conrois* acting together rather than the whole Norman army.

William's army included both knights and infantry from beyond the borders of his dukedom. Predominantly they were from the countries bordering

Normandy, from France and Flanders and from further afield, most notably Poitou and Aquitaine.

Before attacking the English army it is said that William organised his force into three divisions. The left wing was composed of Bretons under the command of Alan Fergant, the cousin of the Count of Breton. William himself commanded the Norman division, the largest, in the centre, and the right wing included Flemish and French soldiers under William fitzOsbern and Eustace of Boulogne. Each division was comprised of cavalry, infantry and archers.

As might be expected the opposing forces were clothed and armed in much the same way. The fully armed Norman knight would wear a coat of metal chain-mail. This included a mail hood to protect the head and cheeks of the face, known as the "*healsbeorg*". The word became corrupted to hauberk and came to mean the complete garment.[21] Many of these reached down to or below the knees, with the skirt split front and back to allow the soldier to mount a horse. The hauberks had elbow-length sleeves and some of them extended over the head to form the *healsbeorg*. In the Bayeux Tapestry William and Eustace of Boulogne are shown with mail sleeves reaching to the wrist and mail leggings. It is possible that padded jackets were worn underneath the hauberk to cushion the effects of heavy blows. They also wore conical metal helmets which sometimes included a nasal-guard.

Their weapons included a straight, double-edged long sword and a lance or spear with a plain ash pole around eight feet long, to the tip of which was added a leaf-shaped, or triangular, iron head. The spear could be thrown or used to thrust at the enemy. The long sword, of which many examples still exist, was around thirty-five inches in length and, although it had a sharpened tip, was used more for slashing than thrusting. Some knights may have carried a mace, which was a studded iron club-head on a straight wooden shaft. Kite-shaped wooden shields were also carried. Decorated with elaborate designs, they were usually faced and possibly backed with leather and had an iron boss riveted to the centre. These were usually slightly more than four feet tall.[22]

The Norman heavy infantry also wore hauberks and helmets and were armed with spears and swords. They too carried shields, round as well as kite-shaped.

The archers, who would not expect to have to become embroiled in hand-to-hand combat, wore no armour (though one figure on the Bayeux Tapestry is shown fully clothed in mail complete with helmet). The archers used what was called a "selfbow" with quivers holding twenty-five arrows. Usually five and a half feet to six feet long, it is reckoned that the selfbow had an effective range against an armoured opponent of around 100 yards. It seems that there were also a number of crossbowmen. According to Gravett these weapons were likely to be somewhat more powerful than selfbows.[23]

The English *housecarls*, and those thegns that could afford it, wore a chain coat similar to the hauberk which was called the "byrnie" and they too had conical helmets and shields. Both kite-shaped and round, convex shields were used. The main difference in armament between the Continental knights and the Anglo-Saxon warriors was the battle axe used by the latter in addition to sword and spear. The Bayeux Tapestry shows two types of battle axe. One is a small weapon which could be swung with one hand. The other, the most famous and the most feared, was the much larger broadaxe, or Danish axe, which was introduced into warfare in approximately AD 1000. It had a cutting blade of ten inches or more which was slightly asymmetrical to assist a downward cut. The edge was made from specially hardened steel forged onto the blade. It was mounted on a thick wooden haft some three feet long. Both hands were needed to wield this terrifying weapon.[24]

Charles Lemmon declares that the representation of the *housecarl* uniform on the Bayeux Tapestry is incorrect. The Tapestry shows them dressed in a similar fashion to the Normans but Lemmon says that in reality they wore short, tight-fitting leather doublets without sleeves, and with iron rings sewn on. They had trousers with straps round the bottom and sandals on their feet. Their hair was long and their helmets, with nose-pieces like the Normans, had long leather flaps that fell over their shoulders. Members of the *fyrd*, Lemmon states, were generally clad in leather doublets and caps. Most of them carried small circular shields and their arms consisted of spears, short axes, scythes, slings and clubs with stone heads.[25]

How these respective armies fought now needs to be considered. This also is a subject which has been over-simplified by many commentators. As so much of what followed began with Freeman, it is worth quoting his views. "The mode of fighting of an English army in that age made it absolutely invincible as long as it could hold its ground. But neither the close array of the battle-axe men, nor the swarms of darters and other half-armed irregular levies, were suited to take the offensive against the horsemen who formed the strength of the Norman army. It needed only a development of the usual tactics of the shield wall to turn the battle as far as might be into the likeness of a siege."[26]

Like most of what Freeman wrote, this limitation of imagination on the part of the English has been repeated many times. Therefore Sir Charles Oman, writing in 1924, declared that the English were capable of little more than "the stationary tactics of a phalanx of axemen".[27] In recent times, however, a number of individuals have explored this subject more thoroughly and a more sophisticated and flexible method of fighting has emerged.

Firstly, we can dismiss the idea that the English were only capable of fighting behind a shield wall. This can be gleaned from John of Worcester, who, in discussing Tostig's raid upon England in May 1066, wrote that Harold "ordered a large fleet and a force of cavalry to be assembled."[28] Peter Rex informs us that in previous battles the English made use of a manoeuvre involving counter-attacks. This was, he has written, undertaken by columns of attack in which two such columns of men might converge to form a blunt wedge which would drive back opposing infantrymen. He further states that such a manoeuvre was attempted by the Earls Edwin and Morcar at Gate Fulford, though in this instance it was unsuccessful.[29] Also, at the Battle of Stamford Bridge, the English attacked the Vikings and the Icelandic chronicler Snorri Sturluson wrote in his great, if flawed, work *Heimskringla* that they "made a cavalry charge on the Norwegians, who met it without flinching." Sturluson explained that the English were unable to force home their charge because they were met by a volley of arrows. So they rode round the Norwegian position and "when they had broken the shield line the English rode upon them from all sides and threw spears and shot at them." Harald Hardrada, after all, was killed by an arrow to the throat.[30]

These extracts demonstrate not only that the English fought on horseback and used archers, they also show that the English were capable of manoeuvre and effective offensive action. This is confirmed by the fact that the Battle of Hastings was probably lost because the English repeatedly broke ranks, and therefore broke up the shield wall, and charged the Normans. Such action shows that they were naturally inclined to take the offensive whenever the opportunity arose.[31]

Equally, as Warren Hollister has pointed out, the English shield wall was not just a defensive formation. At the Battle of Sherston in 1016, the entire English force advanced as a body towards the enemy, moving slowly so as not to break formation.

Emma Mason has also written that the English had recently taken an increasing interest in cavalry and that the war-horse played an important role in late Anglo-Saxon England. The reason why the English fought on foot, it has then been argued, was because of the wearied condition of the English horses after the efforts of the previous couple of weeks. Mason states that the terrain also played a part in Harold's decision to leave the horses in the rear and fight on foot. This would be entirely appropriate if the English were massed upon Caldbec Hill.[32]

We must also take into consideration the words of William of Poitiers. As we will read later, this chronicler had previously fought alongside William and was accustomed to medieval warfare, and he described the Battle of Hastings as "a battle of a new type: one side vigorously attacking: the other resisting as if rooted to the ground."[33] Clearly, then, such tactics were unusual and were forced onto Harold by the circumstances he found himself in.

Part of this discussion is the explanation by Lieutenant Colonel Lemmon of the true purpose of shields: "A constantly recurring phrase in descriptions of the battle is 'the shield wall'; and some writers have asserted that the shields were 'locked'. The suggestion conveyed is that shields could, in some manner, confer on a battle line additional power to resist shock. This is a misconception of the functions of a shield, which were to stop or deflect arrows and other missiles, and to protect the soldier from sword-cuts in hand to hand combat. Against charging horsemen and their lances, shields would be useless."[34] If this is the case, then the remarkable length of the Battle of Hastings, which lasted for possibly six hours, can only be explained because the severity of the slope up which the Normans had to attack did not allow their horsemen to achieve the speed of a full gallop.

We have also read that at the Battle of Stamford Bridge the Norwegians "stretched" their shield wall to ensure that it rested on physical obstacles, which meant that it could not be outflanked. This most likely resulted in the shield wall being less deep than would normally be expected. Being caught without armour and with inferior numbers, the Vikings therefore stood little chance of holding off the English until the rest of their army arrived. But it serves to confirm Frank McLynn's view that "Viking warfare was marked with an obsession with vulnerable flanks."[35]It is also said that this manifested itself at Stamford Bridge by the Vikings pulling their wings right round to form a circle, presumably as their numbers diminished and they could not hold their original line without exposing their flanks.

The English had been fighting the Vikings for generations and their method of fighting was modelled on those tactics which had proven so highly effective for the Norsemen. The *housecarls* that formed the backbone of the English Army were of Viking origin and their principal weapon was the "Danish" axe. We may easily assume, therefore, that the English fought the way that the Vikings did and that the fear of exposing a vulnerable flank was a prominent factor taken into consideration whenever the English chose to adopt a defensive position. Furthermore, a shield "wall" would have possessed little integrity if an enemy could simply sweep round its flank; indeed in such circumstances a shield wall would have been a pointless formation. The significance of this will become apparent when we study the battlefield of Hastings more closely.

Finally there is a view expounded by Matthew Bennett, which may offer an explanation as to why Harold had no mounted troops at the battle. We know that his accession to the throne was not immediately accepted by the northern earls and we are also led to believe that Harold had lost a lot of goodwill amongst his men by withholding the plunder from the Battle of Stamford Bridge. He had good reason, therefore, to doubt the loyalty of his men. "It may be that Harold feared mounted troops might leave the battlefield by their own volition. This was a common problem for medieval generals and one which they solved by insisting that their best troops dismounted to fight alongside their leader."[36]

Whatever Harold's reasoning or practice may have been, on that autumn morning when he knew that the Normans were marching towards him with possibly thousands of cavalry there was only one tactic available to him (at least in the opening engagement) and that was the defensive shield wall, of which there were two types. The first type, which is clearly shown in the Bayeux Tapestry, is that of the men standing sideways, which enabled them to interlock their shields in one continuous wall. This is what would have been adopted at the outbreak of hostilities at the Battle of Hastings when the Norman archers unleashed a fusillade of arrows up the hill. Then when the archers ceased firing and the Norman infantry marched up towards the English line, the front rank of *housecarls* would have stuck their shields into the ground in front of them so that both hands were free to wield their battle axes. This was the second type of shield wall which may have looked like, and to some extent may have acted like, a barricade, which may have given rise to the belief that the English had formed a palisade around their position on Caldbec Hill. This, though, contradicts what is shown on the Bayeux Tapestry where it appears that the axemen and the spearmen worked in teams, with the spearmen providing the cover of their shields for the unprotected axemen.[37]

One thing that does seem beyond doubt about the English army is that Harold fought at Hastings with comparatively few archers. It used to be thought that this was because the English did not consider the bow to be a weapon of war. Other than Snorri Sturluson describing the killing of Harald Hardrada by an arrow at Stamford Bridge, there is no other written record of the English using the bow in warfare. It is known that the English nobility were keen huntsmen and that they were skilled archers, but in battle it was the sword, the spear or the battle axe that they would have carried. However, wrote Terry Wise, "it is highly unlikely that an army of such high quality as the Anglo-Saxon one, and with such recent battle experience against the Scandinavians – who had a strong tradition of the use of a war bow – would have completely ignored the bow as a weapon of war. Nor should the strong Scandinavian influence in England itself be forgotten, and it is more than likely that the men from the Danelaw also had a strong tradition of the use of the bow in war. It can be safely assumed that archers were a recognised part of the normal English army of the 11th century."[38]

Why then does the Bayeux Tapestry show so few English archers? The reason for this has been well covered by historians and the usual explanation is that when Harold marched north to face Harald Hardrada he took with him a very large army, one which included the southern Select *fyrd* and its body of archers. This seems to be supported by the fact that when William landed at Pevensey there was no one defending the coast. Harold rushed back to London on hearing of William's landing and, as we have seen, it is likely that the archers were still on the road when he set off again for Sussex.

This also would have meant that many of the well-armed *fyrd* infantry who had travelled from the south to confront the Vikings did not reach Caldbec Hill in time for the battle, and explains the description of the *fyrd* given by William of Poitiers as being armed with agricultural implements and sling stones – their better-equipped country folk were still on the march.[39]

Another explanation for the comparative dearth of English archers at the Battle of Hastings has been provided by Terry Wise: "The real crux of the matter is that the English army still used archers in the Scandinavian manner – relatively few in number and useful only in the opening phase of a battle, battles normally lasting between two and three hours at the most." Having explained that, Wise then sensibly advises us that it "is not really worth entering into the controversy, as there is no evidence on which to base any accurate numerical estimate." We will leave this subject there.[40]

The impression we get from reading the accounts of the Battle of Hastings is that the Norman army was well-organised and that William was an experienced commander. It may come as a surprise, therefore, to learn that until that day in October 1066 the duke had never led an army in a large-scale pitched battle.[41]

The only comparable encounter was the battle of Val-ès-Dunes in 1047. In this instance, however, the young William fought alongside King Henry I of France and it is normally given that it was Henry who was in overall command. Though this was considered to have been a decisive victory in favour of the duke and the king, William was rarely at peace with his neighbours in the following years, not the least of reasons for this being that King Henry turned against him. William often found himself on the defensive but his general policy was to avoid the uncertain consequences of a pitched battle where posiible.[42] Nevertheless, our interest here lies in the manner in which William conducted his offensive campaigns and for this we have the evidence of William of Poitiers. William clashed repeatedly with Geoffrey Martel of Maine and in his first operations against this neighbouring country he targeted the castle of Domfront, which was then close to the Norman border. The place was too strong to be attacked and so William blockaded Domfront in the hope of starving the garrison into surrender. What is interesting here is that this was no passive siege by William, as William of Poitiers makes clear, "he went out riding by day and night, or lay hidden under cover, to see whether attacks could be launched against those who were attempting to bring in supplies, or carrying messages, or trying to ambush his foragers."[43]

In 1063 Duke William again invaded Maine with his objective being the capture of its capital city of Le Mans. Rather than attempting a direct assault upon the city, William adopted a different approach: "This then was his chosen method of conquest," wrote William of Poitiers. "He sowed terror in the land by his frequent and lengthy invasions; he devastated vineyards, fields and estates; he seized neighbouring strong-points and where advisable put garrisons in them; in short he incessantly inflicted innumerable calamities upon the land."[44] By the beginning of 1064 Maine was in Norman hands.

Even though William was engaged in warfare almost continually from 1048 until 1065, he managed to avoid becoming embroiled in a pitched battle. It has been calculated that William went to war on a minimum of thirteen occasions during this time, and was largely successful, yet was only involved in small-scale engagements. This was because systematic ravaging of the countryside, not fighting great battles, was the principal strategy of attack and included in that was another vital consideration, and one of the main reasons why men went to war – plunder. The soldiers did not need to be told to go plundering.

This, though, was not just William's way of conducting warfare, it was more the western European way, as similar tactics were used by King Henry when he in turn invaded Normandy. Thus, says John Gillingham, "the usual method, indeed the very aim of warfare was to live at the enemy's expense and by doing so compel him to give in to your demands."[45]

As we have read, this is exactly how William behaved when he arrived in Sussex. He landed close to Harold's ancestral home, built castles to establish a secure base, and then he set about pillaging the countryside. As he had brought with him a very powerful force he knew that Harold would have to agree to his terms and allow him to take the English crown, or face him in battle. No doubt William prayed for the former. Whilst waiting on the turn of events he would have been highly active, watching all the roads for any sign of movement by the English. Harold knew William quite well and he must have known that he had little chance of catching him by surprise.

Harold, of course, had a wonderful opportunity to observe William's fighting methods when he turned up on the Continent in 1064, which one person has called his "involuntary reconnaissance patrol". During Harold's enforced stay with William he participated in the duke's invasion of Brittany. What the Earl of Wessex witnessed was, as Gillingham explained, a very typical example of William at war – a campaign in which the duke seems to have been prudently content with a small gain and in which logistical considerations were of primary consideration. "In 1064 there was no sign of an aggressive, battle-seeking, risk-taking strategy."[46]

When Harold learnt that William had landed on the Sussex coast and had shown no inclination to move further inland Harold no doubt drew the conclusion that this was typical of the duke and that he would have little difficulty throwing him back into the Channel. This may be yet another reason why Harold rushed down to Sussex before all his forces had been assembled. He had seen William avoid battle where possible and he possibly thought that merely by placing himself astride the road to London and therefore restricting William's ability to forage for food he would compel the invader to withdraw back to his ships.

With regards to medieval warfare in general, Frank Stenton informs us that "feudal battles were determined more by the event of a simple collision of large masses of men than by their manoeuvres when in the field: the skill of a great feudal captain lay chiefly in his ability to choose his ground so as to give his side the preliminary advantage in the shock of battle."[47] To this Brigadier Barclay added that the skill of a medieval general was not just to choose an advantageous ground but also to bring the greatest number of men in the best fighting condition to that ground.[48] Harold certainly found an advantageous position to resist the initial assault of the Normans but it was William that brought his men to the battle in far better condition.

The last thing to examine is the number of troops who fought on both sides on 14 October 1066. In investigating this, Colonel Lemmon took an average of eleven writers to arrive at a figure of 8,800 Saxons and 8,000 Normans, the latter being divided into 1,000 archers, 3,000 cavalry and 4,000 infantry.[49]

Robert Furneaux went much further and engaged in some complex mathematics derived from the images shown on the Tapestry. He presents his calculations by working forward from the size and composition of the Norman invasion fleet. The images on the Tapestry, he observed, show that the horse transports varied in size. For example one ship carries nine horses and eight men whilst another shows four horses and five men. Having examined the written evidence from the list of ships provided for the Norman fleet he deduced that the average ratio of knights to horses ranges between 1.5 and 3.5. He calculated that the average number of men per horse-transport was eight plus horses.

Furneaux then looks at the infantry transports. The largest vessel depicted on the Tapestry has thirteen shields slung along its bulwark. Presuming that there were the same number of cross-benches, upon each of which was seated four armed men, this gives a figure of fifty-two men. This though was the largest. He therefore reduces the average of the infantry to twenty-five per ship. The result of such deductions is that altogether William took with him a little more than 10,500 men. From this figure we can deduct sailors and camp-followers so that the actual number of fighting men would be around 7,500.

Wace related that his father, who was alive in 1066, said the Normans had 700 less four ships, i.e. 696.[50] Orderic Vitalis gives a figure of 782. Captain James of the Royal Engineers, using Wace's ship numbers, believed that 400 of the ships each carried nine men with horses, and that the remaining 296 carried twenty-five dismounted men. This makes a total of around 11,000 men, which would have included the sailors etc. Furneaux concurs with James, saying that of the approximately 700 ships, 400 carried knights with their horses and esquires and the remainder carried an average of twenty-five men.[51]

Poyntz Wright bases his preferred figure – of around 3,000 infantry, 2,000 cavalry and 800 archers, along with 1,000 sailors – on the length of time it took for the Normans to embark on an average-sized Viking ship and conforms to the troop movements of Robert of Gloucester in 1142.[52] He also remarks on another calculation that has been extrapolated from the number of knights that the Normans on their own would be able to put into the field. This figure is about 1,200.[53]

Admirable though such efforts are to establish how many men fought at Hastings, it is an egregious example of just how little we really know about the battle and the lengths that historians will go to in their efforts to create facts out of supposition. This is highlighted by the fact that, according to the military historian Terry Wise, English warships of the period were manned by sixty sailor-warriors. Are we, therefore, to assume that English vessels were generally larger than the Norman ships, or that the numbers that fought at the Battle of Hastings were greater than is now generally accepted? As with so much of the story of the Battle of Hastings we can never really be sure.[54]

The calculations for the number of English troops at the battle are less convoluted. The highly respected General J.F.C. Fuller did the maths: "... if Harold positioned his army in a phalanx of ten ranks deep to allow two feet frontage for each man in the first rank – the shield wall – and three feet footage for those in the nine rear ranks, then on a 600–yard front his total strength would be 6,300 men, and if in twelve ranks, 7,500."[55]

As it is generally agreed that Harold had at least as many men as William, even possibly more, then the latter depth of twelve ranks would be the one to pick. But to suggest such precision of rank and file is unrealistic amongst soldiers unpractised in such large-scale engagements and, as we know neither the absolute nor the relative size of the two armies, to discuss the size and deployment of the English army is, as M.K. Lawson has put it, "to discuss a range of possibilities."[56]

It is certainly all guess work, but putting it altogether it does give us the approximate number of around 7,500 to 8,000 men aside, which Brown, *The Normans and the Norman Conquest*, regards as "more or less rational guesswork". Most authorities agree on this, but other figures have been suggested. Numbers may seem academic, but they are relevant to our supposition that the battle was most probably fought on Caldbec Hill. Professor Oman, *A History of the Art of War*, gives a bizarre total of 25,000 English and 10,000–12,000 French knights and 15,000–20,000 infantry.[57] How so many men could have squeezed themselves onto either Battle Hill or Caldbec Hill is a complete mystery.

Wilhelm Spatz, *Der Schlacht von Hastings*, gave us 7,000 a side; E.M. Stenton, *Anglo-Saxon England*, went for 7,000 English with slightly fewer French, as did D.C. Douglas in *William the Conqueror*. A.H. Burne, *The Battlefields of England*, opted for 9,000 each at the start of the battle with Harold receiving reinforcements during the course of the day. Barlow, *The Godwins*, says that there were 10,000 actual fighting men out of a French invasion force of twice that number. Peter Rex says that 10,000–12,000 or even more is considered more likely, referring to the Chronicle of St Maixent, which provides the "startlingly reasonable number," for a medieval chronicler, of 14,000.[58] Freeman, most sensibly of all, says of the numbers involved "it is hopeless to do more than guess."[59]

The same figures apply to Caldbec Hill as they do to Battle Hill and indeed provide further support for our contention that the battle was fought on Caldbec Hill. The former is a little narrower than the latter, which would enable the English army to encircle the heights and provide all-round defence. This is certainly how the English defence was organised according to one authority, who says that the English stood in a "closely gathered ring." It would also explain why John of Worcester said that the hill was already over-full and some Englishmen drifted away as there was no space for them.[60]

Wace also gives us some indication of the composition of Harold's army. He says that the "barons of the country whom he had summoned" gathered upon Caldbec Hill. "Those of London had come at once and those of Kent, of Hertford and of Essex, Surrey and Sussex, of St Edmund and Suffolk, of Norwich and Norfolk and Canterbury and Standford, Bedford and Huntingdon, Nottingham, Salisbury and Dorset, from Bath and Somerset. Many too came from about Gloucester and Winchester." In other words from all the Home counties, the south and west of England. Wace tells us that there were none from north of the Humber because of the casualties they had suffered at the hands of Hardrada and Tostig.[61]

It seems possible that Harold received some outside support, though little is known about this, other than the following: "Also the land of the Danes who were allied with them [the English] had sent substantial reinforcements." This means that King Sweyn broke his promise to William that he would remain neutral.[62] It is possible, however, that the references to the land of the Danes could well refer to Northumbria, which had long been settled by the Danes.

Just how many of the English troops were *housecarls* is also entirely unknown. Mogens Rud believes it was around 1,000 and, as we have seen, it is unlikely to have been more. Yet, if it was the case that many of the greater thegns were indistinguishable from the *housecarls*, then the number of such troops might have been considerable.[63]

* * *

The reasons why this chapter has been included in our investigation into the site of the Battle of Hastings are manifold but there are three which deserve a special mention. The first of these is to demonstrate that the *fyrd* was not the disorganised rabble it has so often been portrayed as. The full significance of this will be explained in the next chapter, suffice it to say at this point that this casts doubt upon the long-held belief that the most striking topographical feature shown on the Bayeux Tapestry – a steep-sided hill – was held by ill-disciplined *fyrdmen* who had broken ranks and left the main English position.

The second reason is to make clear that the English army was not restricted to fighting purely on the defensive behind its shield wall. This is important because it confirms our belief that Harold had intended to attack the Normans when all his troops had arrived and that he only stood on the defensive against the Normans because he was taken by surprise at the assembly point on Caldbec Hill.

The third is that the English army would not have adopted a defensive position with an exposed flank when they were already in possession of a far more secure position on Caldbec Hill.

Chapter 6

The Battle of the Hoar Apple Tree

"When King Harold was informed of this, he gathered together a great host, and came to oppose him at the grey apple tree."

The Anglo-Saxon Chronicle

The Battle of Hastings, according to the chroniclers, began at the third hour of the day, in other words 0900 hours, which was three hours after daybreak.[1] Providing the weather was not overcast, there would have been some light in the sky by 0530 hours and the Normans would have been up and on the march as soon as practicable.[2] Yet the Normans had some eight or nine miles to travel from Hastings and, whilst the main elements of William's army could well have reached the foot of Caldbec Hill by 0900 hours, the rearmost troops of the long column would still have been trudging along the narrow track that led from the coast. There may have been some early skirmishing which began at this hour as William's army formed up at the foot of the hill, but the first main attack most probably began closer to 1000 hours.

Frank Stenton regarded the distance which the Normans had to travel and the alleged time at which the battle began and remarked: "The march must have been a toilsome business and the rapidity with which it was accomplished is remarkable."[3]

Being a military man, Brigadier Barclay provides a considered view on these early manoeuvres. He states that by modern (he was writing in 1966) marching methods the Norman column would have been about three or four miles long but as it was probable that William knew exactly where the English were deployed he would have moved with his army "closed up or double banked". In this case his force would have extended to half or perhaps one-third of that distance from front to rear, enabling it to be deployed for action comparatively quickly.

Even so, Barclay believes that the Norman deployment could not have been completed before 0930 or even 1000 hours. "I think there is a tendency to underestimate the time it would take William's men to march six or seven miles," he declared, "carry out the necessary reconnaissance, issue orders, shake out the columns and move up to the 'Start Line'." Lieutenant Colonel Lemmon also believes that it would have taken the Normans an hour to form up into battle array. If Barclay's and Lemmon's calculations are correct, it may well be that the battle did not begin until after 1000 hours, far later than the time usually stated.[4]

Professor McLynn believes that the battle may not have begun until as late as 1100 hours. He says that whilst the battle was a more prolonged affair than most medieval battles (usually acknowledged as being *the* longest) historians have made it "absurdly long" by stating that the first serious clashes took place at 0900 hours.[5]

Regardless of when battle was joined, the dominant factor in the ensuing engagement was the height and severity of the slopes upon which the battle was fought. As will be seen it dictated the tactics and stratagems employed by both sides.

The English formed up around the summit of the hill with most likely the *housecarls* and wealthier thegns occupying the front ranks and the lesser-armed *fyrd* behind. The men in the front rank overlapped their shields to form a continuous wall as so graphically depicted on the Bayeux Tapestry. As a number of the sources remark upon the constricted nature of the English position upon where they stood, it is possible that they formed into not just a single shield wall but into multiple ranks of shield walls.[6]

If the English were to fight a defensive battle, as is usually stated, then their tactics would be simple. From behind their shield wall the men, packed into one massed formation, would swing their mighty battle axes and throw their javelins. If the men held their ground (and their nerve) the enemy would be unable to make much impression upon such a body in hand-to-hand combat alone. The only vulnerability such a formation could have would be if its flanks were exposed.

Such tactics did not require a complex command structure. All each man had to do was stand and fight unless directed by Harold to charge the enemy if a suitable opportunity arose. By contrast, William's army, with its large proportion of mounted troops, was an offensive force and needed careful handling. It's three arms, the bowmen, infantry and cavalry had to be organised, disciplined and controlled to be truly effective.

William, therefore, split his army into three divisions – the traditional three "battles". The main division, led by William himself, was entirely Norman and this held the centre. Of the other divisions, one was a combined French and Flemish force (with a small Norman contingent) under Count Eustace of Boulogne on the right flank, and on the left flank was a mixed body of mercenaries from Brittany, Anjou and Maine. This last division was commanded by a Breton called Alan Fergant. Each division was a well-balanced force of infantry and cavalry though the centre division, under William, was possibly twice the size of the other two. This subdividing of his army meant that each one could be more easily handled and, if one division failed to dent the English shield-wall, one of the other two might succeed in doing so. The archers, it seems, were an independent, composite force of men drawn predominantly from Evreux and Louviers.[7]

It is most likely that the battle began with a volley of arrows, and crossbow bolts, from the Norman archers. Orderic states that the first attack was delivered by the infantry; the *Carmen de Hastingae Proelio* has it that it was the Norman archers who opened the battle and that they aimed at the faces of the English: "First the bands of archers attacked and from a distance transfixed bodies with their shafts and the crossbow-men destroyed the shields [of the English] as if by a hail-storm, shattered them by countless blows."[8]

The English had not seen crossbows before and the bolts, or quarrels, terrified them and it is possible that under the barrage from this new weapon some men started to desert before the battle had really begun.[9]

According to Colonel Lemmon, William's battle plan envisaged three phases – "first phase, a shot of arrows, equivalent in those days to artillery preparation; second phase, assault by heavy infantry to effect breaches; third phase, exploitation of the breaches and pursuit by the cavalry."[10]

The Norman archers used a short bow with an effective range of around a hundred yards. It was most likely from this distance that the first volley was fired. The *housecarls*, forming the front ranks of the English army, raised their shields in an interlocking barrier and few arrows would have found their mark at this early stage, many even passing over the heads of the English line. Volley followed volley but the shield wall remained unbroken. With few arrows being returned by the handful of English bowmen, the Normans soon began to run out of missiles.[11] At around 1030 hours, or possibly later if Brigadier Barclay is to be believed, William called off his archers and ordered the main attack.

To the cries of "Dex Aide!" (God help us!") the Normans marched up the severe slope of Caldbec Hill with, allegedly, the papal banner leading the way. "Out!", "Out!", "Out!" was the English war cry as they banged their weapons rhythmically against their shields.

"The English stood ready at their post," wrote Wace, "the Normans still moving on; and when they drew near, the English were to be seen stirring to and fro; men going and coming; troops ranging themselves in order; some with colour rising, others turning pale; some making ready their arms, others raising their shields; the brave man rousing himself to the fight, the crowd trembling at the approaching danger."[12]

Ahead of the Normans rode a man known as Taillefer, or Cleaver of Iron, who had received permission from William to be the man to strike the first blow. Throwing his sword into the air and catching it again, he galloped into the English line. He may have struck the first blow for William, but it cost him his life as one of the *housecarls* stepped out of the line and brought the exuberant Norman down.[13]

The infantry of all three divisions of William's army attacked simultaneously. As they approached to within forty yards of the English line, the defenders "hurled their javelins and weapons of all sorts;" wrote one man, "they dealt savage blows with their axes and with stones hafted on handles."[14] Now came the first hand-to-hand combat of the day. "The English fought confidently with all their strength," declared William of Poitiers, "striving in particular to prevent the attackers from penetrating within their ranks, which indeed were so closely massed together that even the dead had not space in which to fall."[15] The Bayeux Tapestry shows this first assault being received by the English with the shield wall facing both to the left and to the right, which is presumably intended to depict the all-round defence of the English on the hill.

It has been said that this infantry combat may have lasted for an hour or so. It would have taken a while for the first wave of archers to advance up the hill, discharge their missiles and withdraw out of the firing line. Then the Norman infantry would have the laborious task of marching up the hill, trying to retain a cohesive line as they moved across the broken ground before they locked swords with the English.[16] "The shouts both of the Normans and of the barbarians were drowned in the clash of arms and by the cries of the dying," wrote Poitiers, "and for a long time the battle raged with the utmost fury."[17]

With the Norman infantry unable to make an impression upon the English shield wall, William ordered forward his elite body of knights. The Norman cavalry are shown on the Tapestry delivering their charge, slowly at first and then progressively increasing speed until they are at full gallop. This is exactly how cavalry charges are conducted and so would seem to be an accurate representation of events. The reason for the elaborate and extended portrayal of the Norman cavalry charge is because it glorifies the knights, the nobility and high-ranking members of William's army. These important men, the survivors of whom became rich and powerful landowners in conquered England, are shown charging along in panel after panel.

However, there are two problems with this. The first is, as Peter Rex concedes, that there could have been no shock charge by knights riding full tilt with couched lances, as such weapons would have been quite useless in any charge uphill.[18] The second is that the scene on the Tapestry shows the charge being delivered, and received, on flat terrain. A steep hill is shown on the Tapestry but not until a later panel. This has caused historians much trouble. The scene in question shows a steep hill defended by English soldiers. Against the hill the Norman knights throw themselves, many coming to grief, their horses being overthrown. Most historians believe that this scene is misplaced in the Tapestry and actually relates to later events. So we will leave the discussion of this and move on with the narrative and return to it in due course.

The Normans, though many were experienced fighters, had never come across anything like the Anglo-Saxon shield wall nor had they encountered the terrifying battle axe. By all accounts the attackers were horrified at the shocking wounds the axes made both on man and horse.[19]

This first attack was halted and eventually, as Poitiers described, the English "had the advantage of the ground ... Thus they bravely withstood and successfully repulsed those who were engaging them at close quarters."[20] This statement makes it clear that as the attack lost momentum the English got the upper hand and actually pushed the Normans back down the hill and therefore implies some forward movement by the English, and this contradicts the often-stated opinion that the English army was incapable of anything other than a static defence.

We know that the English were capable of effective offensive action, as displayed at Stamford Bridge, and, as Bradbury points out, the English could never have won any battles simply by standing still. The only reason that the Battle of Caldbec Hill was relatively static is because the steepness of the slope gave the English an advantage they would have lost if they had abandoned the high ground – as indeed they later did. But if they saw the enemy retreating, the English were perfectly able to follow up their success.

It may well be the case that the defensive stance taken by the English, which was forced upon them by the sudden arrival of the Normans, was only the initial formation that Harold planned to adopt. From his alleged words in London, it was clear that he was rushing down to Sussex to throw the invaders that had been terrorising his people into the sea. He could not do that simply by adopting a defensive position on the hill. So he may well have formed his men up behind their shield wall to blunt the first Norman assault before launching his own attack.[21]

The English must have moved a considerable distance down the hill and in large numbers because Poitiers wrote that even the Norman spearmen and archers, who were operating at a distance, came under attack and were wounded and "almost the whole of Duke William's battle line fell back." This included the Bretons on William's left and some of his prized cavalry, "panic-stricken by the violence of the [English] assault".[22]

According to Howard, in their haste to escape the axe-wielding warriors the knights rode through their infantry and archers and carried them away with them in their panic. The *Carmen de Hastingae Proelio*, refusing to acknowledge that the Normans could possibly have been driven back by the English, has it that the retreat was feigned but that "the flight which had first been a ruse became enforced by valour", and the Normans fled.[23]

The invaders were close to defeat at this point. The Norman leaders now came to the fore in an attempt to stop the retreat becoming a rout. The Bayeux Tapestry shows Bishop Odo in particular waving his baton to encourage his men to continue the fight. A rumour even ran through the Norman ranks that William had been killed. William is reported to have thrown back his helmet to show his face to his men and, according to William of Poitiers, William rallied his men with these words: "What is this madness which makes you fly, and what way is open for your retreat … You are throwing away victory and lasting glory, rushing into ruin and incurring abiding disgrace. And all for nought since by flight none of you can escape destruction."[24]

Harold might well have won the battle if he had been bolder in his tactics and counter-attacked with his entire force, rather than just a large part of it. David Douglas certainly thought that Harold missed his best chance of victory.[25] Stephen Morillo believes that Harold may well have ordered a counter-attack as William of Poitiers wrote that the duke saw "a great part of the enemy leave their positions, and pursue his troops."[26] The question then becomes, continues Morillo, if Harold did order a general advance, what happened to it?

Morillo, as do others, suggests that the answer to this may lie in the deaths of Earls Gyrth and Leofwine.[27] Exactly at what time during the battle Harold's brothers were killed is yet another of those subjects that has caused historians much anguish.

In the Tapestry the death of the brothers is shown at an early stage, before the first Norman attack is repulsed. Both are shown as being killed by lances. Guy of Amiens certainly places the death of Gyrth at this time. Gyrth seemingly came face-to-face with William. Gyrth threw a javelin at the duke which only managed to strike down his horse. Now on foot, the duke "fought yet better, for he rushed upon the young man like a snarling lion. Hewing him limb from limb …"[28]

If Harold did order his brothers to lead the counter-attack and both were killed in the front of the English army as it advanced, it could well explain why it failed, and why Gyrth came into contact with William. Lieutenant Colonel Lemmon also thought that this was Harold's main counter-attack but believes that it failed because it was delivered too early. Had the counter-attack taken place later in the day, when the Normans were tired and dispirited, it might well have won the day.[29]

On the other hand, the counter-attack may not have been authorised by Harold. He had witnessed first-hand the effectiveness of the Norman cavalry and his cautious approach appeared to be succeeding. Why then should he abandon his defensive position from which the Normans had already been repelled? Harold did not need a victory that day. He was on home ground and could remain there indefinitely.

Peter Rex does not believe that this episode occurred as early in the battle as is usually thought. He argues that it was only after the third or fourth assault that the English, weary of merely standing fast and taking punishment, gave vent to their frustration in a savage counter-attack. The slope up which the

Bretons had to advance, by this somewhat later stage of the battle, Rex writes, "was by now slippery with mud and blood and littered with the shattered bodies of the dead or dying. The air stank with the reek of blood and emptied bowels, resounding with the groans of the wounded." When the English suddenly charged down upon these attackers, the Bretons' nerve broke.[30]

Yet, at whichever point in the fighting this occurred, this was the moment when the battle swung decidedly in favour of the invaders. William not only stopped the rout of his army but he managed to bring them round to counter-attack the English troops that had chased the Normans down the hill. "Taking new courage from his words", they turned on the men "who had pursued them and wiped them out." In the words of the *Carmen de Hastingae Proelio*, "William led his forces with great skill, holding them when they turned in flight, giving them courage, sharing their danger. He was more often heard shouting to them to follow him than ordering them to go ahead of him." In this deadly fighting William had three horses killed under him. Each time he found another mount and continued to fight. William of Poitiers says that on each of these occasions William killed the man who had brought down his horse. In one incident an English "wrestler" wielding an axe, struck the duke "on the head, and beat in his helmet, though without doing much injury."[31]

This was probably the most critical moment of the whole battle, for two complementary reasons. William had not only turned a near-rout into a limited success, it had shown him how the English could be defeated. He must have hoped that the infantry attack would have been able to make a breach in the English line which the cavalry could exploit. When the infantry failed, the cavalry alone were equally unable to penetrate the English shield wall. The heavy war-horses could not gallop up the steep slopes of Caldbec Hill and the splendid charge would have lost much of its momentum. The horsemen, and their horses, faced with the terrifying swings of the *housecarls'* battle axes, had given way and like the infantry had been forced back down the hill.

But William had managed to turn the tables on the pursuing English. This is where the hill shown on the Tapestry comes into the picture. It is said by most historians that the hill was in fact a small hillock which can be found to the south-east of Senlac Hill. As the fleeing Normans turned round upon the English, the latter found themselves in trouble and they gathered on the little hillock where they tried to fight off the Normans. Eventually all of the men on this isolated hillock were killed. This marked the end of the English pursuit. This, though, is a far from satisfactory explanation and consequently many people have sought to embellish the story.

Because the English defending the supposed hillock do not wear armour it has been deduced by many as implying that these men were members of the *fyrd*. This, it is said, explains the rash pursuit by the English which cost them so dear – it was because it was undertaken by the ill-disciplined members of the *fyrd* against Harold's orders. "They could not see the whole line from their position," wrote one historian, "and may have been under the impression that they had already won and that the whole Norman army was in flight." This idea that it was an unauthorised move by a number of the *fyrd* is entirely without foundation yet readers will find it repeated without caveat by writer after writer.[32]

One historian who has questioned this is Lieutenant Colonel Lemmon. "In this episode of the battle one cannot fail to notice the very strange disproportion between the alleged cause and the recorded effect. A supposed undisciplined rush of some Shire-levies is said to have caused disorganization in the whole of the Norman army which their own chroniclers admit was little short of a debacle. There are strong reasons for supposing that the Saxons made a planned counter-attack on the Norman left; and it may even have been Harold's main counterstroke."[33]

Equally, we are led to believe that the English front ranks were filled with *housecarls* and thegns. Are we to suppose then that the *fyrdmen* pushed past the professional and heavily armed men in front of them to run after the Normans? No one would be so stupid. The advance by the English must have been a far more organised affair than is usually thought. It would have been led by the *housecarls* and thegns and would still have retained as much cohesion as the situation and the terrain would allow. This was no wild charge. The English would have moved downhill with their shield wall still largely intact – and they nearly won the day. But on the slightly easier, and more open, lower slopes of Caldbec Hill they no longer had the advantage of the ground. Once William and Odo had rallied their forces, the advantage swung in favour of the Norman knights. Harold's chance of a quick victory had gone.

Judging from what we have learnt about the tactics of medieval battles and the English inclination for attack, it would seem that the English took upon their defensive position merely to resist the initial Norman onslaught, using the ground to their advantage. With the attack halted the English then countered en masse. This was no unauthorised rush by some ill-disciplined members of the *fyrd*, this was a full-scale counter-attack involving a large proportion of the English force.

In the midst of this fighting Harold's brothers were killed, but the entire Norman army tottered on the edge of defeat and William became personally involved in the fighting. The only thing that saved the invaders was the speed and effectiveness of their mounted arm on the more open and gentler lower slopes of Caldbec Hill.

Most medieval battles lasted no more than an hour or two before one of the opposing forces broke off the engagement and retired to the safety of its own strongholds. But there was no avenue of escape for the Normans. With their ships now surrounded by the English fleet, the invaders had to win or they would certainly die. The English dared not break formation to flee because the Norman cavalry could outpace them. They had seen the fearful consequences of such action when their comrades had chased after the Norman knights only to be slaughtered. The Normans had nowhere to run and the English could not run. So the battle continued throughout the afternoon developing into one of the longest medieval battles ever recorded.

Yet the fighting cannot have been continuous. After the English had been driven back up the hill there must have been a long pause whilst William reorganised and reassured his men. During this lull in the fighting, priests and water-carriers moved amongst the dying and the wounded who had been carried to the rear. Rider-less and panicked horses were caught and calmed. It was necessary to replenish the archers' quivers, check weapons and re-sharpen swords.[34]

The nature of the battle now changed. Harold had seen that he could not follow his usual offensive tactics because the Norman knights were too powerful. The only immediate course of action was for the English to hold the high ground and re-establish the shield wall. Harold's losses must have been very severe to force him to adopt such a stance which, as we know from William of Poitiers, developed into a battle of a new type, with one side rooted to the spot and the other side vigorously attacking. If the English army had been severely reduced in number they could not have held Battle Hill for very long against the Normans, as the attackers would have been able to mount the western slope of the heights but the conical nature of Caldbec Hill would have enabled even a much-reduced force to hold their position higher up the hill.

With the shield wall re-established closer to the summit of Caldbec Hill the English position must have still looked formidable but, as William had made clear to his soldiers, retreat was not an option. They had no choice but to fight or die and, although the first attack had failed, Harold's counter-attack had cost the defenders dear. So, with fresh heart, as Wace describes, "the Normans press the assault, and the English defend their post well; they pierce the hauberks, and cleave the shields; receive and return mighty blows. Again some press forwards; others yield, and thus in various ways the struggle proceeds."[35]

As the battle raged, large numbers were killed on both sides to such an extent, Poyntz Wright wrote, that as the dead piled up they caused "much difficulty" to the attacking infantry and cavalry.[36] One of the defenders, with a hundred of his comrades, rushed down upon the struggling attackers: "He wielded a northern hatchet, with a blade a full foot long, and was well armed after his manner, being tall, bold and of noble carriage. In the front of the battle, where the Normans thronged most, he came bounding on, swifter than the stag, many Normans falling before him and his company. He rushed straight upon a Norman who was armed and riding upon a war horse, with his hatchet of steel to cleave his helmet: but the blow miscarried, and the sharp blade glanced down before the saddle-brow, driving through the horse's neck down to the ground, so that both horse and master fell together to the earth." According to Wace, this English warrior was killed by Roger de Montgomery. "And again a fierce mêlée was to be seen, with many a blow of lance and sword; the English still defending themselves, killing the horses and cleaving the shields."[37]

Poitiers says that "gaps began to appear in their [the English] ranks here and there, where the iron weapons of our brave soldiers were having their effect." How long this part of the battle lasted we have no idea and it has not been investigated in much depth by historians, but what happened next has been the subject of intense debate throughout the decades. This is the "feigned" retreat – a planned move to repeat the earlier action which drew some of the English down Caldbec Hill.

It is described by William of Poitiers as follows, "Realising that they could not without severe loss overcome an army massed so strongly together in close formation, the Normans and their allies feigned flight and simulated a retreat, for they recalled that only a short while ago their flight had given them advantage." The English saw the Normans retreating and, believing that victory was within their grasp, "several thousand" of them rushed down the hill after the invaders. Then "suddenly wheeling their horses surrounded them and cut down their pursuers so that not one was left alive."[38]

Many historians have cast doubt on this story, questioning whether or not such a manoeuvre could be organised on such a scale. Lieutenant Colonel Lemmon believes that this tactic was simply not practical. "The impossibility of passing orders to hundreds if not thousands of individuals, all engaged in separate hand–to–hand combats; and of the simultaneous timing of such an operation should be sufficiently apparent." The reason why the chroniclers "made up" this story, he continues, was that "a 'feigned retreat' was the recognised method by which chroniclers concealed the fact that the troops on their own side had run away."[39]

Bradbury, on the other hand, has demonstrated that the tactic of the feigned retreat was "a common ploy" before 1066 and was used by the Normans on several occasions before the battle on the slopes of Caldbec Hill. At the battles of Arques in 1053 and Messina in 1060, Norman knights, including some of those who fought at Hastings, had indeed performed this exact tactic. It was not a new development in warfare and this manoeuvre had been known and practised in Europe by horsemen since Roman times. Bradbury therefore believes that those historians who consider such a tactic was impossible are "flying in the face of the evidence." All the chroniclers mention the feigned retreats and the fact that Poitiers declared that the first retreat was a genuine flight which almost ended in the defeat of the Norman army whereas the subsequent ones were deliberately planned gives his statement a ring of authenticity.

Bradbury also points out that some have doubted the use of the tactic of the feigned retreat because of the risks involved. A body of troops is always at its most vulnerable when it turns its back upon the enemy. We know that the English had throwing spears or javelins and if the Normans, having been in close contact with the English, were to turn and flee, they would expose their backs to these weapons. It would seem, therefore, that such a tactic would be far too dangerous to be attempted. Yet the *Carmen de Hastingae Proelio* offers a solution to this. The writer says that as the Normans fled they used their shields to cover their backs. The long Norman shields had straps which the knights could sling over their shoulders for carrying so it would be a simple matter to sling their shields further round to cover their backs.

Furneaux also dismisses the claim, made by many, that such a complicated stratagem in the heat of battle would have been too risky because panic is infectious and a feigned flight could well have degenerated into a complete rout.[40]

Despite all the ink that has been spilt discussing the feigned retreats, it is possible that this manoeuvre has been entirely misconstrued. The evidence for this comes from the *Chronicle of Battle Abbey* and is revealed in the following passage: "By a pre-concerted scheme the duke feigned a retreat with his army, and Eustace the valiant count of Boulogne, nimbly following the rear of the English who were scattered in the pursuit, rushed upon them with his powerful troops."[41] What we have here is not some complex manoeuvre whereby the retreating troops turn upon some signal to cut down their pursuers, what the chronicler is describing is something far simpler – an ambush. As the Normans retreated, Eustace was waiting with his men to pounce upon the English. Such a move would be easy to organise. One group is instructed merely to turn and gallop away whilst the other group simply waits until the unsuspecting English run into range and then charge.

It is hard to believe that the English would repeat their earlier mistake and this is not depicted in the Bayeux Tapestry. Yet no authority has refuted the story and it is hard to understand how Harold could have been beaten unless large numbers of his troops broke formation. As William of Malmesbury quite correctly wrote, "The English ... formed an impenetrable body, which would have kept them safe that day, if the Normans had not tricked them into opening their ranks by a feigned flight." It is certainly conceivable that the English were so easily duped because the Anglo-Saxons were accustomed to fighting on foot and their traditional enemies, the Vikings, also fought on foot. They had not previously encountered a large and disciplined body of mounted knights such as they faced at Hastings.

This having been said, it probably was impossible for William's polyglot force to operate such a sophisticated move as one body. "How could the order to wheel about and flee have been conveyed to hundreds, perhaps thousands, of men engaged in personal hand-to-hand combats?" asked Furneaux.[42] Indeed it is equally unlikely that all the Norman knights acted together in unison in their attacks upon the English line. It is more probable that they operated in more manageable groups of twenty or thirty at a time, in other words in *conrois*, as detailed in the previous chapter. Their attacks would therefore be of a localised nature – hand-to-hand combat is always a highly personalised business – in which case it would be a similar number of English that would be drawn out of position to chase the men they had been fighting.

We also know from Peter Rex that the English were accustomed to manoeuvring in wedge-shaped columns and, as the "killing zone" in front of the English line was about thirty yards deep (the effective range of a javelin), it is possible that they would have advanced and retreated frequently within that zone. It is not impossible that the English, used only to fighting against other infantry, were caught out of position during such manoeuvres, being taken by surprise by the speed and capability of the Norman knights.[43]

Another simpler and entirely plausible explanation of the feigned retreats has been put forward by Emma Mason. This, she explains, is because of a misunderstanding of the periodic withdrawals and regroupings which inevitably occurred during the long battle. In other words, the various *conrois* would ride up to the English line and prod or slash at the defenders. From time to time, as the battle raged, individual *conrois* or maybe small groups of *conrois* would withdraw to regroup and recoup before returning to the fray.[44]

Terry Wise emphatically believes that the stories of feigned retreats and undisciplined English pursuits "cannot be taken seriously" and he provides a similar, and just as simple, explanation to that given by Ms Mason: "This phase of the battle seems to have consisted entirely of repeated attempts by the cavalry, possibly supported by the infantry and/or dismounted knights, to break the English shield-wall; a continuous ebb-and-flow movement which would have kept the élite in the English front ranks constantly engaged, yet enabled the Normans to take turn and turn about." It could well be then that as the Norman knights withdrew to recover their strength and reform some of the English they had been engaged with chased after them. The knights, quite naturally, would be forced to turn and defend themselves and the English could well have become surrounded and cut down as a result of their impetuosity. The "feigned" retreats may have been nothing more complicated than this.[45] Peter Rex also points out that as the Norman cavalry, unable to deliver a fully fledged charge, reached the English line they would have wheeled their horses to the left or the right. They then "as a natural consequence" would retreat back down the slope.[46]

Such actions can be witnessed each October when the re-enactors entertain the spectators. The horsemen gallop up the easy slopes of Battle Hill to merrily hack away at their friends on the low ridge. After a few minutes they ride back down the hill, rest for awhile, and repeat the process. Fighting is tiring, even with blunted weapons. This seems to be confirmed by Wace, who wrote "the Normans by little and little fled, the English following them." From this we can see that what Wace is describing is not a single event, it is a gradual process, conducted, as he says, little by little.[47]

With this in mind one can picture more vividly the fighting on the hill. Groups of knights would move into contact with the English infantry. They would slash away at each other for a while and then the Normans would fall back down the hill. Occasionally the English would rush after them only for the knights to turn their horses round and cut down the isolated group of infantrymen. This would be repeated from time to time all along the line. This accounts for Poitiers' statement that "gaps began to appear in their [the English] ranks here and there, where the iron weapons of our brave soldiers were having their effect."

The Normans continued to attack the English, with the duke heavily involved in the fighting. Though the Normans were gradually wearing down the English troops, William of Poitiers says that the English line "was still formidable and very difficult to overwhelm."[48] The battle still hung in the balance.

By now it was getting late in the day and William desperately needed a breakthrough. Harold could afford a drawn engagement which could be renewed the following day. Harold could call on more men to join him on Caldbec Hill, indeed as he had rushed so precipitously down from London to face William it is highly likely that there were other men already on their way to join him.

So far, Bradbury says, "the hill had blunted the impact of the cavalry and had made it more difficult for the archers to shoot with effect. The shield-wall manned by heavy infantry, well armed and well disciplined, proved a match for the Norman cavalry as well as their infantry." But now, as the day wore on, the tide began to turn in William's favour.

The gruelling contest had dragged on for hours and as losses mounted the English line shrank bit by bit until there were no longer enough men to occupy the whole of their position on top of the hill. This meant that the Norman knights could mount the summit and would no longer be fighting uphill. At last, from the height of their saddles, they could slash down upon the English warriors. This clearly had a demoralising influence upon the defenders and gave the attackers a tremendous boost. As William of Poitiers says the English were becoming exhausted but as for the Normans, they attacked with increased vigor.[49]

There was good reason for the Normans to be pressing harder against the English line. If Harold remained alive by sundown and his forces intact upon the hill, William was in real trouble. If William retreated through the night to Hastings the English would be on his back the whole way. He would experience enormous difficulties trying to embark his men into the longships with the English hacking away at them, and if he did manage to escape to sea with some of his troops they would be met in the Channel by the English ships. "Awareness of this danger," wrote Mason, "would give renewed impetus, born of desperation, to the successive attacks he [William] directed against the shield wall as he tried to force the collapse of the English by nightfall."[50]

Acutely aware, therefore, of the perilous situation he was in, William staged a massive assault on the English line with his entire army. Up until this point he had used his archers, infantry and cavalry independently and none had achieved a decisive breakthrough. Now, owing perhaps to diminished numbers rather than to an early attempt at co-operation, he employed them simultaneously.[51] He set his field, wrote Furneaux, with his archers in a long loose line, leaving gaps through which the knights could ride. The archers were ordered to fire high into the air over the head of the front ranks to assail the lighter-armed troops behind the housecarls.[52]

Upon William's command the archers moved forward and unleashed their remaining arrows. The defenders would have responded to this by raising their shields above their heads. Though the shields would have protected the English, raising them above their heads meant exposing their bodies as well as making it more difficult for them to wield their weapons, especially the two-handed battle axe. At the same time, therefore, the Norman infantry and cavalry rushed forward to attack the front and both flanks of the English line. Though usually accepted without question, this would seem to be a very difficult, if not dangerous, operation to perform. It would certainly require very accurate shooting and in practice the archers must have had to stop firing before the infantry and cavalry got close to the English line.

The French historians Leprévost and Bernage offer a slightly different interpretation of the tactics of the Norman archers at this stage of the battle: "He [William] brought forward his archers who were almost intact and had been preserved for just such an eventuality – the next stage of the battle would be in their hands. Half of them were positioned on the slope just as they had been at the outset of the battle. The other half crept up the hill until they were only a few paces from the Saxons, where they hid behind the piles of bodies ... the first group loosed their arrows high into the air forcing the Saxons to lift their shields to protect themselves against the plunging fire.

"At the same moment the other archers opened up with their bows level, shooting a hail of metal into the unprotected enemy ranks. Time and time again the action was repeated, sowing panic among the Saxons who did not know how to protect themselves against the hail of death raining down on them. They raised and lowered their shields in an ineffective defence. Dead or wounded the English fell, until the archers ran out of arrows to fire."[53]

Whichever tactics were used, the archers certainly seemed to have had a considerable impact and paved the way for the massed attack of the heavy infantry and in particular the cavalry: "Reaching the crest of the ridge, the horsemen pushed home their advantage against the English ranks, now shortened and concentrated round the crown," wrote Furneaux, "which enabled the knights from the west to gain the ridge and ride against the English right." With the Norman knights now able to operate on the hilltop, the shield wall must have quickly disintegrated, and once the wall had broken the end would have been swift. It is possible that at this stage, as the Normans pressed home their newly won advantage, Harold's brothers Leofwine and Gyrth were killed, and it has been said that the bodies of all three Godwinson brothers were found close to each other after the battle. This, though, would contradict the view of Guy of Amiens and others that Leofwine and certainly Gyrth had died far earlier, possibly in the disastrous first advance.[54]

Where they were stationed on the hill is also questionable. Whereas some historians believe that each brother would have been given command of one of the wings of the English army (Gyrth the left and Leofwine the right), others think that they stood and fought alongside the king and were killed in the same attack that resulted in the death of Harold. Yet another view, as we have seen, is that if they had been killed early on in the battle and Harold had not, then the most likely scenario is that Harold's brothers were in a different part of the line than the king.[55]

The death of the two younger Godwinson brothers was not fatal to the English cause, but the death of Harold most certainly was. Most people believe that Harold was killed at the climatic end of the battle, and indeed most of the chroniclers state this as does the Bayeux Tapestry. Yet, like so much about the Battle of Hastings, this is far from certain.

William of Jumièges wrote that the death of Harold occurred right at the start of the battle: "Harold himself was slain, pierced with mortal wounds during the first assault." He is the only one of the early writers who makes this claim (though one slightly later history, the *Historia Ecclesiastica* by Orderic Vitalis, supports this).

Historians have felt unwilling to dismiss William of Jumièges' statement but because it does not comply with the accepted chronology of the battle there have been ludicrous attempts to make it fit. These include suggestions that William of Jumièges really meant that Harold was not killed in the first assault but "in the first rank", or "the first attack in the final assault", or that it was a simple copyist's error – what Bradbury calls all the usual excuses when the evidence doesn't fit. Neither would the English have succumbed just because their king had been killed. They quite probably understood that if they stood firm they were far safer than if they turned their backs on the enemy and tried to run away, especially if they had witnessed the Norman cavalry cutting down their countrymen when they chased them down the hill. There are also the words of the largely ignored twelfth-century *Vita Haroldi*, "at the first attack of the Normans, King Harold, pierced with numerous blows, is thrown to the ground amongst the dead."[56]

Whilst almost all later writers have chosen to dismiss this, if Harold had been killed in the first attack it would explain both the lack of enterprise and lack of discipline displayed by the English throughout the battle. Almost every historian has commented on Harold's poor showing at the battle of the Hoar Apple Tree and his early death might well explain this.

Nevertheless, the weight of probability is that Harold's death occurred late in the day as William threw all his troops at the English line in a last desperate effort before night intervened. William of Poitiers says that the English position still remained difficult to surround, which indicated that no part of the ridge had yet been taken[57] and, according to Colonel Lemmon, it was only because the ranks of the *housecarls* had become thinned towards the end of the day that the Norman knights were able to reach Harold.[58] Having accepted that this is the most probable of the various alternatives, we now have to consider the manner of Harold's death.

The Bayeux Tapestry is presented chronologically and it appears to show a soldier with an arrow in his eye followed by a soldier being hacked down by a knight on horseback. The words "Harold Rex" are sewn immediately above the first of these two figures but these are not the only words in the sentence, which continues "was killed" ("*interfectus est*"), which is sewn above the second figure. Needless to say, this has led to a divergence of opinion amongst academics. Some claim that the first figure is Harold, some that it is the second, and some that both figures are of Harold showing him being struck in the eye and then finished off with the sword.

Peter Poyntz Wright is unequivocal on this subject. He states that the traditional view that Harold was killed by an arrow in his eye is a "misconception that stems from an incorrect interpretation of the Tapestry." This, he continues, was because of Abbot Baudri of Bourgeuil in a poem written about thirty-five years after the battle.

Charles Gibbs-Smith also supports this view. He correctly indicates that the Tapestry is presented in a series of scenes and the associated texts are frequently too long for the scenes to which they refer. He therefore states that the words *Hic Harold Rex interfectus est* above the warrior with an arrow in his eye are part of the previous scene and should not be confused with the scene depicting Harold being cut down. Gibbs-Smith also observes that the man with an arrow in his eye carries a spear whereas the figure being cut down is armed with a battle axe. Harold, it is presumed, would be carrying an axe rather than a spear.

The previous scene that Gibbs-Smith refers to shows the battle for the Saxon standard which, of course, was where Harold stood, so any attempt to try and separate these scenes is really quite invalid. All that the Tapestry is attempting to portray is the fight around the centre of the English line and the eventual death of Harold.

Nevertheless, historians have devoted an astonishing, some may say an inordinate, amount of time to this subject. Amongst those historians that have studied the Tapestry in excruciating detail is David Bernstein. He has found that a close examination of the panel showing Harold's death reveals visible stitch marks by the head of the second figure. The interpretation of this, which is supported by Bradbury, is that originally there was the shaft of an arrow in the eye of the second figure, which has been removed for some inexplicable reason. Though this sounds highly improbable, it is certainly possible that Harold was hit by an arrow and, in his weakened and vulnerable state, was then struck down by one or more of the Norman knights. The relevant scene in the Tapestry was restored in the nineteenth century so it may be that this is when the arrow shaft was stitched out.

Peter Poyntz Wright has also looked closely at the Tapestry, and he deduces that "a careful examination of the stitch-holes of the original embroidery shows that the arrow was originally shown passing above the helmet, not entering the eye; it was distorted when this part of the Tapestry was restored and made to look as though the face was wounded."[59]

If we turn to the written sources we note that William of Malmesbury wrote that Harold's "brain" was "pierced by an arrow" before one of the knights hacked his thigh with a sword as he lay on the ground." Henry of Huntingdon wrote that "the whole shower sent by the archers fell around King Harold and he himself sank to the ground, struck in the eye." Thus badly wounded, "a host of knights broke through and killed the wounded king." The graphic description of the death of Harold given by Guy of Amiens can probably be discounted, though for the sake of balance it will be included. The duke saw Harold fiercely hewing to pieces the Normans and called Eustace of Boulogne, Hugh of Ponthieu and a knight called Giffard. They moved in on Harold: "The first, cleaving his breast through the shield with his point, drenched the earth with a gushing torrent of blood; the second smote off his head below the protection of the helmet and the third pierced the inwards of his belly with his lance; the fourth hewed off his thigh and bore away the severed limb: the ground held the body thus destroyed." Amusingly, the word "thigh" may be a euphemism and it was a somewhat smaller part of Harold's anatomy that was severed![60]

Professor Frank Barlow was unconvinced with this: "There is no acceptable story of how the Normans won the battle. The simple truth may be that they were still losing it, or at least had achieved no decisive advantage, when, to their surprise, the English fled, Harold having fallen, unrecognised by his foes, in some skirmish."[61]

Regardless of the circumstances of Harold's death, when he was cut down it inevitably spelt defeat for the English. "The flying rumour 'Harold is dead!' spread through the fray," ran the words of the *Carmen de Hastingae Proelio*, "and forthwith proud hearts were tamed by fear."[62] If either of the king's brothers had still been standing the English might have fought on, but with the death of Harold they were left leaderless. The *housecarls* would have stood and fought to the bitter end with their lord but with Harold dead they had no reason to sacrifice their lives.

"The English army realised beyond doubt that they could no longer resist the Normans," wrote William of Poitiers. "They knew that they were reduced by heavy losses; that the king himself, with his brothers and many magnates of the realm had fallen; that those who still stood were almost drained of strength; that they could expect no help. They saw the Normans not much diminished by casualties, threatening them more keenly than in the beginning, as if they had found new strength in the fight; they saw that fury of the duke who spared no one who resisted him; they saw that courage which could only find rest in victory. They therefore turned to flight … some on looted horses, many on foot; some along the roads, many across country." The Normans followed in hot pursuit.[63]

The rout of the English is the last scene on the Tapestry that remains (the final scenes of the Tapestry have been lost; it is assumed that it would have shown the coronation of William). It shows Normans with sword, spear and bow chasing a small group of English. The bottom margin shows the English dead, some headless, one with a severed arm, stripped of their armour.

With no further pictorial record to help us after this point we have to rely on the chroniclers to describe the pursuit. We know that the Andresweald reached as far as Caldbec Hill so the men would have slipped away into the woods as quickly as they could, though according to William of Poitiers many of the English "lay on the ground bathed in blood, others who struggled to their feet found themselves too weak to escape, while … many left their corpses in the depths of the forest."[64] But, as with everything relating to the battle, even the pursuit of the English is subject to dispute.

The main problem with the various accounts of the pursuit relates to the famous "*Malfosse*" incident which, according to Paul Hill, has sent historians "into a 900–year spin".[65] This is supposedly a rearguard action by a large number of the English, which may have been taken in conjunction with a considerable body of reinforcements that had just arrived in the area.[66]

For their stand they chose a good defensive feature in front of which was a ditch or gully. The Norman knights came up against this position and in the deceptive light of early evening they failed to see the irregularities in the ground. They charged at the English and crashed headlong into the ditch where many of the Normans came to grief. William of Poitiers provides a very detailed description of this incident though he does not name the place where it occurred or attempt to identify its location. The name *Malfosse* comes from the *Chronicle of Battle Abbey* and whilst this means "evil ditch" it could have been so named for a variety of reasons – because it was where so many died, or because it was a burial ditch, or because of its physical characteristics. The chronicler devotes as many words to this part of the pursuit as he does to the actual battle.

This, says Bradbury, might be because the chronicler had picked up some vivid tale, perhaps from local gossip, and tied it in with an account of the battle. "A final disaster was revealed to all," reads the *Chronicle of Battle Abbey*. "Lamentable, just where the fighting was going on, and stretching for a considerable distance, an immense ditch yawned. It may have been a natural cleft in the earth or perhaps it had hollowed out by storms. But in this waste ground it was overgrown with brambles and thistles, and could hardly be seen in time; and it swallowed great numbers, especially of Normans in pursuit of the English."[67]

Guy of Amiens makes no mention of the *Malfosse*. All that he says in the *Carmen de Hastingae Proelio* is: "It was evening; already the wheeling heavens were turning day to twilight when God made the duke the victor. Only darkness and flight through the thickets and coverts of the deep forest availed the defeated English ... Ever vigilant, the son of Hector pursued the fleeing with slaughter ... Till it was fully day he spent the night in varying conflict, not overcome by sleep, nor suffering himself to dream."[68]

It is difficult to believe that the Normans would have chased the English through the night. They were in entirely unfamiliar and hostile territory and likely to be ambushed by the enemy in the deep forest. It is rare for pursuits to continue after nightfall and this can comfortably be dismissed. Furthermore there can have been little profit in the pursuit being taken up on the following day as the enemy would have dispersed all around the countryside or have fled half way to London. William also knew that he had won a battle but had not yet won the war. He dared not let his troops get out of hand in a protracted pursuit in case the English regrouped and returned to the offensive. In fact the *Malfosse* incident really confirms this. After losing so many men in a hidden ravine or at least one that was difficult to see in the growing darkness William would never have permitted his men to risk further disaster. The battle he had spent all day winning could be lost in a reckless pursuit.

The duke, by most accounts, does not take part in the pursuit after the *Malfosse* incident, however long or short it may have been. Once he had completed his victory, William of Poitiers wrote, "the duke rode back to the main battlefield, and he could not gaze without pity on the carnage ... The bloodstained battle ground was covered with the flower of the youth and nobility of England."[69] Duke William camped for the night on the battlefield amongst the dead to demonstrate that the field, and thus the victory, was his.

* * *

It has been estimated that William's casualties amounted to more than 30 per cent of his original force and the English losses higher still.[70] This time, in order to arrive at a representative figure, people have tried to compare the battle with other engagements where the casualty figures are known. Thus we have estimates of the number of casualties based on estimates of the numbers engaged – estimates of estimates! What we do know is that whilst most of the English leaders had perished it seems odd, as Furneaux observes, that no notable Norman, Frenchman or Breton appears to have been killed or severely wounded other than Count Eustace of Boulogne, who was wounded in the fighting at the *Malfosse*, even though the Tapestry depicts a number of Normans or their allies being slain.[71]

The seeming survival of so many leading Normans may be the most telling statistic of all. It implies that the day-long struggle was not quite as bloody as is believed, particularly for the Normans. One can imagine that the severity of the slope so neutralised the effectiveness of the Norman cavalry that there was little they could do once they had urged their mounts up to the English line. If they had been able to press home their attacks and become embroiled with the powerful *housecarls*, they must inevitably have incurred heavy casualties. But with the English swinging their terrifying battles axes as their horses struggled slowly up the hill, it is unlikely that the Norman knights, after they had released their spears, would have approached the English line too closely. That job would have been left to the infantry. It is most likely that it was only when the English line had shrunk because of the losses in the actual or feigned retreats that the Norman knights could operate effectively, and it was only then, when the advantage had swung decidedly in their favour, that they dashed in amongst the English.

If we look at the actions undertaken by William after the Battle of the Hoar Apple Tree they show that his army cannot have been much reduced in numbers, as he was able to brush aside all resistance when he later marched upon London. Nevertheless, William acted very cautiously at first. He no doubt hoped and prayed that the English would now accept his right to the throne. Another such battle might not go so decidedly in his favour.

Fearing a renewal of hostilities, William withdrew from the battlefield to his camp at Hastings on 16 October. He was in a perilous position in a hostile country with supplies running low. But William received warning that a large English force was assembling at Dover which he knew he had to dispose of immediately, so, after an anxious week of inactivity, William left a garrison at Hastings and marched eastwards along the coast.

Dover proved less of a problem than anticipated and the place surrendered as soon as it was threatened. Here William learnt that the grandson of Edward Ironside, Edgar Aethling, had been proposed as Harold's successor, and London was preparing to resist the invaders. Over the course of the next few days

William remained at Dover, during which time he and a large part of his force was struck down by an epidemic (which may have been dysentery or gastro-enteritis). When he eventually renewed his offensive, he had to leave behind some 1,700 men.[72]

On 31 October he captured Canterbury, the ecclesiastical heart of the country, and sent a large detachment to cut off all the main routes into London. William marched with the rest of the army to Winchester, with his fleet tracking his movements along the coast to Chichester or Portsmouth, and occupied the old Wessex capital.

With London surrounded and the other two most important cities in the hands of the invaders, the leading English figures, including the Archbishop of Canterbury and Edgar Aethling, submitted to what they considered was the inevitable. They invited William to accept the throne. It was, as Wulfstan of Worcester remarked, "as though with Harold had fallen also the whole strength of the country." William was crowned King of England on Christmas Day and "the Lord, the ruler, brought to fulfilment what He had long planned for the English people: He delivered them up to be destroyed by the violent and cunning Norman race."[73]

Chapter 7

The Sources

"The sparseness of the sources means that numerous aspects are uncertain and many controversial."

David Bates, *William the Conqueror*

What we have related so far is a fairly straightforward account of the Battle of Hastings, and the events that precipitated it, albeit with its many confusions and contradictions, the only significant difference being that we have placed the battle on Caldbec Hill instead of the traditional site of Battle Hill. In compiling this account we have drawn upon medieval sources and more recent studies. What we will now do is look more closely at those sources and their interpretations to see if they can provide us with clues to where the battle may have been fought.

We have seen that there is little certainty about many of the events that led to William's great victory on 14 October 1066. The reason why there is such uncertainty is not just because of the fog of war or the mists of time obscuring our view, this we expect. The difficulty we have in discerning the facts is that the primary sources available to us were predominantly produced for the conquerors. History is always written by the victors but so complete was the Norman Conquest, both socially and politically, that few contradictory voices could be raised. This does not mean that all that was written in the years following the battle was biased or factually incorrect, however, as Morton and Muntz point out, the "intention" of the composers of these original works was "to deceive posterity in some degree, while refraining if possible from verbal untruth."[1]

Historians have debated the merits or deficiencies in the documents which are regarded as near-contemporary accounts of the battle. Andrew Bridgeford's view of these sources is that "each has its own limitations; none has any inherent right to be regarded as inviolable truth." Equally, as Doctor Stephen Morillo declares, "The primary sources for the battle ... raise interesting problems of interpretation because of their variety of style and point of view." M.K. Lawson accepts that amongst the great fascinations of the Battle of Hastings are "the complexities which inevitably arise when dealing with sources about which there will never be complete agreement." R. Allen Brown, for his part, advises us to regard the sources with "increasing scholarly caution". Richard Huscroft says that the sources for the Battle of Hastings are "abundant but problematic", Lieutenant Colonel Lemmon warns us that the chroniclers "have so embroidered their narrative with romantic matter that it is difficult to arrive at the truth" and David Bates advises us to "read these sources carefully, and often sceptically." Harriet Wood adds to this by reminding us that there may well have been other primary accounts of the battle that have been lost, and intriguingly some of the medieval writers alluded to earlier documents from which they have drawn their information.[2]

Despite these cautionary warnings, our objective is to try and extract from these sources evidence that will help us locate the place where the battle was fought. Those passages which do not assist with this enquiry are not investigated here for reasons of simplicity.

We will begin with what is possibly the earliest of these sources, the *Gesta Normannorum Ducum*, which is said to have been written in 1070 by William of Jumièges, seemingly at the request of the Conqueror. This writer was a monk at one of the principal Norman abbeys, probably at Rouen, with no military experience. In his dedicatory note to King William, the monk indicates that the first part of his narrative has been excerpted from several works, which he abbreviated and reinterpreted. The rest is "partly related by many persons trustworthy on account equally of their age and their experience, and partly based on the most assured evidence of what I have witnessed myself, from my own store." But much of this information seems to have been based on hearsay, rather than eyewitness reports.

He has little to say about the actual battle and the events immediately preceding it. "With favourable wind and sails billowing aloft, he [William] crossed the sea and landed at Pevensey, where at once he built a strongly entrenched fortification. He entrusted it to his warriors and speedily went to Hastings, where he quickly raised another one. Harold, hastening to take the duke by surprise, gathered innumerable English forces and, riding through the night, arrived at the battlefield at dawn." As we can see, there is no mention of Harold assembling his forces at one point and then moving off again to occupy another. He rode directly to the battlefield.

The *Gesta Normannorum Ducum* was later added to and amended by other historians, principally Orderic Vitalis (more of whom later) and Robert of Torigni. The combined work is regarded as one of the most important narrative sources for the history of Normandy and England, with the various texts intermingled to make a continuous narrative.

That which refers to the Battle of Hastings is quite brief, and reads as follows: "The duke, taking precautions in case of a night-attack, ordered his army to stand to arms from dusk to dawn. At first light, having disposed his troops in three lines of battle, he advanced undaunted against the terrible enemy. The battle began at the third hour of the day, and continued amid a terrible welter of carnage and slaughter on both sides until the late evening. Harold himself was slain, pierced with mortal wounds, during the first assault. When the English learned that their king had met his death, they greatly feared for their own lives and turned about at nightfall and sought refuge in flight. When thus the Normans saw the English fleeing they pursued them obstinately through the night till Sunday to their own harm. For high grass concealed an ancient rampart and as the Normans fully armed on their horses rode up against it, they fell, one on top of the other, thus crushing each other to death ... The most valiant duke returned from the slaughter of his enemy to the battlefield at midnight. Early next morning, on Sunday, having looted the enemy and buried the corpses of his own dear men, he set out for London."[3]

In this, amongst the earliest of our sources, what we learn of the site of the battle is that Harold rode through the night and arrived on the battlefield at dawn. It says nothing about a rendezvous point from which Harold, with his army assembled, then marches to take up another position. It implies that Harold marched throughout the night to the assembly point and that it was there that the battle took place. The nature of the terrain is not discussed apart from the disaster during the retreat in which long grass and an ancient rampart are mentioned.

The longest prose account of the Norman campaign (as distinct from the longest physically, which is of course the Bayeux Tapestry) is the *Gesta Willelmi ducis Normannorum et regis Anglorum* compiled by William of Poitiers. He was born in about 1020 and in his youth had served under Duke William as a soldier, and so he was familiar with the duke's methods of making war. He had subsequently taken holy orders at Poitiers after which he returned to the Duke as his chaplain, finally becoming Archdeacon of Lisieux. He was self-evidently William's man and everything he wrote must be viewed in this light.

He did not accompany William on the 1066 campaign but, as his account was written about five years after the battle (in around 1071), he would most likely have been told about the engagement from those that had been involved. His work is therefore generally regarded as reliable, though it is necessarily written from the Norman perspective and its intention was to glorify Duke William's achievements. As William of Poitiers conceded in his own words he wished to "celebrate the glory of King William". His comments on the actions of the English should, therefore, be treated with this in mind. In their presentation of this work, Douglas and Greenaway remark that "many problems connected with it still await solution" and, as Harriet Wood points out, many of William of Poitiers' statements are clearly incorrect.[4]

As our interest now lies in the battle rather than the campaign as a whole, the following is a translation of William of Poitiers' narrative which begins on the morning of 14 October:

> In the meanwhile, trusted soldiers, sent out as scouts on the duke's orders announced the imminent arrival of the enemy, because the king in his fury had hastened his march, particularly because he had learnt of the devastation around the Norman camp. He intended to surprise them and to crush them in a nocturnal or surprise attack. And in case they took flight he had armed a fleet of seven hundred boats to ambush them on the sea. The duke hastily ordered all those who were in the camp to arm themselves, for many of his companions had gone foraging that day ...
>
> He [William] advanced with his troops in the following highly advantageous order, behind the banner which the Pope had sent him. In the vanguard he placed infantry armed with bows and crossbows; behind them were also infantry, but more steady and armed with hauberks; in the rear, the cavalry squadrons, in the midst of which he took his place with the elite. From this position he could command the whole army by voice and gesture.
>
> If an author from antiquity had described Harold's army, he would have said that as it passed rivers dried up, the forests became open country. For from every part of the country large numbers of English had gathered. Some were moved by affection for Harold, all by love of their country, which they wished to defend from strangers, even though the cause was unjust. Considerable help had been sent from the land of the Danes, to whom they were related. But, frightened of attacking William, whom they feared more than the king of Norway, on equal terms, they camped on higher ground, a hill close to the forest through which they had come.
>
> They immediately dismounted and went on foot, drawn up one close to the other. The duke and his men, in no way frightened by the difficulty of the place, began slowly to climb the steep slope. The terrible sound of the trumpets announced on both sides the beginning of the battle. The eager boldness of the Normans gave them the advantage of attack ... The English were greatly helped by the higher position which they held; they did not have to march to the attack, but remained tightly grouped.[5]

Here then we have a number of specific descriptions of the battlefield. The first is that the English "camped on higher ground, a hill close to the forest through which they had come." It is impossible to describe Battle Hill in this way, as it is far lower than the forest (the Andresweald) through which they had travelled. Such a description, nevertheless, would fit Caldbec Hill perfectly, as it was indeed close to the forest and higher. The severity of the slope is repeatedly stressed, thus we have the Normans "in no way frightened by the difficulty of the place" having to slowly climb the steep slope. The English were "greatly helped by the higher position."

Clearly Harold, an experienced and successful warrior, had chosen a formidable position upon which to fight. We know that Harold had witnessed William's capabilities as a war leader having fought alongside him during his time in Normandy. He knew that William's best troops were his mounted knights and that to fight them in the open fields would lead to disaster. The higher the position, the more difficult it would be for the Norman knights. Not only was it a high position that William of Poitiers described, it was also upon a hill with slopes so steep that the Normans could not rush upon the English but could only "climb slowly". None of these descriptions fit the gently sloping, low rise of Battle Hill.

The *Anglo-Saxon Chronicle* is one of the few primary sources that was not written by the Normans. Thought to have been founded by King Alfred towards the end of the ninth century, it was not one manuscript but in fact a group of English vernacular annals assembled at three different monastic centres, these probably being Abingdon, Worcester and Peterborough.[6]

There are, as a consequence, three different versions of the events of each year. The three surviving *Chronicles* spanned the years 1042 to 1079 (though one version, designated "E", continued until 1154). After December 1066 every chronicler worked under a Norman king and must therefore be subject to Norman influences.

The Battle of Hastings is given a degree of treatment in only two of the versions, the versions identified as "D" and "E"; the "C" version preferring instead to highlight the Battle of Gate Fulford and, in particular, the great English victory at Stamford Bridge. The description of the Battle of Hastings below is the one given in version "D".

"Then Count William came from Normandy to Pevensey on Michaelmas Eve, and as soon as they were able to move on they built a castle at Hastings. King Harold was informed of this and he assembled a large army and came against him at the hoary apple tree. And William came against him by surprise before his army was drawn up in battle array. But the king nevertheless fought hard against him, with the men who were willing to support him, and there were heavy casualties on both sides."

The "E" version merely states: "Meanwhile Count William landed at Hastings on Michaelmas Day, and Harold came from the north and fought with him before all the army had come, and there he fell and his two brothers Gyrth and Leofwine."

It would seem from the *Chronicle* that all we need to do is identify the site of the "hoary apple tree" and we have the site of the battle. The *Chronicle* does not

THIS PLAQUE IS TO COMMEMORATE
THE VISIT TO PEVENSEY OF
HER MAJESTY QUEEN ELIZABETH II
ON 28TH OCTOBER 1966
AND THE LANDING OF
WILLIAM DUKE OF NORMANDY
ON 28TH SEPTEMBER 1066

The commemorative plaque outside Pevensey Castle marking the landing place of the Normans in 1066.

An aerial view of Pevensey Castle. The old Roman walls made a perfect base for the Normans, within which they erected their first wooded castle. It is presumed that where the medieval castle now stands is where that first wooden one was positioned. In the eleventh century the sea lapped up to the foot of the Roman walls.

The summit of Tent Hill on the 1066 Country Walk from Pevensey to Hastings where, allegedly, the Normans camped overnight.

A photograph showing part of the ancient track which led to the London–Lewes road that crossed Caldbec Hill. Members of the *fyrd* would have marched along this track to the concentration point of the English army on the hill.

An aerial view of Battle Abbey and its grounds showing the relationship between Battle Hill and Caldbec Hill, which is in the background, identifiable by the white windmill on its summit.

Two views looking up Caldbec Hill from the direction in which the Normans would have advanced, i.e. from the south. The difficult and steep terrain is quite evident. The windmill marks the summit of the hill.

Caldbec Hill's eastern slopes are just as steep as the other faces.

Looking along the length of the traditional battlefield. The difference between the steep and difficult terrain of Caldbec Hill and the gentle, smooth slope of Battle Hill is quite remarkable.

The western part of the traditional battlefield. Battle Abbey can be seen on the right.

Members of the *fyrd* moving across the lower slopes of Battle Hill to take up their positions at the annual re-enactment.

The site of the Watch Oak on the side of Caldbec Hill where, according to legend, Edith Swan-Neck watched the battle unfold.

In these aerial views, the open, flat expanse of ground on the right flank of Battle Hill is shown. These clearly demonstrate how easy it would have been for the Norman (or Breton) cavalry to surmount or even turn this flank. The small area of rough, wooded ground at the foot of Battle Hill as shown below is the so-called hillock.

The watercourse at the bottom of Caldbec Hill: N 50 54 972, E 00 29 505. This could well be the one depicted on the Bayeux Tapestry that caused the Normans such difficulty.

Austin's suggested battle site at Pye's Farm. The treeline is considered by Austin to be where the English line was formed.

This photograph shows the place suggested by Nick Austin as the *Malfosse*. It is situated to the east of Pye's Farm.

This is a view of Nick Austin's suggested battle site. As can be seen this flank is open and poorly defined. It would be difficult to defend such a flank, particularly against cavalry.

Freeman's Malfosse: N 50 54 964, E 00 29 514.

An aerial view of Caldbec Hill from the north-west to show its relationship with what is now widely accepted as being the *Malfosse*. The *Malfosse* is marked by the row of trees running diagonally across the bottom of the photograph.

This picture shows the spot on Caldbec Hill where the victory cairn, the Mountjoy, was probably erected after the battle. Note how the slope falls steeply away.

The area near the summit of Caldbec Hill is still known as Mountjoy.

The Bayeux Tapestry panel showing William (carrying the Mace) being told by the Norman scouts that the English army has been spotted.

The continuation of the above scene, depicting the Normans observing the English from a hill top. This is the only hill shown on the Tapestry before the controversial "hillock" scene.

Battle is joined. Note that the fighting is shown on level ground, not uphill. The all-round nature of the English defensive formation is depicted by the men in the shield wall facing both left and right.

As the battle continues the fighting becomes more confused.

The start of the most significant scenes in the battle. In the centre can be seen the watercourse and to the right is the start of the "hillock", which is shown at the top of the next page.

The continuation of the scene showing the English defending the hill. The Normans are driven off
in confusion, believing William has been killed. He lifts his helmet to show his face to his men and
therefore rallies his troops. What is significant with these scenes is that the action on the hill,
following which the Normans are driven off, is before William rallies his troops, not afterwards. This
clearly contradicts the traditionally accepted accounts.

say that Harold moved away from this position and then fought. As we can be fairly certain where the old grey apple tree once stood we can be equally certain about the site of the battle.[7]

Moving on to a slightly later document, we have the *Chronicon ex Chronis*. Though previously it was thought it had been compiled by a Worcester monk known as "Florence", the general view now held is that much of the chronicle was written by another Worcester monk called John. This is the most detailed of the "English" sources. It was written in the 1120s but it is believed that it drew upon now-lost older English documents, possibly a version of the *Anglo-Saxon Chronicle*.[8] The passage below starts as Harold receives the news that William has landed at Hastings.

"Thereupon the king led his army towards London by forced marches and although he knew that all the more powerful men from the whole of England had already fallen in two battles, and that half his army had not yet assembled, yet he did not fear to go to meet his enemies in Sussex with all possible speed, and nine miles from Hastings, where they had earlier built a fortress for themselves, before a third of his army had been drawn up, he joined battle with the Normans. But inasmuch as the English were drawn up in a narrow place, many slipped away from the battle line and very few of a constant heart remained with him. Nevertheless he made a stout resistance from the third hour of the day until nightfall, and defended himself with such courage and obstinacy, the enemy almost despaired of taking his life. When, however, numbers had fallen on both sides, he alas! Fell at twilight."[9]

All that can be learnt from Florence/John of Worcester is that the English position was a "narrow" one. This, of course, could apply to Battle Hill but equally it could relate to other sites and would suit Caldbec Hill, which is slightly narrower than Battle Hill, admirably. Perhaps the most telling point made by this writer was that he said the battle was nine miles from Hastings, which would put it on Caldbec Hill and not Battle Hill, which is only eight miles from Hastings.

The *Carmen de Hastingae Proelio* (the Song of the Battle of Hastings) provides us with a highly detailed account of the battle. Unfortunately no one is entirely certain when it was written. It had been assumed that it had been compiled by Guy, Bishop of Amiens (nephew of the Count of Ponthieu, the man who had captured Harold and handed him over to William in 1064), as it is known that this individual did compose a verse on the battle, and that it had been written in 1067 or 1068. Bishop Guy died in 1074 or 1075, so if the document that exists was indeed written by him then this would make it an extremely valuable source, even though Harriet Wood observes that it was only written for "entertainment".[10] More recent study has cast doubt on this and there is one school of thought which believes that the *Carmen* was written much later than this. Professor R.H.C. Davis insists that it is "neither an original source nor the poem by Guy of Amiens" but is a literary exercise of the second quarter of the twelfth century. Not everyone agrees with Professor Davis.[11] Part of the problem is that the original poem produced by Guy was lost just a few years after it had been written and the document which we now know as the *Carmen* was rediscovered in 1826.

The relevant passages in the *Carmen* are as follows: "The duke said: 'Where is the king?' 'Not far off', answered the monk. He said to him in his ear: 'You can see the standards!' I bear many words which I hold unfit to be repeated, yet I will report what it would be harmful to conceal. He hopes to be able to take you by surprise; by sea and by land he is planning great battles. He is said to have sent five hundred ships to sea to hinder our voyage back. Where he goes he leads forests of spears into the open country, and he makes the rivers through which he passes run dry! Perhaps you fear the number? But the greater number lacking greater strength often retires worsted by very few ... He kept silence for a little and then, causing himself to delay there, he drew up the armed ranks by a command. He dispatched the foot in advance to open the battle with arrows, and set crossbowmen in the midst so that their speeding shafts might pierce the faces of the English (these wounds given, they might fall back). He hoped to establish the knights in the rear of the foot but the onset of the battle did not allow this; for he perceived companies of the English appearing not far off and could see the forest glitter, full of spears.

"Suddenly the forest poured forth troops of men, and from the hiding-places of the woods a host dashed forward. There was a hill near the forest and a neighbouring valley and the ground was untilled because of its roughness. Coming on in massed order – the English custom – they seized possession of this place for the battle. (A race ignorant of war, the English scorn the solace of horses and trusting in their strength they stand fast on foot; and they count it the highest honour to die in arms that their native soil may not pass under another yoke.)

"Preparing to meet the enemy, the king mounted the hill and strengthened both his wings with noble men. On the highest point of the summit he planted his banner, and ordered his other standards to be set up. All the men dismounted and left their horses in the rear, and taking their stand on foot they let the trumpets sound for battle.

"The humble and God-fearing duke led a more measured advance and courageously approached the steeps of the hill".

From the *Carmen* we can learn that the English could be seen with their spears glittering in a forest and that they poured forth from the trees to occupy a hill near the forest. This makes much sense. It was the middle of October and the nights would be cold. The men would form their bivouacs in the forest where they could cut down branches to form cover from the elements and twigs for their fires. They would not spend a night out in the open hillside if it could be avoided. As Bradbury observes, Caldbec Hill was right on the edge of the Andresweald and if they emerged from the forest the first hill they would come across would be Caldbec, which was after all the appointed meeting place.[12]

We also know that the ground was steep and so rough that it was untilled. Again this does not correspond to Battle Hill. Its gentle slope is quite suitable for farming (though this does not mean that there was farming in the district at that time) and there is no evidence that indicates it was wooded in 1066, whereas the wooded nature of Caldbec Hill is known about from the Domesday Book. However, the reference to the valley could indeed refer to the low ground between Battle Hill and Telham Hill, but equally it could be ascribed to the ground between Caldbec Hill and Battle Hill.

Catherine Morton and Hope Muntz, in their translation of the *Carmen*, make an interesting comment on the passage which opens the battle where it is said that William despatched his crossbowmen and directed them to shoot in the faces of the English to drive them back:

> The military detail in this passage is of great interest. The duke's purpose is, seemingly, to check the enemy's further advance, so that he may anticipate the seizure of the hill – causing panic with his missiles, notably his bolts while the enemy is in the act of concentration upon Caldbec. Since the range of these weapons was not great, it would be necessary for the foot to advance beyond the lower hill to achieve this. They would then fall back on that position, the duke in the meantime having brought up the knights in support. The text may, however, be construed to mean that only *balistantes* [cross-bowmen] in the centre were to retire, opening a way for the knights to press home the attack ... The duke's presumed objective, in this case, would have been to carry Caldbec Hill, pushing the English back in disorder from the high ground and so assuring himself freedom of manoeuvre.[13]

It is interesting to note that the reference to the rivers running dry is so similar to that given by William of Poitiers that it appears to have been taken from the *Gesta Willelmi ducis Normannorum et regis Anglorum*, or indeed William of Poitiers may have copied it from Guy of Amiens or whoever it was that wrote the *Carmen*.

In terms of the location of the site, the fact that Battle Abbey stands on Battle Hill is usually given as definite proof that the battle was fought at that place and there is a document concerning the building of the abbey, *The History of the Foundation of Battle Abbey*, which is generally referred to as the *Chronicle of Battle Abbey*.

It is, strictly speaking, two manuscripts, which were bound together by the monks of Battle Abbey, possibly in medieval times, though this is unproven. The first twenty-two folios deal with the Norman invasion, the battle and the reason for the founding of abbey, in one individual's handwriting, followed by a different, and much lengthier, section in another hand, which concerns the lands belonging to the abbey, its rights and privileges. H.W.C. Davis believes that the first chronicle is in fact the later of the two and is a revision of the second, main text, which means that it has even less validity than it is usually accorded.[14]

This document, as Elenor Searle has explained, is not really a chronicle at all. It was written, as its author tells us, not to recount history but to commit to writing pieces of evidence about the abbey's lands and to explain the background to and prosecution of a series of lawsuits.

The main legal debate was a dispute which came to a head in the 1150s between Bishop Hilary of Chichester and Abbot Walter de Luci of Battle (who was the Abbot of Battle between 1139 and 1171). The abbey claimed the rights of a Royal Peculiar which gave it exemption from Episcopal control. No bishop welcomed such exemption and the Bishop of Chichester was no different and he was keen to bring this wealthy establishment under his control. (The abbey had originally been granted rights over all the land within one and a half miles of the abbey, putting it on a par with Canterbury Cathedral.)[15] The dispute between the abbot and the bishop reached such a pitch that de Luci was temporarily excommunicated.

The monks did not have a problem with their status during the reign of William the Conqueror or his son William II, the problem was how to maintain this with later kings who had no emotional associations with the abbey. Somehow they had to find a way of demonstrating that their establishment was special and deserved to retain its privileges. The result was the forging of a number of charters to provide written "proof" of their claims. These charters were drawn up in 1154 and the chronicle followed a number of years (possibly around thirty years) later.[16]

The charters are extant today and, according to Searle, we can see that they are forged. Forgeries of the twelfth century were not uncommon, wrote Searle, "but usually we can only guess at the forgers' motives. In the Battle chronicle the veil is for a moment lifted, and we can see the living world in which the abbot came to pass where forgery was his last, best hope of victory." The evidence was put in the form of a story rather than just as a document or deed because "where there was uncertainty or ambiguity, the best testimony as to a privilege or possession was often the tale of its donation."[17] Thus we have the story of the founding of the abbey under William's orders. It is unfortunately entirely fabricated.

Yet the reason why modern historians assume they know where the battle was fought is because they accept without question the statements in the *Chronicle of Battle Abbey*. William, as we have seen, supposedly made a vow regarding the building of a monastery before the battle and following the incident in which

William put on his armour back to front. His followers saw this as a bad omen and they were dismayed by this, but William responded with these words: "I ought on no account to go to battle this day but, committing myself trustfully to my Creator in every manner, I have given no heed to omens; neither have I ever loved sorcerers. Wherefore now secure of his aid and in order to strengthen the hands and courage of you, who are for my sake about to engage in this conflict, I make a Vow, that upon this place of battle I will found a suitable free Monastery."[18] This was heard by a monk, called William Faber. He asked William if the monastery could be dedicated to the blessed bishop St Martin. Needless to say, according to the chronicler, the Duke agreed.

As Freeman "suspects", the vow comes from the chronicler, not the Duke, "William was hardly already thinking of the exemption [i.e. the alleged statement about the monastery being "free"] of the abbey of Battle from the jurisdiction of the Bishop of Chichester" when he was about to take part in the most desperate encounter of his life.[19]

As we know the years passed by and no such monastery was built; the chronicler had to find some way of explaining this, which he does as follows: "The illustrious King (William) was fully occupied, as we have mentioned, and although he never actually forgot his vow, yet because of his preoccupations of this period, he put off its fulfilment (amongst other things) for a long time. However his conscience was urging him from within, while from without the monk William 'the smith' kept reminding him assiduously, no easy thing to do. At last, since the monk was nearby, the king committed the building of the abbey to him as he had wished, commanding him to fetch some brothers from his own church and set speedily in hand the establishment of a suitable monastery on the battlefield.

"Accepting the alacrity, the monk went quickly to Marmoutier and brought with him into England four monks from there; Theobald, nicknamed 'the old', William Coche, Robert of Boulogne, and Robert Blancard, men outstanding in character and piety. They studied the battlefield and decided that it seemed hardly suitable for so outstanding a building. They therefore chose a fit place for settling, a site located not far off, but somewhat lower down, towards the western slope of the ridge. There lest they seem to be doing nothing, they built themselves some little huts. This place, still called Herste has a low wall as a mark of this.[20]

"Accordingly, when the solicitous king inquired meanwhile about the progress of the building, it was intimated to him by these brethren that the place where he had decided to have the church built was on a hill, and so dry of soil, and quite without springs, and that for so great a construction a more likely place nearby should be substituted, if it pleased him. When the king heard this he refused angrily and ordered them to lay the foundations of the church speedily and on the very spot where his enemy had fallen and the victory been won."

This explains the chronicler's reason for declaring that the abbey was built on the Conqueror's specific instructions but why bother to go into such detail about where the building work originally began and the fact that the work then had to be stopped and restarted on the present site? Does this mean that some people had already challenged the monks over the position of the monastery, and therefore cast doubt upon its claim to special privileges?

The rather convoluted description of the building of the monastery is certainly quite strange. It almost seems as if the site of the battle was not the acknowledged fact it is perceived to be today. It was just an ecclesiastical building which King William had agreed to found as a penance for the blood that was shed during his unauthorised invasion of England. But no, declared the monks, the monastery is particularly special, for it was built on the very spot where William won his crown, the altar being erected exactly where the last Anglo-Saxon king of England fell. It is powerful stuff. Who could therefore deny that the monastery was very special indeed and one not to be constrained by the normal regulations? Who dare defy the word of the Conqueror?

If we also consider the statement made in the *Chronicle of Battle Abbey* that the battle site was not suitable for such an outstanding building we have something of a contradiction with the steep-sided, commanding position described by William of Poitiers. What better place could there be upon which to build a great church than the imposing ridge which Harold had tried to defend?

As it happened the forged documents passed muster and de Luci won the dispute. However, in the 1230s the whole debate was renewed. Needless to say the chronicle was produced as evidence as before. This time no one believed a word of it and the abbey's case collapsed and was never revived. It is utterly remarkable that even though this document was dismissed as being bogus more than 700 years ago historians still choose to believe that the battle was fought on Battle Hill simply because that is where the monastery was built. Jim Bradbury is almost a lone voice in questioning this blind assumption.

If the chronicler is known to be unreliable, Bradbury asks, "can we trust his story of the abbey's foundation on the spot where Harold was killed?" The answer is clearly negative. "We should have reservations about swallowing the tale without question," continues Bradbury. "It is some cause for concern that the altar story does not emerge until a century after the event; it is surprising that no earlier writer knew of and repeated such a vivid detail."[21]

We will conclude our investigation into this aspect of the *Chronicle of Battle Abbey* by considering the reported words of Walter de Luci. With reference to the charter he remarked to King Henry II that "we should all ourselves be Charters, for we are all feoffees [trustees] from that conquest made at Battle." In other words, we all know that the charter is not genuine but does it really matter how or where the abbey was built or that the abbey is claiming a few special privileges for itself when all the leading Normans, including Henry himself, had benefitted enormously from the Conquest of England?

The other notable inclusion in the *Chronicle of Battle Abbey* is the use of the name *Malfosse* in describing the incident at the end of the battle in which large numbers of Norman knights came to grief in a deep ravine or ditch. To Eleanor Searle a ditch filled with bodies suggests a *Malfosse* of a different sort. "It may well have been the site of a mass grave, the knowledge of which had come to light in the hundred years or more following the battle, and had been identified with the no doubt authentic disaster of the narratives of the battle. There had been no kinsfolk to claim the Norman dead, and, in the duke's hurry to consolidate his first victory, a mass grave was surely the best that could be afforded." As Searle points out, the field given the name *Malfosse* had been the site of reclamation projects and arable cultivation in the twelfth century and it seems likely that, as the district was brought under cultivation, the graves would have been uncovered. It is not surprising that the ditch containing the mass grave became associated with the place where the Normans perished at the end of the battle.[22]

If Seale is correct and the *Malfosse*, which we understand to be at Oakwood Gill, was where the Norman dead were buried, this would further reinforce our belief that the battle was fought on Caldbec Hill, as there is not the slightest possibility that William's men would have been able to move all the bodies that far, especially as the Normans returned to Hastings just two days after the battle, nor would such action make any sense. Nor are these two events mutually exclusive. If many men were killed at the *Malfosse* why move them elsewhere? What better place could there be for the mass grave than the place where many of the Norman dead already lay?

The next work to consider is the *Historia Ecclesiastic agentis Anglorum,* which was compiled by Orderic Vitalis, a monk and historian of St Evroul. As with so many of the early sources, there is some doubt about when it was written. The dates vary from between 1099 and 1122 and between 1123 and 1141. It is divided into three parts, the first section of which (books i and ii) purports to be a history of Christianity from the birth of Christ and are regarded as historically valueless. The second part deals with the Conquest. It is said by Marjorie Chibnall that it is based on the *Gesta Willelmi,* which Vitalis also helped to write, and on other now lost *pancartes* (cartularies or collections of charters) of various Norman monastic houses as sources.[23] So despite its later date it can be regarded as one of the primary sources.

The first part of this work to note is where Vitalis discusses the Battle of Stamford Bridge. "A hard-fought battle ensued, in which there was great effusion of blood on both sides, vast numbers being slain with brutal rage. At last the furious attacks of the English secured them the victory, and the king of Norway as well as Tostig, with their whole army, were slain. The field of battle may be easily discovered by travellers, as great heaps of the bones of the slain lie there to this day, memorials of the prodigious numbers which fell on both sides." This, remember, was nearly eighty years after the battle, yet the evidence of the battle could still be seen. It is odd that no such remarks were made about the Battle of Hastings.

Orderic is also the first person to use the name Senlac for the location of the battle: "the English troops, assembled from all parts of the neighbourhood, took post at a place which was anciently called Senlac, many of them personally devoted to the cause of Harold, and all to that of their country, which they were resolved to defend against the foreigners. Dismounting from their horses, on which it was determined not to rely, they formed a solid column of infantry, and thus stood firm in the position they had taken ... Although the battle was fought with the greatest fury from nine o'clock in the morning, King Harold was slain in the first onset, and his brother Earl Leofwine fell some time afterwards, with many thousands of the royal army.

"Towards evening, the English finding that their king and the chief nobles of the realm, with a great part of their army, had fallen, while the Normans still showed a bold front, and made desperate attacks on all who made any resistance, they had recourse to flight as expeditiously as they could. Various were the fortunes which attended their retreat; some recovering their horses, some on foot, attempted to escape by the highways; more sought to save themselves by striking across the country. The Normans, finding the English completely routed, pursued them vigorously all Sunday night, but not without suffering a great loss; for, galloping onward in hot pursuit, they fell unawares, horses and armour, into an ancient trench, overgrown and concealed by rank grass, and men in their armour and horses rolling over each other, were crushed and smothered. This accident restored confidence to the routed English, for, perceiving the advantage given them by the mouldering rampart and a succession of ditches, they rallied in a body, and, making a sudden stand, caused the Normans severe loss."[24]

It is interesting to read that Orderic states, as does William of Jumièges, that Harold was killed in the first attack. If this is true, and as we have seen it might well explain the English army's seemingly restricted performance in the battle and the lack of discipline which they displayed, then this means that the description of Harold being killed on the spot where the High Altar of the monastery was placed is false.

With regards to the supposed vow made by William to found a monastery on the site of the battle, Orderic wrote that William only made that decision "after he had gone to war, triumphed over his enemies and received a royal crown at London."[25]

We also, of course, have the famous Bayeux Tapestry, which Colonel Lemmon considered to be "undoubtedly" the oldest of all the sources and

Edward Freeman regarded as being the "highest authority" of all the original sources.[26] Whilst this may or may not be the case, it is almost certainly a product of the last third of the eleventh century and so can justifiably be considered as a contemporary artefact, though Harriet Wood reminds us that "as with so much else, we don't know when it was worked or by whom; we can only guess."[27] It is a far larger item than might be thought and provides a great deal of information. Along its 231-foot length it depicts 626 human figures, 202 horses, 55 dogs, 505 other animals, 49 trees, 37 buildings and 41 ships.[28]

If it is indeed the oldest of the surviving sources, upon what evidence or information was it manufactured? It cannot have been based on any of the surviving written documents, as Wolfgng Grape explains: "No extant Norman source mentions the village of Bosham, from which Harold sets out on his travels, or the episode in which he rescues some Norman soldiers caught in the quicksands of the River Couesnon. Alongside the main participants in the historical narrative, the Tapestry names three men: Turold, Waldard and Vital ... The point is that these names do not appear in any written record of the conquest. It follows, therefore, that the Tapestry rests on a separate Norman source, now lost."

Grape is convinced that this long-lost account was seen by the Tapestry designer in written form and that the Tapestry narrative is an attempt to rewrite history in the interests of William's half-brother – Odo, Bishop of Bayeux.[29]

In addition to Grape's excellent work, there have been 400 or more books devoted to examining the Tapestry since the early nineteenth century, yet it remains an enigma which, according to those others that have studied it in meticulous detail, "still raises numerous questions."[30] This is, of course, because being a visual representation it is more open to interpretation than a text document and as Frank McLynn has realised it "becomes more mysterious the more one looks at it."[31]

It was also customary in eleventh-century narrative art to borrow traditional pictorial formulas and insert them into new contexts. Thus the scenes in the Tapestry which portray the battle, and those which might help in our search for the battleground, are likely to be in some form of stylised representation. They are, as McLynn has put it, "iconographic rather than documentary".[32] The lengthy scenes depicting the Norman cavalry charging into battle, for example, are unquestionably "formulaic".[33]

Yet the Tapestry does have some words of explanation embroidered on it which may help in our research. One of the sections is described as "scouts from the two forces spot each other". This shows the mounted Norman scouts on a much higher hill than those of the English. This could well be Telham Hill, which at 460 feet is higher than both Battle Hill (275 feet) and Caldbec Hill (353 feet). Andrew Bridgeford, in his examination of the Tapestry, writes that the English scout "peers out through lush foliage" with his hand shielding his eyes as he looks southwards into the sun. The scout sees the Normans approaching and returns hastily across what Bridgeford sees as "rough terrain" in order to report back to King Harold.[34] Though we cannot be certain which places are being portrayed in these scenes, we know that the lush foliage and the rough terrain could not be ascribed to the land in front of Battle Hill, which is considered to have been largely treeless at that date, but could easily be a representation of the countryside around Caldbec Hill which, even today, is rough and wooded.

From that point onwards all the fighting is shown on undulating ground – woven as a sort of wavy line. The English are depicted standing close together to form their famous shield wall. They are shown facing left and right, no doubt to indicate that the Normans were attacking them from all directions. As we know, many historians believe that the English shield wall if it was deployed on Battle Hill was formed along the ridge in a straight line. The Tapestry contradicts this. If, however, the battle was fought on conical-shaped Caldbec Hill the English would have been deployed around the hill, just as is portrayed in this scene of the Tapestry.

The Tapestry shows the confusion of battle with the English and the Normans intermixed in hand-to-hand combat. This continues until about halfway through the battle when what many interpret as being an isolated group of English are shown holding a hill. Against this hill the Normans come to grief, with dramatic images of knights and horses crashing to the ground. It is hard to accept that this is supposed to be an isolated group causing such problems for the Normans, especially as the next scene depicts the famous retreat of the Normans in which it was thought that William had been killed. Every single published account of the battle states that the Normans had been driven back from the main English position, not from some small hillock. What the Tapestry it trying to demonstrate is that the Normans attacked the English army, which was stationed on top of a steep hill. Bradbury agrees that what the Tapestry designer is attempting to show is the main hill of the battle in two views in just the same fashion as he presents the English shield wall. "In which case," he writes, "we do not need to search the ground for isolated hillocks."[35]

After that, the rest of the battle continues on the undulating ground. It has been said that the undulating ground is meant to represent the rough nature of the terrain or the ridge upon which the English were stood.[36] It is particularly interesting to note that the Tapestry does not show the supposed *Malfosse* incident during the retreat of the English after the death of Harold, which, if it was so significant, seems a remarkable omission. What it does show, however, is the English retreating over high ground away from an unusual tree. Could this be the men running away over Caldbec Hill? And could that unusual tree be the famous hoary old apple tree which gave the battle its name?

A somewhat later source, possibly written at some point between 1160 and 1174, is Robert Wace's *Le Roman de Rou*. Wace was later made a canon of Bayeux Cathedral by Henry II. Wace's story is written in verse chronicles and it follows the Bayeux Tapestry so closely that it is clear he must have had access to it. He describes in detail supposed attempts at negotiation by William on the eve of the battle and then writes: "The duke and his men tried no further negotiation, but returned to their tents, sure of fighting on the morrow. Then men were to be seen on every side straightening lances, fitting hauberks and helmets; making ready the saddles and stirrups; filling the quivers, stringing the bows, and making all ready for the battle."[37]

He adds to our early knowledge of the battle site with a number of points. On the day before the battle, Wace records Harold creating some form of ditch to defend his encampment: "He [Harold] had the place well examined, and surrounded it by a good fosse, leaving an entrance in each of three sides, which were ordered to be well guarded." It is reported that each side fears the other will attack at night and both prepare for the battle. This aspect of the campaign is emphasised by Wace by repeating the preparations made by Harold: "Harold knew that the Normans would come and attack him hand to hand; so he had early enclosed the field in which he placed his men. He made them arm early, and range themselves for the battle; he himself having put on arms and equipment that became such a lord."[38]

Once again there is nothing to indicate that the English moved from their assembly point. The suggestion that the English had dug some kind of defensive ditch is interesting. Though most scholars have dismissed this as impractical, what it does indicate is that the English had time to prepare their position, and possibly even strengthen it in some way. If elements of the English had been gathering on Caldbec for the previous day or so it is far from unrealistic to suggest that they would have sought to protect themselves by erecting some kind of defensive work whilst they waited for Harold and the main body of the army to appear.

It is usually stated that the English scouts spotted the Normans from the vantage point of Caldbec Hill. This was the place where the English army had spent the night and as Harold knew he was in close proximity to the Normans he, quite sensibly, had prepared the ground so as not to be surprised during the night. If the English had seen the Normans as they crested Telham Hill (they could not have seen them any earlier, as Telham Hill is the highest point between Caldbec and Hastings) then they would surely not have left their prepared position. Although Battle Hill is closer to Caldbec than it is to Telham, Harold would be taking an immense gamble in leaving his much higher, well-prepared position for another in the hope of reaching the second position and assembling his forces in battle array before the enemy was upon him. This is such a risky manoeuvre that it defies comprehension.[39]

Wace also relates William's speech to his men before the battle: "The duke stood on a hill, where he could best see his men; the barons surrounded him and he spoke to them proudly." After this he puts on his armour and then the battle begins. There is nothing in Wace to say that the Normans then moved onto the battlefield. The way the document reads is that the speech is given at or close to the battlefield. It is usually stated that these incidents occurred on Telham Hill but this could equally apply to Battle Hill and, if Wace is to be believed, would be more appropriate to Battle Hill, which is considerably closer to where the troops would have been drawn up at the foot of Caldbec Hill if the battle took place on the latter hill.

Moving onto the battle itself, Wace specifically details an incident during the fighting which relates to the nature of the ground.

This incident occurs after the first Norman attack: "In the plain was a fosse, which the Normans had now behind them, having passed it in the fight without regarding it. But the English charged and drove the Normans before them, till they made them fall back upon this fosse, overthrowing into it horses and men. Many were to be seen falling therein, rolling one over the other, with their faces to the earth and unable to rise. Many of the English also, whom the Normans drew down along with them, died there. At no time in the day's battle did so many Normans die, as perished in that fosse. So those said who saw the dead."[40] Although historians have sought to portray the ditch at the rear of the hillock at the bottom of Battle Hill as being the one referred to by Wace, it is far too small to have caused such casualties. There are, however, three long watercourses running across the lower slopes of Caldbec Hill.

William of Malmesbury was born in Wiltshire in about 1095. His father was a Norman and his mother came from England. William became a Benedictine monk at Malmesbury Abbey, and while working in its library he became interested in history. He wrote his *Chronicle of the Kings of England* between the years 1123 and 1135. He was considered to be a comparatively diligent historian for his time, yet his writing is extremely pro-Norman, having almost nothing good to say about Harold or the English. The only passage in his work that mentions anything relating to the ground is in relation to the feigned retreats: "In this manner, deceived by a stratagem, they met an honourable death in avenging their country; nor indeed were they at all wanting to their own revenge, as, by frequently making a stand, they slaughtered their pursuers in heaps: for getting possession of an eminence, they drove down the Normans, when roused with indignation and anxiously striving to gain the higher ground, into the valley beneath, where, easily hurling their javelins and rolling down stones on them as they stood below, they destroyed them to a man. Besides, by a short passage, with which they were acquainted, avoiding a deep ditch, they trod under foot such a multitude of their enemies in that place, that they made the hollow level with the plain, by heaps of carcasses. This vicissitude of first one party conquering and then the other, prevailed as long as the life of Harold continued."[41]

We can draw from this that the English gained an eminence, one so steep that they were able to roll stones down upon the Normans. Traditionalists point to this eminence being the hillock at the bottom of Senlac Hill. This small rise, however, could hardly furnish many stones nor would they gather much momentum in the short drop to the ditch.

Amongst those considered as having produced prime source material, though distant from the events of 1066 by half a century, was Henry of Huntingdon in his *Historia Anglorum, The History of the English People 1000–1154*. Henry was born in around 1088 to a Norman family. The *History* was started at some point shortly after 1123 but offers us little of interest about the Battle of Hastings; in fact Henry devoted more words to William's rousing speech before the fighting began than to the entire battle itself. The only point of note is that he places the *Malfosse* incident during, not after, the battle. These are his words: "So Duke William instructed his people to simulate flight, but as they fled they came to a large ditch, cunningly hidden. A great number of them fell and were trampled. While the English were continuing in pursuit, the principal line of Normans broke through the central company of the English. When those who were pursuing saw this, they were obliged to return over the said ditch, and the greater part of them perished there."[42]

In conclusion, none of these prime sources specify where the Battle of Hastings was fought other than the discredited *Chronicle of Battle Abbey*. They do, though, provide a few clues and their descriptions of the ground indicate that the hill upon which the English formed their battle line was steep and difficult, that it was close to and higher than the Andresweald forest and even that it was nine miles from Hastings. We know that the English army concentrated by the hoar apple tree and that is where they made their stand. The weight of evidence from the sources, therefore, lies heavily in favour of the battle having been fought on the high, steep-sided Caldbec Hill.

Chapter 8

The Interpretations

"Hypothesis is as dangerous as it is unavoidable in any account of the whole business of the Norman Conquest."

R. Allen Brown, *Proceedings of the Battle Conference on Anglo-Norman Studies, 1980.*

"The study of [the battle of] Hastings," wrote M.K. Lawson, "must ultimately be a study of the characteristics and the strengths and weakness of the sources, and of what interpretations of the battle they seem to render most plausible".[1] J.J. Bagley, however, warns us that "historians are ever disputing with each other about the interpretation of facts, and each new generation, shifting the emphasis made by its predecessor feels it essential to re-write history."[2] Having, therefore, looked at the prime sources we must now investigate how the Battle of Hastings has been interpreted by the historians of more recent generations.

It was not until the eighteenth century that the first "modern", i.e. rigorously investigated, histories began to emerge. Amongst the first of these was the 1767 publication, *The History of England from the Invasion of Julius Caesar to the Revolution in 1688,* written in seven volumes by David Hume. The Battle of Hastings is in volume 1. His description of the battle is commendably brief and adds nothing that is not presented in the original sources. With regard to the battlefield all he states is that Harold "had seized the advantage of a rising ground, and having likewise drawn some trenches to secure his flanks, he resolved to stand upon the defensive." Hume does not deviate from, nor expand upon, the original sources and therefore makes no mention of Harold having left his encampment to take up an alternative position. He does, however, mention that Harold had dug trenches to secure his flanks. If nothing else, this does indicate that the English army had occupied their position long enough to be able to complete a fieldwork of this nature.[3]

The next genuinely significant work was E.A. Freeman's monumental, multi-volume, *The History of the Norman Conquest of England,* written in 1873. He uses his imagination to conjure up far more drama than Hume, and his description of the battlefield is very thorough and considered. Freeman set the standard and his book is still regarded by many as being the most detailed scholarly study of the battle. Where he has led, others have followed and many subsequent histories have remained faithful to his interpretation.[4] He had studied the ground carefully and in June 1869 he walked the battlefield with Captain R. James of the Royal Engineers, whose father Major General Henry James was Director General of the Ordnance Survey. The result was that Freeman was able to publish volume three of his great work with a large map reproduced by the Ordnance Survey.[5] This map showed not only the *Malfosse* situated almost immediately to the rear of the English line but also a three-deep line of palisades at the foot of the main English position, which he describes on two occasions in his survey of the battlefield: " He [Harold] occupied the hill; he surrounded it on all its accessible sides by a palisade, with a triple gate of entrance, and defended it to the south by an artificial ditch ... The whole height was alive with warriors; the slopes strong in themselves, were still further strengthened by the firm barricades of ash and other timber, wattled in so close together that not a crevice could be seen."[6]

It was simply not possible for the English to have constructed such defences if they had moved down from Caldbec Hill earlier in the day. Freeman therefore does not subscribe to the idea that the Hoar Apple Tree was on Caldbec, he believes that it was on Battle Hill and that Harold marched straight to Battle Hill on the 13th.

He does unfortunately contradict himself as he then writes that "it does not appear that any long time passed between Harold's occupation of this hill fortress and the battle itself. The spot was not one in which a large body of men could remain for any length of time; on the other hand the invaders could not keep themselves altogether inactive, neither could they pass by the English position without attacking it ... Immediate battle was absolutely inevitable on both sides."[7] So, on the one hand Harold "occupied and fortified as thoroughly as the time and the means at his command would allow a post of great natural strength which he made into what is distinctly spoken of as a castle" but on the other, "everything in our narrative leads us to believe that the battle followed almost immediately on the arrival of Harold." Both statements cannot be correct.[8]

Freeman had clearly examined the Bayeux Tapestry in compiling his work and he interpreted the scene showing the English on a steep hill as being an English outpost ahead of the main battle line. "Some way westward from the abbey is the point where the slope is gentlest of all, where the access to the natural citadel is least difficult. But here a low, detached, broken hill, a sort of small island in advance of the larger peninsula, stands out as an outpost in front of the main mass of high ground."[9]

He refers to this mound again when he discusses the Bretons giving way and being chased by some of the English: "A body of English troops was now rash enough, in direct defiance of the King's orders, to leave its post and pursue. These were of course some of the defenders of the English right. They may have been, as is perhaps suggested by a later turn of the battle, the detachment which guarded the small outlying hill. Or they may have been the men posted at the point just behind the outlying hill, where the slope is easiest and where the main Breton attack would most likely be made."

Though scholars have now in general rejected the possibility of the English having erected a palisade, the outpost as identified by Freeman on the little hillock ahead of the English line has been accepted by some. The whole basis of the English defence, we are led to believe, was to remain closely together to prevent the Norman knights getting amongst them. A relatively small body of men placed so far ahead of the main position would have been surrounded from the start of the battle. The Normans would have had no need to assault them and could simply have placed a number of knights to watch them in case they came down from their position to attack the advancing Normans. Alternatively the Normans could have overwhelmed the outpost before advancing against the main English line as it would have been too far away to have been reinforced or supported by the main body and the isolated troops would have been slaughtered in full view of their comrades.

The fact is that none of the sources mentions any such hillock and, had it not been for the representation of a hill being embroidered on the Tapestry, Freeman and subsequent authors would never have considered an isolated outpost at all.

Jonathon Duncan wrote his history of *The Dukes of Normandy* in 1839 and he too believed the story of the palisade: "the English front of battle stretched over a line of hills, fortified on all sides with a rampart of stakes and hurdles formed of osier."[10]

Mark Anthony Lower, one of the most notable early historians of the battle and the man who first translated the *Chronicle of Battle Abbey*, presented a paper to the Sussex Archaeological Society in 1852 in which he made a number of observations regarding the battlefield. He identified the *Malfosse* as being next to a place called Winchester-croft, which was north-west of the town. Though not exactly precise in his description, this seems to be what is now known as Beech stream, which is at the bottom of Caldbec Hill. Lower also believed that the *Malfosse* incident may have taken place during, not after the battle. If these two statements are correct then the battle could not have been fought on Battle Hill but they most certainly point to Caldbec Hill.

Lower was also of the opinion that, following Wace, the English built a barricade around their position. "We can well understand how the army could in a few hours erect a fortification of some strength by such means, when we remember that the ordinary mode of constructing houses of the meaner sort in Saxon times by driving large stakes into the ground."

By the time of the twentieth century, History, as a social science, had become firmly established. It became accepted practice for historians to analyse every available source and to declare the use of those sources in the composition of their works. The challenge of the historian was that of interpreting those sources.

As the site of the Battle of Hastings was evidently where the abbey had been built, none of those historians even thought of questioning such an incontrovertible fact. Book after book was published, each of which endeavoured to add more meat to the bare bones left to us from the eleventh and twelfth centuries.

In so doing, the academics have enriched our understanding of medieval warfare, both Norman and Anglo-Saxon. The motivations and consequences of the Norman Conquest have also been explored at enormous length and historians have expanded our knowledge of the weapons, armour, tactics and moral values of that era. They have also interpreted every aspect of England's most famous battle. But in doing so have attempted to fit the known, or surmised, actions into or upon the presumed battle site. This is not a case of incompetence; it is merely one of neglect. The battle was fought on Battle Hill, because that is where the abbey was built.

Around the turn of the century Frank Merry Stenton made his contribution to the Norman Conquest historiography with his *William the Conqueror and the Rule of the Normans*. He was a little more circumspect in his comments than Freeman and he adheres quite firmly to the accepted sources. With regard to the ground upon which Harold made his stand, he wrote that: "It is plain from all the narratives of the forthcoming encounter that the ridge in question was quite unoccupied [i.e. uninhabited] at the time of the battle; and when the English chroniclers wish to describe its site they can only tell us that Harold and William came together 'by the hoar apple tree'."[1]

The renowned soldier-historian Major General J.F.C. Fuller wrote the first volume of *A Military History of the Western World* in 1954. In this he states that "Harold encamped his men on or near a rise in the downs [*sic*] marked by a 'hoar apple-tree' ... If surprise was Harold's aim, then, in all probability he encamped in the [Andresweald] forest, and only occupied the 'hoary apple-tree' position early on the following morning."[12]

Lieutenant Colonel Charles Lemmon, who lived just a few miles away from Battle at St Leonards-on-Sea, wrote *The Field of Hastings* which, as its name implies, looks closely at the battlefield. He also gives this explanation of Caldbec Hill: "Harold's method of putting his plan into operation emerges in his selection of the rendezvous, the Hoar Apple Tree, which there are good reasons to believe grew on Caldbec Hill on the northern edge of the town of Battle. The selection of this rendezvous was instrumental in determining the site of the battle, and consequently, in after years, that of the Abbey and the town of Battle. Harold appears to have chosen it for four reasons: it was a short march from Hastings, a nodal point of communications; a point which the Norman army must pass on its march to London, and it was covered by an excellent defensive position. Once there, he could consolidate his army and then pounce on the Norman base at Hastings, secure in the knowledge that should William move first, the Saxon army was in a strong position astride his route, and could not be passed ... These facts make it possible to say with some certainty that Caldbec Hill was the appointed rendezvous."[13]

It is interesting to note that Lemmon also considers that it was Harold's decision to concentrate his army on Caldbec Hill which led to his downfall, as it was too close to the Norman camp. The result was that William was able to catch Harold with the latter's army still forming. This reinforces the view that those who suggest that the English army's assembly point was even closer to the Norman camp – on Battle Hill, or even at Crowhurst as one person has proposed – are likely to be wrong. Lemmon, a retired officer of field rank, considered that "Harold would have been wiser to assemble his army on the North Downs and only to have advanced from there once his army had completed its concentration."[14]

In his 1966 publication *Conquest 1066*, Rupert Furneaux wrote the following: "The great natural strength of the position where Harold ordered his army to assemble, and where he stood his ground, has been taken to prove that he always intended, having marched to meet William, to fight a defensive battle. There can be little question that Harold knew the place of the 'Hoar Apple Tree' and had assessed its advantages for such an eventuality during his sojourn in Sussex during the summer, but he could not have counted, when he left London, on the Normans sallying out of their entrenchments to attack him." Furneaux believed that Harold probably intended to attack William just as he had Hardrada but when he saw the Normans moving upon him he decided to take advantage of the ground his forces already held. "The appointed assembly-place was ideally suited for defence," continued Furneaux. "He intended to stand on the impregnable redoubt which nature provided; the crest of the slope against which nature provided; the crest of the slope against which the Norman horsemen would dash themselves in vain."[15]

Norman Denny's and Josephine Filmer-Sankey's *The Bayeux Taspestry*, also published in 1966, makes little attempt at detailed interpretations. The makers of the Tapestry, they said, "have handed down to us a terrible and wonderful picture of the savagery and confusion of war ... the details do not greatly matter."[16]

In 1972 Catherine Morton and Hope Muntz translated and edited Guy of Amiens', *Carmen de Hastingae Proelio* and included a discussion on the battle.

This includes a quote from H.B. George's *Battles of English History* as follows: "If detailed narratives are to be fitted into their historical place, the first question that suggests itself is why battles were fought where they were. The exact site is usually a matter of deliberate choice on the part of one combatant or the other, the assailant seizing his enemy at a disadvantage ... or the defendant selecting what seems to him the best position in which to await attack; and what position is most favourable obviously depends on the tactics of the age. Of the latter, Hastings and Waterloo furnish conspicuous examples ..."

The authors make the point that Harold chose the ground at the Battle of Hastings, even though the "D" version of the *Anglo-Saxon Chronicle* states that William came upon Harold unprepared.[17] They also point out that the Bayeux Tapestry shows the English receiving the first Norman attacks in perfect formation and that none of the Norman chroniclers say that William surprised the English. They reconcile these opposing views by suggesting that words of the *Anglo-Saxon Chronicle* "sound suspiciously like an excuse for defeat."

We know that the ground upon which the battle was fought did not favour the Normans in any way. We also know that the English forces spent the night before the battle in the immediate vicinity of the eventual battlefield and that the Normans had to travel all the way from Hastings to make contact with their enemy. Everything, therefore, indicates that, as H.B. George states, one side chose where the battle would be fought and that side was clearly the English. That being the case, as it must surely have been, the most logical position to accept battle was on top of Caldbec Hill.

Though Morton and Muntz argue in support of Battle Hill as the site of the battle, they do offer an interesting explanation of one of the key sentences in the *Carmen*. When William is informed that the English have been spotted he orders forward his archers to engage the enemy, settling cross-bowmen in the midst, with instructions to aim at the faces of the English and then retire. "The military detail in this passage is of great interest," Morton and Muntz observe. "The duke's purpose is, seemingly, to check the enemy's further advance, so that he may anticipate the seizure of the hill – causing panic with his missiles, notably his bolts, while the enemy is in the act of concentration upon Caldbec. Since the range of these weapons was not great, it would be necessary for the foot to advance beyond the lower hill to achieve this. They would then fall back on that position, the duke in the meantime having brought up the knights in support. The text may, however, be construed to mean that only the *balistantes* in the centre were to retire, opening a way for the knights to press home the attack, with archers upon the two flanks ready to enfilade any attempted counter-attack. The duke's presumed objective, in this case, would have been to carry Caldbec Hill, pushing the English back in disorder from the high ground and so assuring himself freedom of manoeuvre."

Morton and Muntz also come down in favour of it being William who was taken by surprise rather than Harold. When William's scouts catch sight of the English his knights are out foraging. As they state, we learn later in the *Carmen* that Harold's advance guard, at least, was mounted. "It would seem, therefore, that it was the sight of armed bands of horsemen on Caldbec, with the advance-guard of the English close behind them at the edge of the forest, that forced William to change his plans ... 'Florence' of Worcester's story that there were heavy desertions among the English early in the day may denote the initial effect of *ballistae*, but William could not dislodge the enemy [from Caldbec]."

With regards to Guy of Amiens, own words, there is a passage later in the *Carmen* which describes the death of Harold. Duke William spots the English king "far off on the steeps of the hill". This sounds nothing whatsoever like the Battle Abbey ridge, where no point could be considered particularly far away.

In his 1974 publication, *The Enigma of Hastings*, Edwin Tetlow devotes much space to debunking the alleged holy justification for William's invasion. The significance of this is two-fold. Firstly, it casts doubt upon the veracity of all the sources which support the papal approval of the invasion of England and, secondly, it challenges the assumption that before the battle William swore to build a monastery if he were victorious. Though Tetlow does not think to question the battle site, he is unequivocal in his condemnation of the falsification of papal support for the conquest. "This is the theme of all Norman propaganda about the Conquest," he wrote, "that William had every right to cross the English Channel with his powerful force to strike a usurping Harold off his throne." The purpose, he continued, "was nothing less than to make a *post facto* justification of the invasion and seizure of an independent kingdom."[18]

The fact that Harold's oath was used as providing the legal basis for William's invasion cannot be entirely discounted. At least some element of the story simply must be true and Tetlow believes that he knows what that is. He believes that Harold paid a visit to the Continent in the autumn of 1056. Proof of this is provided by a document which survives to this day. This is a diploma issued at St Omer on 13 November of that year by Baldwin, Count of Flanders. Amongst the witnesses and signatories were both Harold and Guy of Ponthieu, the man who supposedly captured Harold. "This raises the possibility that Harold in fact made only one visit to Europe and went to St Omer not as Guy's captive but as his guest," writes Tetlow, "and that the creators of the Tapestry conveniently altered dates and circumstances in concocting their story of Harold's visit to William, which quite probably never took place at all." It was, according to Tetlow, "a skilful adaptation and extension of true facts."[19]

The first volume of William Seymour's *Battles in Britain 1066–1547* was published in 1975. Seymour agrees with Freeman that Harold always planned to fight a defensive battle: "The alternative would have been to catch the Normans off balance, as he had done the Norsemen, but here there could have been little hope of surprise and he might well have given William the chance to make use of ground of his own choosing and more suitable for his cavalry." He disputes the idea of any form of defences being erected around the English position, but he does believe that Caldbec Hill was "likely" to have been the concentration point for Harold's forces, though he does concede that the hoar apple tree may have been on Battle Hill. "It is," he writes, "yet another detail of which we cannot be sure."[20]

Seymour also tells us that in the first phase of the battle the Normans were overwhelmed by the weight of missiles hurled at them by the English. It is generally accepted that the English front was made up of *housecarls* yet it was most probably the *fyrd* that were armed with missile weapons – slings, bows and javelins. There are two possible explanations to this apparent paradox. One is that some of the *fyrd* were out in front as skirmishers but it seems unlikely that small numbers of such troops could have produced the firepower to "overwhelm" the Norman infantry. The other explanation is that the *housecarls* stood lower down on the slope and the *fyrd* behind them threw their missiles over the heads of the men in front. This could only happen if the slope upon which the men were stood was sufficiently steep. If they were stood upon Caldbec Hill such a tactic would be possible. If they were stood on Battle Hill it would be difficult for the missile-throwers to see or aim at the enemy and dangerous for the *housecarls* placed in front of them.[21]

David Howarth in his *1066, The Year of the Conquest*, published in 1977, also uses the Battle of Waterloo as an analogy, describing Harold's position as "having a peculiar likeness to the position Wellington chose at Waterloo." It is certainly true that Battle Hill is not dissimilar to the ridge of Mont St Jean but Wellington's position at Waterloo has never been regarded as being steep. Howarth himself then confirms this by explaining the similarities he has observed, "the gentle ridge with a lane along the top, the muddy valley, the main road cutting across it and the forest in the rear." Where then are the untilled "steeps" up which the Normans toiled slowly? These are not to be found on Howarth's gentle ridge.

Howarth also discusses the English assembly point of Caldbec Hill. "The place was actually on the watershed where the road came out of the Hastings triangle. There was an obvious reason for the choice: beyond that place there were two roads to London, and had he assembled farther away he could not be certain of intercepting William. It was certainly too near to be safe: it was open to attack at any moment William cared to choose. But this was not a mistake if Harold expected and intended to fight as soon as he arrived there, and there is every evidence that he did." This being the case, there is no explanation as to why, when the Normans had been sighted, Harold abandoned this position for one undeniably inferior and one that was nearer to the approaching enemy. As Howarth then writes, Harold had spent the night encamped on Caldbec Hill amongst his men: "… he had chosen his position and taken it before William could stop him, and he expected to fight the next day."

In 1979 Peter Young and John Adair wrote *Hastings to Culloden* in which they gave a fine description of Caldbec Hill: "This camp was not chosen at random; it effectively barred the way to London. It is true that there was a Roman road from Hastings to London by way of Bodiam and Maidstone. This route, however, was impracticable for an army unless the Brede estuary could be circumvented, and this could only be done by taking the prehistoric track way to Caldbec Hill, crossing the Brede at Whatlington, and then regaining the Roman road. If this road was defended, for example at Whatlington, an army could still reach London from Caldbec Hill by way of Lewes. If Harold was to make certain of opposing a Norman march on London it could only be done by confronting them at this particular fork in the road."[22]

The contentious move by Harold from the heights of Caldbec Hill to the lesser elevation of Battle Hill has proved difficult for historians to explain. In the 1979 publication *1066 Year of Destiny* Terry Wise avoided this problem by skipping directly from Harold's forces being on Caldbec Hill to them forming up on Battle Hill, giving no reason or explanation of why these men had suddenly changed location.[23] What Wise does bring to the reader's attention, however, is a very well-considered point about the deployment of the Norman army.

Anyone who has stood at the foot of Battle Hill will note how close the summit is. Visitors to the grounds of Battle Abbey are advised by the information boards on the site that the line of the existing buildings roughly marks the place where the English shield wall would have been formed. We are led to believe from almost every account that the English quietly waited on the hill while the Normans de-filed from their march and sorted themselves out into their respective divisions. "Why Harold allowed William to deploy his army at such close range will never be known," remarked Wise. "The English could have charged down upon their enemies while they were still only half deployed, with the remainder piled up along the narrow trackway to the rear." This is certainly what most commanders would have done and it can safely be said that William was too cautious and experienced a commander to have put his army into such a dangerous position.

If the battle had been fought on Battle Hill, then Harold's failure to attack the Normans when they were at their most vulnerable would certainly have been inexplicable. As we have already seen, the only reason why the English stood their ground was because the ground they stood upon was Caldbec Hill, the long slopes of which would have made such a manoeuvre hazardous – as was demonstrated so dramatically in the battle itself.[24]

Also in 1979 Eleanor Searle presented a paper to the Battle conference with the title of *The Abbey of the Conquerors: Defensive Enfeoffment and Economic Development in Anglo-Norman England*. In this Professor Searle provided the most plausible reason yet suggested for the construction of Battle Abbey.

Dismissing, of course, the claims of the Battle Abbey chronicler, she states, with regard to the abbey's location, that it "dominated the route of a successful invasion. It was placed here to ensure that no-one else might do the same." That is to say, whatever the penitential or commemorative character of the new abbey, "it fitted shrewdly into the strategy of defence that determined the unusually early settlement of the south-east Channel coast."[25]

Following the Conquest, William divided Sussex into five corridors of land running north to south called Rapes. These compact, virtually independent lordships were expected to prevent invasion and the Norman lords built mighty castles which controlled access from the coast to London.

The Rape of Hastings was granted to the Count of Eu (one of William's cousins), who was asked to accept the *banlieu* of Battle abbey as an independent rape within that of Hastings. The reason for this is that the Hastings rape was only lightly settled in 1066 and there were only a few manors inland from the coastal plain. Anything that could attract more people to settle on the land would increase its defensive potential. The building of a great abbey was an obvious magnet which would draw in immigrants, and the reason for its independence was that it offered newcomers the chance of settling on the land free from the constraints of the count and his court.

The significance of this is that on the previously unoccupied areas there was no ancient traditional hereditary right to the land as there was in areas of the country already settled. The right of succession was dependent on the favour of the Count of Eu and so could easily be lost or removed. Offering settlers the chance to hold land under the abbot of Battle, free of the constraints of the Norman knights, was clearly appealing. Remarkably, the Battle Abbey charter also claimed that "any person guilty of theft, manslaughter, or any other crime, should, through fear of death, take refuge in this Abbey, he should receive no injury [and] all its tenants should be everywhere exempt from toll and from every custom of earthly service."[26] The result of this liberal approach, as is recorded in the *Chronicle of Battle Abbey*, was that "many persons were brought out of the neighbouring counties, and some from beyond the seas, who prepared themselves habitations according to the distribution of the abbot and the monks. These, *who are in other respects free*, have from that time been accustomed to pay the abbey the fixed charge for the land."[27]

Searle summarises her explanation as follows: "It was into this pattern of isolated, free peasant assarts [cleared land suitable for cultivation] overlaid with the web of feudal enfeoffment and responsibility, then, that Battle Abbey was set, like a 'go' stone on a partially filled board. But it was meant to be free of the responsibilities and the dependences of the knights of Eu. It was set down, not in order to contribute to settlement and defence *through* the count, but to be his equal."

We must remember that ecclesiastical buildings in medieval times were defensive structures. Churches, built with tall bell-towers and often surrounded by moats, were places of refuge for the local population. The abbot of a great abbey was expected to lead the local resistance if invaders struck, and in Sussex this indeed occurred during the Hundred Years War with France. During this period Battle Abbey certainly fulfilled the role set down for it by William, and the magnificent gatehouse and crenellated walls the visitor sees today are a reminder of the days when, as Searle makes clear, Battle Abbey was a leader of the coastal defensive system.

The abbey was built therefore in the most suitable spot to block an enemy advance from the coast and to encourage settlement in the adjacent area. Battle Hill and its immediate environs was far better suited to such a development than the steep and difficult Caldbec Hill.[28]

It is in the light of Searle's explanation of the purpose for the building of the abbey that we can understand far better the reasons for the compilation of the *Chronicle of Battle Abbey*. The abbey's prosperity depended on it being able to retain control over its extensive lands but, by the mid-twelfth century, with the Hastings Rape more heavily populated, there was no longer, in terms of its role in coastal defence, a need for it to be independent. The abbot, therefore, could not claim that its original purpose was still valid. Some other reason had to be found, thus the story of its peculiar importance on the site of the battlefield and William's vow was concocted.

Amanda Clarke's *A Day that Made History* written in 1988 gives a clear description of Harold's move to Battle Hill. "He intended to make a surprise attack at dawn, firstly by wiping out any foraging parties and then going in to take the main army. His plan relied on the element of surprise and was virtually a repeat of the tactics he had used so effectively nineteen days before at Stamford Bridge. As Harold's men were preparing for battle, a scout arrived in the Norman camp to warn William that the English were near. William quickly called in his foraging parties and set off with his army to attack Harold. This aggressive move by the Normans forced Harold to change his plans. "Realizing that a surprise attack was out of the question, Harold decided to take advantage of his strong defensive position and allow William to come to him. However, instead of remaining on Caldbec Hill, the King decided to concentrate his forces on a small ridge half a mile to the south." The contradictions here are obvious and Clarke is unable to reconcile the decision of Harold to take advantage of his strong defensive position with his move to the small ridge further south.[29]

In R. Allen Brown's 1985 book, *The Normans and the Norman Conquest*, we have an author who is unequivocal in accepting that the monks built the abbey on the correct spot. "We know the site of the engagement: we know with an unusual degree of precision where it was fought, and thus, with the aid of the generous literary and artistic evidence, we have a good chance of knowing *how* it was fought also." Even though he accepts that "the Conqueror's vow before the battle to found his penitential abbey on the battlefield is now discredited", he says that he has "no reason at all to disbelieve the tradition preserved at Battle." His opinion is that the abbey must have been built on the correct site because that is the traditionally accepted view. Brown qualifies these positive statements, however, by declaring, as we have already noted, that the only really undisputed fact about Hastings was that the Normans won.

Brown also dismisses the *Malfosse* incident. "For this," he writes, "there is no contemporary authority. The story obviously has its beginnings in William of Poitiers who reports a stand by some fleeing English taking advantage of 'a broken rampart and a labyrinth of ditches' … But in this there is no '*Malfosse*' ridden into by Norman knights; for that we have to wait for Orderic Vitalis in the earlier twelfth century … while the dread but romantic name '*Malfosse*' first appears only in the suspect Battle Abbey Chronicle." Having declared that Battle Hill is where Harold made his stand he then acknowledges that the position was "something less than ideal". He describes the hill as low, constricted and one from where retreat would be difficult. This hardly seems to comply with the descriptions provided by the prime sources.[30]

Peter Poyntz Wright, in his *The Battle of Hastings* published in 1986 and republished under the title *Hastings* ten years later, becomes confused over the choice of battlefield, which at least indicates that he had investigated the ground well. He concedes that "if Harold had meant to surprise William, it seems unlikely that he envisaged an encounter near the Caldbec assembly point; he may have hoped to achieve his surprise attack by a forced march the next day, perhaps leaving some of his baggage at the edge of the forest. Nevertheless his choice of Caldbec as an assembly point was a shrewd one, because in the event of surprise he had his army in the best defensive position the neighbourhood provided." The last point is hugely significant and it is one he reiterates later: "he [Harold] chose the Hoary Apple Tree both as a familiar rallying point and one as easily defended in the event of an attack." Poyntz Wright also subscribes to the view that the defenders may have erected some kind of defensive structure having "hammered a few stakes into the ground to protect the end of each flank."

A more recent appraisal is provided by David Crouch in his *The Normans: A History of a Dynasty*. In this book, the author, ignoring the usual statements that the English assembled at Caldbec Hill on the 13th, writes that "Harold reached what was to be the field of battle soon after the cold dawn of Saturday, 14 October 1066." He then states that Harold "had the luck" to come up against the Normans when his troops were in a strong defensive position! As we have seen, Harold was a Sussex man and the Hoar Apple Tree was a well-known spot. It seems highly unlikely that luck played a part in the position adopted by Harold for his battle.

Crouch's description of this "strong defensive position" is that it was "a wooded east-west ridge at the end of a spur of the Weald with a steep southward slope lying across the road northwards out of Hastings. The valley in front was wet and rough with sedge, features that were bound to hinder the Normans."

Finally, he says that William's only recorded words were, in reality, "a prayer to the effect that: 'I'll found an abbey here if I survive!'" Crouch fails to mention either William's recorded address or the fact that the only reference to the building of the abbey are from the discredited *Chronicle of Battle Abbey* a century after the event.

Other aspects of the battlefield can be inferred from his description of the deployment of the Norman army. There was not enough space for the "ordered and well-marshalled companies" that William would have wished to arrange before he attacked. The battlefield was therefore relatively confined. He also writes that the steepness of the slope all "along the front" allowed the Norman Knights no chance to charge, or even manoeuvre in front of the English line. Crouch, therefore, conforms to the traditional view of the English position being on top of a steep-sided hill, yet anyone who stands on the lower slopes of Battle Hill will see wide open spaces ideal for cavalry. He makes no reference to the *Malfosse*.

One historian who appears to have given particular thought to the nature and location of the battlefield is Jim Bradbury. As he wrote in his book, *The Battle of Hastings*, "the *best* evidence for the location of the battle is not at all definite about the accepted site, and we should recall that none of the eleventh-century sources was the work of an eyewitness, or probably of anyone who ever visited the site." The italics are Bradbury's. He goes on to explain what he means: "The early chronicles in fact do not clearly identify the location, and there are some comments which are a little worrying to the acceptance of the traditional site." The comments he refers to in particular are those in the "D" version of the *Anglo-Saxon Chronicle* disclosed earlier, which states that Harold assembled a large army and William came against him at the Hoar Apple Tree. "It does not say they assembled there and then moved on a mile and fought, but that is where they fought," continued Bradbury. "This also indicates that it was no chance location, but one that was well known and selected well in advance as a meeting point, perhaps with the prime intention of preventing a Norman march northwards to London."

Bradbury points out the oddity that even though no one has thought of investigating the site of the battle, the location of the apple tree has been thoroughly examined and settled to most people's satisfaction. This is a place where the boundaries of three hundreds met, and such old trees often marked important boundary points of that kind. It is odd, Bradbury remarks, "that historians have settled the position of the tree, but never considered that the 'D' version might be correct."[31]

Bradbury then goes on to consider the site of the apple tree, Caldbec Hill: "It is an eminently suitable position for the sort of battle the chronicles describe. Caldbec is a hill with slopes steeper than those at Battle. In fact Caldbec, 300 feet above sea level, dominates the area and ... Caldbec Hill was right on the edge of the heavily wooded land. Domesday Book allows us to say this with some hope of being accurate, since it indicates which parts were cultivated. The Battle chronicler says there were woods around the abbey, but from Domesday it seems likely that if troops emerged from 'forest' they would first come on to Caldbec, which after all was the appointed meeting place."

He also examines Orderic's use of the name Senlac. As has been mentioned before, the *Historia Ecclesiastica* is the first document to call the battlefield Senlac Hill. Bradbury has pointed out that this has been universally applied to Battle Hill, but without any evidence, and that there is no reason to think that Senlac Hill means Battle Hill based on any earlier documents.

Yet Bradbury tells us, quite correctly, that there was a lake at the base of the northern slopes of Caldbec Hill at a place close to Oakwood Gill on the edge of the wooded area. It is here where another feature of the battlefield is located – the *Malfosse*. This place will be investigated in detail later; for now Bradbury's words are sufficient: "it fits as well and perhaps better with a battle fought on Caldbec than on Battle Hill."

Bradbury also points out that at the place where the Bayeux Tapestry moves to the story of the battle it shows three trees, the first that have been portrayed since the Normans were seen cutting timber for building their ships. This, says Bradbury, seems to confirm that woods were in the vicinity of the fighting.

Bradbury also considers the claim made by Poitiers that "William came against him [Harold] by surprise before his army was drawn up in battle array." Bradbury discounts this: "Had both armies been on the march, Harold would have been in no more disarray than William. If he were ready to deploy on Battle Hill he would have been in better state than William. The suspicion recurs that William caught Harold at the assembly point [of Caldbec Hill]."

Bradbury repeated many of these observations as recently as December 2010 in *Heritage* magazine: "We do know that the English assembled at nearby Caldbec Hill. The earliest source on Hastings was the *Anglo Saxon Chronicle* which stated that William came against Harold 'at the hoary apple tree'. The author who places the battle on the abbey hill is the monk who wrote the *Battle Abbey Chronicle* a century after the event. Either the Normans attacked Caldbec Hill, as the *Anglo Saxon Chronicle* suggests, or else the English moved on from their assembly point to the traditional hill site and were attacked there by the Normans ... Study of old and new maps gives some indication of the nature of the land, including lakes, woods and pathways relevant to understanding the troop movements. Caldbec Hill fits better with mentions of woodland and a lake in Duniford Wood and Oakwood Pool."[32]

He concludes his analysis of the battle ground by declaring that he would be "perfectly happy if some other proof appears which confirms the traditional location. It is simply that if one looks at the evidence objectively, questions have to be raised."

M.K. Lawson, in his exceptionally well considered book *The Battle of Hastings 1066*, published in 2002, firmly rejects the idea of Caldbec Hill being the site of the battle. He does accept, however, that "wherever his flanks lay, Harold would have been aware of the danger of their being turned by the French horse." He is also very clear in his contention that "the complexities of the written sources are unlikely ever to be resolved."[33]

Frank McLynn in his 1998 book *1066 The Year of the Three Battles* wrote, "It is clear that Harold did not intend to advance against William's main force until his own expected reinforcements had come up, and meanwhile was quite content to take up a defensive position on Caldbec Hill near the 'hoary apple tree' which had been agreed in London as the rendezvous point for later reinforcements and units not proceeding directly with Harold. The location was at the southern exit from the wooded hills, and some scholars even think the subsequent battle was fought there and not on Battle Hill, the traditional site."[34]

In the study of *The House of Godwine* in 2004 by Emma Mason, she refers to Caldbec Hill as being a well-known landmark and "a place where his [Harold's] army could rest overnight, concealed by the surrounding countryside." She also refers to one of the drawbacks associated with Harold abandoning Caldbec Hill to move to Battle Hill: "The only easy route to and from the [Battle] ridge was along a narrow isthmus which would make any retreat hazardous." Mason also reminds us that John of Worcester hinted at defectors being displeased with the narrowness of the site. In addition she considers the "substantial" element of Danish mercenaries mentioned by William of Poitiers. These men deployed on higher ground, on a hill near to the wood from which they emerged. Here they dismounted from their horses and lined up on foot in a dense formation. Mason thinks that the place where the Danish stood was not a hill but was the isthmus leading back to Caldbec Hill, and that they were stationed there by Harold to protect the flanks of the main English position. The isthmus could not be described in this way, however, as it is no higher than Senlac Hill until it starts to climb Caldbec Hill, nor was it particularly close to the Andresweald.[35]

In the 2004 publication *Harold & William: The Battle for England 1064–1066*, Benton Rain Patterson finds a solution to the seemingly illogical move by Harold from Caldbec Hill to the inferior Battle ridge by situating the English camp at the foot of Caldbec Hill. Whilst he details the English march from London down to Caldbec Hill he does not explain why the English camped on the low ground, nor does he take into consideration the fact that the ground at the foot of Caldbec Hill was, and still is, swampy and would have made a very damp place to bed down for the night. He also ignores the fact that the Norman foot soldiers, according to the sources, had to toil up the steep slope because in his description of the battle he has these men *running* towards the English line. On Battle Hill this is entirely possible; on Caldbec Hill this is simply impossible.[36]

The alleged approval of William's invasion of England by Pope Alexander is robustly challenged by Paul Hill in his 2005 book *The Road to Hastings*. The notion of the "extraordinary blessing" given to the invasion of one Christian country against another "has always sounded faintly absurd", as has the granting of a papal banner which was normally only raised against Muslims and pagans or a rebel against papal authority. Though it is usually stated that Stigand was just such a rebel, there was no apparent unease in 1062 when papal legates sat in council with Archbishop Stigand, and despite his "uncannonial" appointment to the senior post in the English church he remained in office for four years after the Conquest. Hill is quite clear that Battle Abbey was built by William only because he had to do so in order to square relations with Rome following his unauthorised invasion. In this light, the idea put forward so strenuously by the chronicler of Battle Abbey that William was passionate about the exact spot where the abbey was built does seem incongruous. In reality William never bothered to visit the monastery and he was probably only concerned that the abbey should be built at a suitable point astride the road from the coast.

Hill also makes the following statement: "At Caldbec Hill, the site of the grey, or 'hoary' apple tree, a known meeting point in the shire, a surprise was sprung upon Harold before he was ready ... So, for all his speed, Harold had been caught out at his forming-up point. Somewhere to the north, marching through the thickly wooded Sussex countryside, were reinforcements expecting to rendezvous with the king at the Caldbec Hill forming up point."[37]

Harriet Wood, in her 2008 work *The Battle of Hastings: The Fall of Anglo-Saxon England*, discussed without reference to the source (or sources), the claim made by others of the "serious accusation that Harold's choice of ground was poor." This is further reinforcement of our contention that those who have declared Harold had chosen Battle Hill to fight his battle on are misguided.

Nevertheless, Wood, like Hill, is quite categorical in her belief that there is no substance to the claim that William promised to build an abbey on the battlefield if he should be victorious. As we have read earlier, it is thought that William ordered the construction of the abbey following the arrival of the papal delegation in England in 1070 and the insistence on a penance being paid by those who had fought at Hastings. They were required to perform a year's penance for each man they had killed. If they did not know how many English they had killed they were allowed to commute the penance by gifts to the Church. The archers, oddly, were required to observe a triple Lent. There were different sentences for crimes committed against civilians after the battle.[38]

Wood believes that the building of an abbey was William's personal penance: "Battle Abbey was not completed and dedicated until 1094; the legend, originated and maintained by the monks of Battle that William had vowed a monastery on the site of the battle before it had ever taken place, has now been demolished." The alleged papal sanction of William's invasion and his promise to build an abbey on the site of the battle should he prove successful are what Wood calls "part of the fable of the conquest".

Finally, we must not ignore the Internet. Whilst we have all learned to turn to websites with extreme caution the World Wide Web does, with its informality and its low production costs, enable those with no academic training and limited resources to express their opinions, and with respect to the Battle of Hastings to offer alternative views to those of the mainstream. The one site which does deserve consideration here is www.secretsofthenormaninvasion.com. It has recently been self-published in the form of an e-book.

This has been compiled by Nick Austin, who claims not only to have found a new site for the Battle of Hastings but also a new site for the Norman landing, which he reckons was at Wilting. The old route from Wilting towards London ran through Crowhurst and it is here that Austin believes the battle was fought. He supports his belief by indicating that the Domesday Book shows Crowhurst to have been wasted. Austin also uses the words from the *Chronicle of Battle Abbey* referred to earlier: "They studied the battlefield and decided that it seemed hardly suitable for so outstanding a building. They therefore chose a fit place for settling, a site located not far off, but somewhat lower down, towards the western slope of the ridge. There lest they seem to be doing nothing, they built themselves some little huts. The site *(i.e. the battlefield)*, still called Herste, has a low wall as a mark of this." The italics are Austin's.

It is true that an ancient wall has been found by Austin at Crowhurst and, whilst Austin's arguments are interesting, a study of the suggested site at Crowhurst reveals that it is far too extensive to have been securely held by some 7,000–10,000 men and they certainly would not have been packed tightly together as the sources indicate. It is also simply too far from Battle, being some two miles away. Whilst it only takes a few moments today by car to travel this distance, by foot it is more than thirty minutes away from where the abbey was eventually built. It is unrealistic to imagine that the Marmoutier monks could possibly have walked such a distance to build their abbey when more suitable sites exist much closer to Crowhurst. Also, though it was four years after the battle when the monks arrived to start their project, they must have been given some information concerning the site of the battle by people living in England and some physical evidence of a battle having been fought in the area between Caldbec Hill and Battle Hill must have still been present. No one could have got the place so badly wrong. Such cannot be said of the relationship between Caldbec Hill and Battle Hill, which are separated only by a shallow valley.

Unfortunately for Austin's theory, Crowhurst is referred to in the *Chronicle of Battle Abbey* entirely separately and is called Croherste. Herste cannot therefore also be Croherste.[39]

Finally, Austin makes much of the fact that according to the Domesday Book the manor of Crowhurst was wasted and that therefore the battle must have been fought there. Crowhurst was not the only place to have suffered at the hands of the Normans but if, as we have read, the Normans camped in the vicinity of Battle on the night of the 13th then they must have been somewhere near Crowhurst. An army of some 7,000–10,000 hungry men camped there would have quickly laid waste to the area. It is not evidence that the battle was fought at Crowhurst. He does not take into account that at Battle the great monastery was being built at the time of the Domesday Survey (1085–6). This would have meant a considerable influx of builders and craftsmen of different sorts, which would have encouraged a rapid development of the area – more so than in any of the other villages wasted by the Normans.

Nevertheless, Austin is convinced that Battle Hill is not where the battle took place. "If Harold had fought this battle at the Abbey site he would have had a very small chance of success against the Normans, because they could destroy the Saxons with their horse in open country," he writes. "Harold had seen and fought with them in France. He knew their leader and he knew their fighting strategy. William's men fought with war horses. These horses were massive compared to a man on foot and Harold knew his men were used to fighting on foot. These horses were the equivalent of today's tanks against infantry. Standing men in a field had little chance against a ton of horse in full gallop with an armoured knight on its back."

Where Austin's argument really falls down is that Pye's Farm, Crowhurst, where he assumes the English were drawn up, is simply too close to the Norman camp. The distance between Pye's Farm and Wilting, which Austin believes was where the Norman's built their two wooden castles, is only two miles. William would never have waited passively a couple of miles away whilst Harold assembled a large army, nor indeed would Harold have contemplated such an operation.[40]

Austin's theory has also been dismissed by English Heritage, who point out that the Crowhurst site itself would have been a far more convenient place to construct such a large building. The builders had to undertake a considerable amount of terracing to provide a level platform for the abbey on Battle Hill, which would not have been necessary to nearly the same extent at Crowhurst. No one would create work for himself in this way. "Any account of the Abbey's foundation needs to explain why this difficult location was chosen," observed Roy Porter, English Heritage's Territory Properties Curator for the South.[41] That is exactly the point. Battle ridge, difficult though it may be, was chosen because Caldbec Hill would have presented the builders with far more technological difficulties than the site they eventually selected.

From this brief investigation of the historiography of the Battle of Hastings we can draw together a few common threads. The first of these is that the assembly point of the English army was almost certainly Caldbec Hill. It is also likely that Harold was caught unawares at the assembly point by William's lightning strike on the morning of 14 October. Though the general view is that Harold moved down from Caldbec Hill there is no consensus as to why he did this. It seems a strange act to undertake if he intended to fight a defensive battle, as Caldbec Hill offered him greater advantages against the Norman knights. If he was moving to attack the Normans and was taken by surprise whilst on the march at Battle Hill then it means that he had set off without sending any scouts forward to observe the movements of the enemy, which seems extraordinary. No commander would be so foolish.

We also know that there was probably no papal support for the Conquest nor any promise made to build a monastery on the site of the battle. The main reason why the abbey was built was to block the invasion route from the south coast to London and it was granted special privileges to enable it to attract settlers so that there were people to help defend the area from invasion. The insistence of penance being paid by the papal representatives in 1070 probably led to William claiming that the new monastery would be dedicated to those who had lost their lives at the battle.

Chapter 9

The Battlefield

"By no means the least of our witnesses is the battlefield itself."
M.K. Lawson, *The Battle of Hastings 1066*

"It is moving, exciting indeed, for a person of the twentieth century to stand on the slopes of Caldbec Hill and, feeling the breeze brushing the face, receive with its noiseless impact the imagined sounds of events in the second week of October so long ago," wrote Edwin Tetlow in 1974, describing the assembly of the English army in 1066, "the clatter of iron-armed riders and walkers, the shouts of command, the ribaldry and the forced humour, the neighing of ponies whose senses tell them that once again danger lies ahead as an army gathers."[1]

Was Caldbec Hill merely the concentration point of the English army or was it also the place where King Harold made his last stand against the invaders? With none of the original sources specifying precisely where the Battle of Hastings was fought, it is incumbent upon us to examine the area around present-day Battle to see what clues there may be on the ground. Surprisingly, not every historian has done this. "Many popular accounts exist of the tremendous struggle," wrote Mark Anthony Lower in his paper "On the Battle of Hastings", "but they are chiefly copied one from another with little or no reference to original documents, and written in total ignorance of the geographical features of the locality."[2]

This was a theme taken up by Freeman who, in considering the original sources, remarked that with William of Poitiers "his topography is soon lost in his rhetoric", that the Bayeux Tapestry "gives but little idea of the general site"; Wace "could not have seen the ground" and William of Malmesbury and Henry of Huntingdon "seem to have had little notion of the general position."[3]

Despite its limitations as mentioned by Freeman, the one original artefact which provides us with some evidence regarding the battlefield is the Bayeux Tapestry. Without question the most telling images concerning the topography of the battlefield are the alleged watercourse, or ditch, and the hill in the scene that follows the incident at the watercourse. The image of the watercourse had been considered by many writers and, predictably, their interpretations have varied. David Wilson saw it as "a defensive work of sharpened stakes[4], whereas R.A. Brown thought that the image was that of "tufts of marsh grass".[5]

The present authors remain neutral on whether or not these images are those of stakes or tufts of grass but we cannot refrain from observing that the horses that are shown being upturned do so after the feature, not stumbling into it. By examining earlier scenes in the Tapestry it is certain that what is being shown here is a small expanse of water. But it is a very small feature and, as we have noted, it does not appear to be an impediment to the progress of the Norman knights. It would seem, therefore, to be nothing more than an attempt at portraying a stream running across the lower part of the battlefield or to indicate that the lower part of the battlefield was swampy.

The wording on the Tapestry offers little guidance. All that is embroidered above this scene, which is actually the last act of a much longer scene that gives a general picture of the fighting, are the words, "Here English and French fell together in the battle".[6]

We should not read too much into this scene or the subsequent one which portrays a hill being defended by the English. The generally accepted view is that the two scenes are to be read together. Supposedly, the Norman knights coming to grief between the swampy ground and the hill are in fact the ones that were pushed back and forced to flee by the English in the first great counter-attack. In this version of events the English "were driven up on to a hillock where they were soon overpowered," though one historian, Paul Hill considers that this has now become a "moot point".[7]

How all this can be inferred from the Tapestry is quite inexplicable. Unfortunately for this theory, the retreat and rallying of the Normans occurs in the Tapestry *after* the hillock scene. If it was supposed to show the Normans turning back on their pursuers and driving them onto the hillock after being rallied by William and Odo then it is shown completely out of sequence. Furthermore, the numbers do not add up. We are told that it was a significant proportion of the English that were killed in this action, yet the hillock in question on the lower western sector of the Battle Abbey grounds is far too small to have held more than a few hundred men.

What the designers of the Tapestry were endeavouring to show is the savagery of the fighting over wet and difficult terrain. We cannot know who was expected to view the Tapestry but we can be fairly certain that it would include people that had not been present at the battle. The designers, therefore, had to show the viewers exactly what the brave Normans had to contend with when they overcame the stubborn English – and this they have done. They show the impenetrable shield wall, the terrible fighting with the Normans being cut down by the battle axes of the *housecarls*, the swampy and difficult terrain and the steep hill where the English stood and from where the attackers were repeatedly driven back.

If any should doubt this, they should look at the next scene which shows the Norman knights retreating and being rallied by Bishop Odo and then by William who lifts his helmet to prove to his men that he is still alive. The Tapestry makes perfect sense if read in this way without the cerebral contortions that others have undergone in trying to extract precise information from what is simply a general representation.

Whilst on this subject, the question needs to be asked as to why the Tapestry designers would show a small hillock as being such a prominent feature but not the main English position which we know was on a considerable steep-sided hill? It has been said that the manner in which the designers portrayed the main hill was with the curly line upon which most of the fighting is undertaken.[8] This can easily be discounted by looking back through the Tapestry and it will be seen that similar curly lines are shown many times.

The conclusion is really quite obvious. The English troops held a hill up which the Normans attacked. Both sides lost many men in the ensuing fighting and eventually the Normans broke and fled down the hill where they were finally rallied by Odo and William. That is the accepted version of events and that is exactly what is shown on the Tapestry.

The difficulties experienced in analysing the battlefield were recognised by Doctor Stephen Morillo: "Views of the battlefield abound, though the lines of sight are cluttered with contentious issues."[9] Likewise Richard Huscroft saw that "the battlefield itself gives rise to as many questions as answers."[10]

In considering the respective characteristics of the two hills we must look at the possible positions which the English army could have adopted at the start of the battle. R. Allen Brown, for instance, reproduces a map by General E.R. James which shows the English flanks refused (i.e. curved or turned back); Colonel Lemmon's map portrays the English in a straight line. As we have seen, the Vikings, the most successful warriors of the early medieval period and the perennial enemy of the English, were always careful to secure their flanks and we can be fairly certain that Harold would have had similar concerns. The problem with the Battle Hill position, as Terry Wise points out, is that if the English flanks were refused "this would have meant placing men on lower ground and sacrificing the advantage of high ground." This then means that Harold placed his men in a straight line with his flanks exposed, which seems quite unlikely. Such issues would not have been a concern on Caldbec Hill. The almost conical shape of Caldbec Hill means that Harold could have distributed his men to protect not only his flanks but also his rear. This is another very strong reason why Harold would have been unwise, and indeed most unlikely, to have abandoned Caldbec Hill in favour of a position which posed so many problems.[11]

It is usually stated that the front of the English position was held by the *housecarls*; but what of the flanks and rear? The diagrammatic illustrations provided by the likes of Howarth and Brown accurately depict the contours of Battle Hill and in doing so they show how flat and accessible the western flank and rear of the position was – yet they do not ask why the Normans would deliver attack after attack over many hours against the front of the English position where the fierce *housecarls* were stationed when the flank and rear offered such clear advantages. Once again, it simply defies belief.

Diagram A, which is reproduced from David Howarth's book, shows this very clearly. On this diagram the English line is drawn across the Battle ridge but with both flanks and rear horribly exposed. Diagram B shows the same English line with the flanks refused. It is immediately obvious that the Norman knights would have been able to mount the western summit of the hill, and nullify any advantage the position might have offered.

Diagram C portrays that same line transposed onto Caldbec Hill. The reader can see that not only is the slope in front of the English line far steeper than that of Senlac Hill but that the rear is particularly well protected with woods, and a very steep slope rendering the English left flank quite secure. It can also be seen that the marshy and steep terrain in front of the English left would have made deployment very problematic for the Normans. Diagram D shows the English line with the flanks refused. Rather than such a position allowing access to the summit, such a position would have drawn the English line higher up the hill.

This vulnerability to an attack upon its flank and rear is one of the greatest problems associated with the traditional battle site. After William repeatedly attacked the English positions head-on with his infantry and cavalry and had been repulsed every time, it is utterly inconceivable that William would not have sought a way round the English position. Every historian that has examined the Battle of Hastings has remarked on its almost unprecedented duration. For hour after hour the Normans assaulted the English positions with no perceptible diminution in the enemy's ability to hold its ground.

There is no way that William would have continued to batter away at the English positions without result and with mounting casualties and not have sought a way round the flank of Harold's lines. If the battle had been fought on Battle Hill and if William had taken the trouble to investigate the terrain upon which he was fighting, he would have found that Harold's rear was easily accessible and offered almost level ground upon which his knights could operate with impunity.

The duration of the battle is particularly telling. This is normally ascribed to the equality of numbers on the opposing sides, and an unstoppable force meeting an immovable rock. Yet we must not forget that Harold and his men, after fighting one of the bloodiest battles in English history, had travelled 190 miles from York and then another fifty or sixty miles to Sussex in just thirteen days.[12] Apart from the fact that some of the best English warriors must have fallen at Stamford Bridge and many others would have been carrying wounds, the men would have been very, very tired. That the battle lasted so long can only be ascribed to the difficulty which the comparatively fresh Normans experienced trying to fight up such a rough and steep hill.

* * *

Topographically, Battle Hill would not be a bad place to position a small army. Caldbec Hill, however, would be far, far better. Firstly, it is higher than Battle Hill. Secondly, its sides are much steeper. Thirdly, its slopes are much rougher, and fourthly the top of the hill is narrower and less open on its flanks. Fifthly, and possibly most importantly, the slopes at the rear of the hill are extremely steep and they lead down to the place identified by most authorities as the

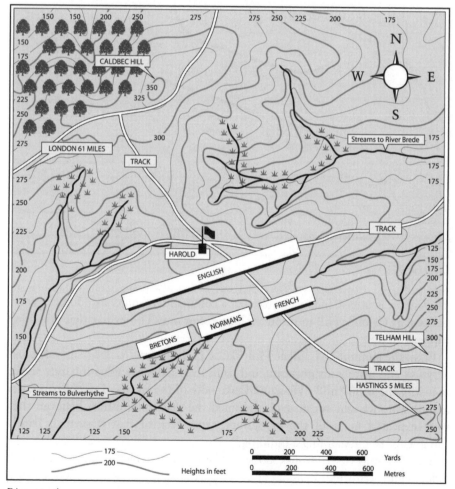

Diagram A.

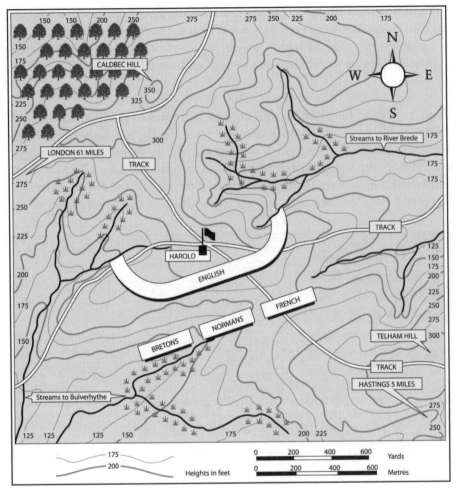

Diagram B.

Malfosse. It is utterly inconceivable that a commander would abandon as good a position as Caldbec Hill in favour of an inferior one. Things like that just don't happen.

From the summit of Caldbec Hill, Battle Hill is clearly visible below. It looks very low and utterly insignificant and from the Caldbec heights it barely seems to justify the term "hill". We should take note of the words of the Marmoutier monks who, we may recall, had examined the place where they believed they were expected to build the monastery "and decided that it seemed hardly suitable for so outstanding a building."

The skyline as viewed from Caldbec Hill is dominated by the ridge along which Telham Hill is situated. If, as has been recorded, the opposing forces spotted each other from the high grounds of Telham Hill and Caldbec Hill, why would Harold

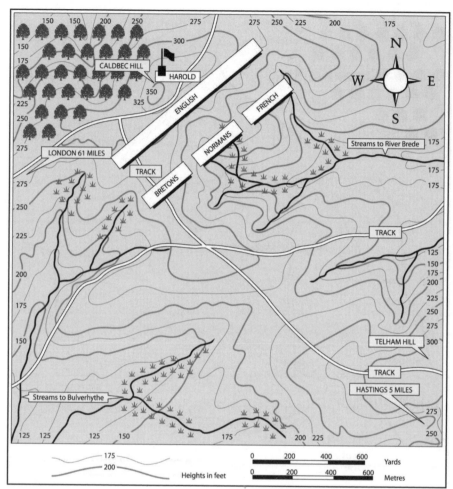

Diagram C.

move his army all the way down to Battle Hill simply to adopt a defensive position? This is particularly puzzling when it is appreciated that Battle Hill is almost equidistant from the two other hills. This means that the English, instead of drawing themselves together on Caldbec Hill, decided to race down the hill in a bid to reach Battle Hill before it could be seized by the Normans. The Normans were already in marching order and had easier ground to cover. They might well have reached Battle Hill first, leaving the English in complete disarray. This makes no sense whatsoever. As Lieutenant Colonel Bourne would no doubt agree, the Inherent Military Probability is steadfastly opposed to such a move.[13]

We know that Harold was an offensive commander. It was not his way to wait upon events, however sensible that might have been. He had marched to meet his enemy, to drive him back to his boats. But William was far more astute than

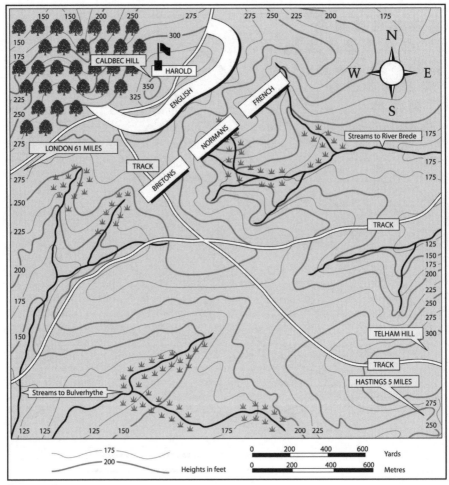

Diagram D.

Hardrada. Harold would not catch him unawares. Indeed, William was expecting Harold to arrive at any moment and if Harold was not careful he might find himself caught by William with his army still in transit and unprepared. So, sensibly, he took up a position which offered him both the best defensive position around and the ideal launching pad for an attack upon Hastings – and that was the hill upon which the Hoar Apple Tree stood. By concentrating in such a strong position Harold could bide his time until his army was fully assembled and then he could attack William at his own time of choosing. It was not a place he would abandon just because the enemy had marched into view.

Freeman was quite certain of this, though he believed that Harold always planned to fight on the defensive. "He [Harold] formed his plan, and he carried it out. He determined to give battle, but he determined to give battle on his own ground and after his own fashion ... The nature of the post which he chose [demonstrated] what Harold's plan was. It was to occupy a post where the Normans would have to attack him at a great disadvantage."[14]

Freeman, unlike most writers, did not believe that Caldbec Hill was the concentration point for Harold's army, but he did believe that the place Harold marched to was the place where he intended to give battle. For Freeman, there was no march to one place and then onto another nearby. Quite rightly, that made no sense to him. "His [Harold's] march was strictly a march to the actual spot on which the battle was to be fought ... He halted on a spot which commanded that road [the London road] and which also commanded the great road eastward from William's position."[15]

Colonel Lemmon, on the other hand, gives cogent reasons why Caldbec Hill was chosen by Harold as the assembly point. "Besides the bifurcation of the main trackway [to London], local roads from the east and west met there, making it a very convenient place for assembling the Fyrd, which would be coming in from all directions. It has been established that in Saxon times the boundaries of three Hundreds met near Caldbec Hill; and there are fourteen known examples in the counties of England of a 'Hoar Apple Tree' marking a boundary or serving as a landmark in former times. These facts make it possible to say with some certainty that Caldbec Hill was the appointed rendezvous."[16] It is most likely that the tree was intentionally planted there to mark this intersection of boundaries as it would be clearly visible from a considerable distance around. In addition to this Peter Rex considers that it might also have been the meeting place of a Hundred Court. There is also a strong local tradition (which should never be ignored) that the windmill which sits proudly on Caldbec's summit marks the site of the Hoar Apple Tree.[17]

According to William Seymour we know that the selected rendezvous "was a hoar apple tree and that it stood just beyond the southern boundary of that massive forest called the Andresweald."[18] If it is the case, as every commentator had stated, Telham Hill was the place where the Normans were when the opposing forces spotted each other, then we can identify where the English were – because the English were seen emerging from the trees. If the English position was just beyond the southern boundary of the forest then it must surely be Caldbec Hill.

It has been noted that the hill on which the battle was fought was steep and "untilled". Lieutenant Colonel Lemmon has looked at Battle Hill and has written that "the top of the ridge was probably rough untilled ground; but from Domesday Book it can be deduced that the eastern slopes, as also the southern slopes with the land extending southwards, therefrom, were cultivated." This is known, continues Lemmon, because this latter area, called "Santlache", consisted chiefly of a detached portion of the Saxon manor of Bollington by

Bulverhythe. So not only do we learn that most of the battlefield was cultivated but that only the top part of the Battle Hill was untilled. If the fighting had taken place on Battle Hill this cultivated area is where the English would have been standing with their front ranks stretching down the gentle slope beyond the rough ground and it would not have affected the Norman advance, or even been noticed by them. This would therefore seem to add further evidence that would eliminate Battle Hill from being the battle site.[19]

In the discussion about whether or not Harold intended to fight an offensive or defensive battle, one obvious question needs to be clarified. This is that if Harold intended to march upon the Normans why did he chose an assembly point that was so close to William's camp that it was fairly certain that his forces would be seen by the Normans as they gathered there over the course of a day or two? On the eve of Stamford Bridge, by comparison, Harold had camped sixteen miles from the enemy, who were therefore oblivious to his presence until he was almost upon them the following day. The only answer can be that Harold knew his concentration point was so strong that he did not fear a Norman attack, and if William did not come to face Harold then the king was ideally situated to attack William when his forces had all assembled. Unfortunately for Harold, William was quicker off the mark than he had anticipated. "All in all," wrote Andrew Bridgeford, "the decisive battle looked like it was going to come rather too quickly for King Harold of England. He would have preferred more time."[20]

Few others since Freeman have questioned Caldbec Hill as being the assembly point of the English army and there are a number of reasons given for this. It has been said that Harold knew the area well and that is why he selected that part of the country to fight his battle. It is true that Crowhurst and the surrounding district fell within his personal demesne but Harold, as his father before him, was Earl of Wessex, which covered almost all of southern England. He had also spent much of his short life at Edward's court and on campaign in Wales. He would know the most important places within his lands but to suppose that he knew a relatively insignificant hill amid the undulating landscape of the Weald is stretching credibility a little too far.

By contrast, Harold almost certainly knew the place of the Hoar Apple Tree. Not only was it at the junction of the roads to London and Lewes, it also marked the boundary between three administrative districts. This meant that the place had an administrative significance and as a consequence would have been familiar to those who had to administer Harold's lands, and by extension Harold, Earl of Wessex, himself.

* * *

Many writers have declared Battle Hill to be ideally suited for a defensive engagement. However, investigations of Battle Hill have shown that the front of

Harold's alleged position on the hill had a gradient of 8 per cent, reducing to about 4.5 per cent on the east flank and just 3 per cent on the west, which reflects how slight the slopes were.[21]

However, R. Allen Brown, unlike many commentators, believes that the accepted site of the battle on Battle Hill was far from the perfect position most writers claim it to be. Brown believes that the successful tactics employed by Harold at Stamford Bridge dictated his actions at Hastings and that he hoped to catch William unprepared. He states that as Harold intended to strike at the Norman army at Hastings he cannot have selected the eventual site of the battlefield in advance. His criticisms of the Battle Hill position are that there was no way of withdrawal save the narrow isthmus which is now Battle High Street and that the space on the ridge was too confined for the size of Harold's army.

A far from resounding endorsement of the traditional site of the battle is also delivered by Frank Stenton: "Towards the south, the quarter from which William was approaching, the contours are much less pronounced, and on the left front of this position the ground falls little more than 50 feet in the 400 yards between the site of Harold's standard and the lowest part of the road from Hastings. In such a position Harold's only chance of victory lay in the possibility that his army would be able to keep its close formation – its 'shield-wall' – until the Norman host had exhausted itself in attack."

If we are to believe those historians who claim that Harold had selected Battle Hill in advance because of its particular suitability as a defensive position then why did he chose a spot with such a gentle slope in its front where his "only" chance of victory lay in maintaining formation with his disparate force for a protracted engagement, something he could hardly be certain of?[22]

Stenton also comments on the story of the English front being defended by palisades. If it is true that the English did in fact reinforce their post then, as he points out, this would have been a difficult task if their position was on Battle Hill: "The strength of the position was determined not so much by the general elevation of the ground which at no point reaches 300 feet above sea level, as by the fact that it was surrounded by country very hilly and much broken by streams," he wrote, "… nor in practice would it have been easy for Harold to collect sufficient timber to protect a front of 800 yards on the barren down where he made his stand." We know that the Andresweald ended on the northern edge of Caldbec Hill, which would make the cutting of timber and its placement in the nearby ground a straightforward matter. But to have to transport the stakes all the way down Caldbec Hill and up and over Battle Hill was not impossible but it was highly impractical. If the English did construct a palisade then the battle cannot have taken place on the treeless slopes of Battle Hill.[23]

Throughout history hand-to-hand combat has rarely proven to last long. At close quarters it soon becomes apparent that one side is the stronger, either though greater numbers, determination or superior tactics, and the other side gives way. This did not happen at Hastings, and there are a number of reasons why.

Firstly, the English and the Normans were evenly matched in terms of numbers. Secondly, the nature of the terrain did not permit any sophisticated tactical manoeuvres. The flanks of the English position were secure and the rear was steep and heavily wooded. Infantry could have attacked the English rear but the Norman cavalry would not have been able to retain any cohesion or establish any momentum, though it is possible that such an attempt was made, which is discussed later. The Normans had therefore little choice but to deliver a frontal attack.

Up such a steep slope as is presented by Caldbec Hill the advantage clearly lay in the hands of the defenders. As long as they held their ground they could not be defeated.

The Normans, on the other hand, could not give up. They were isolated in a foreign country. It was also said that William had ordered his ships to be destroyed so that his men knew that there was no escape and defeat would mean certain death. So the battle continued, probably spasmodically, for hour after hour. It was only tactical naivety, indiscipline or the loss of their leaders that cost the English the battle.

If the battle had been fought at Battle Hill other options were available to the attackers. Whereas the eastern flank was quite steep, the rear of the hill was flat and the front of the position was far from severe. Not only would this have permitted the cavalry to charge directly at the English front line at almost full gallop but if this did not work it would have been possible for the knights to make their way round to the defenders' rear.

It is utterly inconceivable that the Normans would have continued to batter fruitlessly against the solid ranks of the English, suffering as they must have done considerable casualties to the fearsome battle axes, if there was any other choice available to them. This seems to be confirmed by William of Poitiers when he says that until the last desperate charge by William towards the end of the day the English position still remained difficult to surround. Senlac Hill, with its flat rear, would have been surrounded at an early stage of the battle but Caldbec Hill has no such weakness.[24]

Another clue which could help identify the true site of the battle might be gleaned from the fact that we are told by William of Poitiers that before the battle William delivered a speech to his men.[25] This was delivered from a slight hill and it would appear that it was this hill where he took up his command position under his banner, the Leopards of Normandy. This, according to Poyntz Wright, was "in full view of the battlefield and in sight of Harold's phalanx on top of the opposite ridge."[26] He gives this place as just north of Telham Court at TQ 753152, though this, of course, is supposition. Equally, if the English forces were arrayed upon Caldbec Hill then we have the perfect little hill opposite, and that of course is Battle Hill.

If indeed it was on Battle Hill that William raised his standard then we may have an alternative explanation for the building of the abbey on this site. According to the *Chronicle of Battle Abbey* William said that "upon this place of battle I will build a suitable free monastery." Could it be that the Marmoutier monks did actually erect the abbey in exactly the correct place – the place where William vowed to build a monastery if he won the battle – on Battle Hill where he was stood? This, in fact, may explain everything. Although the words of the Battle Abbey chronicler have been discounted it is possible that, in those religious times, William did make a vow of some sort before the battle. It is perfectly understandable, it is the kind of thing many of us have done – promised we would do something good if we were successful or achieved some particular goal. If William told the monks to build their monastery "upon this the spot" when he made his promise then they would have been entirely correct in placing it on Battle Hill and it is only because of the distortions of the *Chronicle of Battle Abbey* that people have been misled into believing that the battle was fought there. Freeman, interpreting the passage in the *Chronicle of Battle Abbey*, says that before the battle began William asked where Harold was stood. A soldier called Vital told him that Harold stood among the thick ranks which crowned the summit of the hill as that was where he had seen the king's standard. It was then that William vowed to build the monastery on the very spot where Harold had raised his standard.[27]

Four years later, after the papal legation insisted that William paid a penance for the bloodshed he had caused, he may well have given the instruction that the monastery was to be built upon the spot where Harold's standard had stood. We all know how messages can become misconstrued when passed on from one person to another and it is far from inconceivable that the information given to the monks at Marmoutier was that the monastery was to be built where the king raised his standard. Of course, since the time of the battle it was William and not Harold who was king. If the monks, having located the general area of the battlefield, found some local people and enquired where the king raised his standard, they might well have been directed, in all innocence and sincerity, to Battle Hill as that was the place where the king, i.e. William, did indeed raise his standard.

Interestingly, this person Vital (who is named on the Tapestry) was one of those who had been sent out earlier to spy on the English. William asked Vital "what he had seen and where the English usurper was to be found." If Harold had moved from Caldbec Hill, as so many believe, to take up a position on Battle Hill then Vital would have no better idea than William where Harold had moved to and where he now stood. It would seem to confirm the view that Harold stood and fought at the assembly point. The final observation to be made on this subject is that if William was sat on his horse looking up to the English position, why was he unable to see the king's banner flying above the ranks of his army? It is difficult to believe that from the bottom of Battle Hill William would be unable to see Harold's banner on the summit above. If, on the other hand, William was stood, or sat on his charger, at the bottom of the much higher Caldbec Hill, then indeed it would not be particularly easy to see a banner placed on the very summit.

* * *

It is necessary at this stage to provide a brief description of both Battle Hill and Caldbec Hill. The traditionally accepted site for the Battle of Hastings is now the preserve of English Heritage. The top of the site is home to both the remains of Battle Abbey and an independent school. This comparatively flat area is surprisingly large, indeed far too large to contain an army of 8,000 men with a frontage of just 1,000 as is generally stated, which is why, as we have seen from the above diagrams, the English right flank was horribly exposed. This, though, is difficult to gauge today with all the abbey buildings and the houses that have been built either side of the London Road, and, whilst some levelling of the hill occurred in the construction of the A2100, the flatness of the terrain cannot be dismissed.

The summit of Battle Hill was altered when the abbey was built. The builders needed to build on level ground and they moved the earth around accordingly. How this affected the ground upon which the abbey was built we do not know with complete accuracy. Though we accept that this must have altered the nature of the top of the hill, Caldbec Hill was still a far more significant feature.

If we wander around the grounds of the abbey today we can see that the ground was levelled twice (it is almost stepped) to provide a flat, or flattish, platform for the builders. The ground below the first step, which constitutes the main part of the battlefield, forms nothing more than a gentle incline. In the days before the paved roads and smooth highways which we know today, everyone was used to walking and riding across country or along narrow, bumpy lanes. A gentle gradient such as can be seen at Battle Hill would be entirely unremarkable, yet it is the very steepness of the slope up which the Normans attacked which is repeatedly remarked upon.

The hillock, considered by Freeman to have been an outpost, is far too advanced and such an idea can be easily dismissed. It is, though, a pronounced feature, indeed the ground here is the most difficult around the whole front of the traditional battle site. However, the visitor will note how small the hillock is and will therefore be surprised that it could be considered by historians to represent the feature shown on the Tapestry.

If we then leave Battle Abbey and walk towards Caldbec Hill, the site of Freeman's *Malfosse* is easily identified (N 50 54 964, E 000 29 514). It is a significant feature, steep and dangerous. From here it is a long, hard walk up Caldbec Hill. The ground is still difficult and is cut up with watercourses and streams, tributaries of the River Brede. In many areas it is still muddy and swampy. If the incident during the battle occurred when the retreating Normans crashed into a ditch then such an obstacle can be found at N 50 54 972, E 00 29 505. Because of its length, this is far more likely to result in the loss of large numbers of mounted men stumbling into it than the much narrower ditch to the south of the above-mentioned hillock in the plain beyond Battle Hill.

The name Caldbec is, quite simply, cold bec, or cold spring, which Mark Anthony Lower said in 1852 "is yet seen bursting from a cavernous recess on the spot."[28] Caldbec Hill, or at least its summit, has another name, as Lieutenant-Colonel Lemmon explained: "Before leaving the battle area, the Duke must have given orders to erect, on Caldbec Hill, the customary cairn of stones to commemorate his victory; for the locality has been known as Mountjoy ever since." If the battle was fought on Battle Hill, why would a victory cairn be erected on some other hill?

"A Mountjoy," Lemmon writes, "is defined by Boyer (historian 1667–1729) as 'a heap of stones made by a French army as a monument of victory'. The name Mountjoy is uncorrupted Norman. France and Belgium each possess a town called Montjoie, and Spain one called Monjouy. Monjoie was also a warcry: 'There is no one who does not cry "Monjoie" (*Chançon de Roland*, line 1525). The Mountjoy on Caldbec Hill has long since disappeared; it was erected presumably on the highest point which is now marked by a concrete Ordnance Survey datum."[29]

It is also said that on Caldbec Hill the Normans lit a beacon to announce their great victory.[30] This is also noted by Mark Anthony Lower, who wrote that *Mont-joie* was "a heap of stones made by a French army as a monument of victory." Tradition asserts, Lower continues, that it was on the summit of Caldbec Hill, "where the windmill now stands that the Normans sounded the trumpet of victory."[31]

Standing next to the windmill is an Ordnance Survey datum, showing that even today Caldbec Hill is a place of geographical importance, just as it was 900 years ago. The steepness of the slope all around is immediately apparent, particularly the rear of the English position, which would have rendered it almost impregnable from attack.

It is a short walk down Caldbec Hill to Oakwood Gill, which is now thought to be the *Malfosse* (N 50 55 292 E 000 28 236). However, one thing is quite certain and that is that there is no way the English could have outpaced the Norman cavalry all the way from Battle Hill, over Caldbec Hill and down to Oakwood Gill. If this is the *Malfosse* then the battle must have been fought on Caldbec Hill.

The *Malfosse* is one of the very few specific geographical features referred to in the primary or near-contemporary sources. It is mentioned by William of

Poitiers, though not by name, and by Orderic Vitalis in his contribution to the *Gesta Normannorum Ducum*: "When thus the Normans saw the English fleeing they pursued them obstinately through the night till Sunday to their own harm. For high grass concealed an ancient rampart and as the Normans fully armed on their horses rode up against it, they fell, one on top of the other, thus crushing each other to death. It is said that almost 15,000 men perished there."[32]

Whilst we can disregard the number of casualties, this account does point to the action at the *Malfosse* as being a significant engagement. The identification of the site depends primarily on a series of medieval records which refer to the "Maufosse". This we know is now widely accepted as being Oakwood Gill, as this is the natural feature that most closely conforms to the chronicle descriptions of a "deep ravine". It is situated some 600 yards to the north of Caldbec Hill.

Bradbury, for one, believes that the accepted location of the *Malfosse* "fits as well and perhaps better with a battle fought on Caldbec than one [fought] on Battle Hill." As he explains: "The *Malfosse* has been identified on the ground with reasonable certainty, and is just to the rear of Caldbec Hill, exactly where one might expect a last ditch resistance after the army had been forced to leave its first line of defence on the hill. It is quite a way back from Battle Hill."

As the compilers of the booklet *The 1066 Malfosse Walk* concede, if the battle had been fought on Battle Hill "it is hard to conceive of infantry outrunning cavalry for approximately one mile."[33] It also means that the English ran down from one hill, up a steep hill and then back down a steep hill. This does not seem either practical or logical and is actually a little more than one mile in distance over the ground. Men running for their lives are hardly likely to take the most difficult route, which is why for a long time it was thought that the English retreat had been in a north-westerly direction.

Lunar conditions on the night of 14 October were such that the moon did not rise until midnight, it was less than half-size, and kept close to the horizon. Lieutenant Colonel Lemmon cites an experiment which was carried out near Battle when the lunar and solar conditions were the same as on the day of the battle which proved that it was dangerous to ride across country at 1800 hours and impossible at 1815 hours. By 1830 hours the darkness was so intense that objects a few feet away were invisible. The *Malfosse* must therefore have been fairly close to the battlefield, further reinforcing the view that it was at Oakwood Gill at the foot of Caldbec Hill.

Not everyone thinks that the *Malfosse* incident took place after the battle, but that it was one of the key moments of the battle itself. Wace, for instance, believes that the incident was in fact the action that took place during the first retreat of the Norman left wing when they were pursued by the English: "In the plain was a fosse which the Normans now had behind them, having passed it in the fight without regarding it. But the English charged and drove the Normans before them till they made them fall back upon this fosse, over-throwing into it horses and men."[34]

M.K. Lawson also concedes some ground on this point. Referring to the *Chronicle of Battle Abbey* and the accounts by William of Poitiers and Orderic Vitalis, he questions whether or not the *Malfosse* incident occurred during the battle or during the retreat. "One might well, however, wonder," if these accounts, "do necessarily all refer to events at the same location."[35]

This was first considered by Mark Anthony Lower when he translated the *Chronicle of Battle Abbey*, "between the hostile armies a certain dreadful precipice, caused either by a natural chasm of the earth, or by some convulsion of the elements. It was of considerable extent, and being overgrown with bushes or brambles was not easily seen; and great numbers of men – principally Normans in pursuit of the English – were suffocated in it." This pit, the chronicler informs us, "is still called *Malfosse*." The most significant phrases in this account are that the *Malfosse* was situated *between* the two armies and that it was a dreadful precipice of considerable extent.[36]

Rupert Furneaux, having searched the Battle Abbey battlefield in an effort to locate this fosse between the two armies, eventually decided that it must be the ground to the south of the, by now famous, hillock that has exercised so many writers. "Like other visitors before me, I pondered the problem as I walked over the battlefield ... I looked, therefore, for such a spot in the centre of the battlefield. On the slope of the ride rose a mound or hillock, now covered by trees and shrubs. Beneath it, the ground was wet and boggy. Walking over to it I saw that it offered a trap to the unwary. In the centre of the group of hillocks lay a deep and noisome dell ... It was easy to imagine the fleeing horsemen galloping over its deceptive slopes and falling into its 'fosse-like' depths."[37]

It is certainly true that the southwards-facing slope of the hillock is as he describes. Yet this does not cover an extensive area and for large numbers of Normans (or probably we should say Bretons) to have perished they would have had to be following each other in fairly close order, which is not in the nature of a desperate retreat. It also seems strange that the fleeing horsemen would have ridden up a steep hillock to try and get away from the English when there were acres of completely flat land between Battle Hill and the start of Telham Hill over which they could have easily ridden away from their pedestrian pursuers. Jim Bradbury also dismisses the hillock in the abbey grounds as being that portrayed in the Tapestry, as "it hardly fits, and is very small."[38]

However, if Furneaux had walked over to Caldbec Hill he would have found not one but two fosses – three if you count Freeman's *Malfosse* – which cut right across the foot of the hill and might not be easily avoided by the desperate Norman cavalry. One of them (N 50 54 972, E 00 29 505) is at the bottom of a slope in the undulating ground, but any one of these could certainly be the place described by Wace.

Apart from the "noisome dell" there is no feature which could be regarded as deep or extended across Battle Hill. The ground in the plain below Battle Hill is so flat that it seems inconceivable that horsemen could come upon any feature that they had not seen well in advance. Jim Bradbury certainly believes that "the mid-battle incident, with a site of ditches and so on, would fit better with Caldbec [Hill] than Battle [Hill]."[39]

It is difficult to draw any firm conclusions on this subject as there is conflicting evidence in abundance. Rather than deny or accept any particular version of events we will assume that an incident or incidents of this nature took place both during and after the battle. The first of these, then, occurred during the fighting when the English delivered their counter-attack. The losses sustained by the Normans and their allies in this incident helps understand why they almost lost the battle at this stage. The second incident took place during the English retreat at Oakwood Gill.[40]

To conclude this investigation, it is worth noting that the man who identified Oakwood Gill as the *Malfosse*, C.T. Chevallier, indicated that Caldbec Hill was the most logical site for the battle, possibly inadvertently, in the summary of the paper he delivered to the Sussex Archaeological Society when he first made his findings public: "It was on Caldbec Hill, and not on the Abbey Ridge, that the traditional name of Mountjoy shows the victory beacon to have been lighted. *William would not indeed have been sure of victory until that summit was in his hands.*"[41]

There is also one aspect of the ground mentioned by William of Poitiers which needs to be taken into account. This is where he refers to the Danish auxiliaries being posted by Harold on higher ground near to the wood from which they had just emerged. There is no such "higher ground" next to Battle Hill, nor is there any higher ground close to Caldbec Hill, the summit of which is the highest point for some considerable distance. The only explanation which we can put forward is that Caldbec Hill rises from the south-west and the ground immediately to the east of the summit forms a kind of shoulder before dropping steeply away. As the English line would have extended down the hill from the summit below this point, it might be the case that the Danes were posted on this shoulder – this higher ground – to guard Harold's eastern flank. This post would indeed be near to the wood through which they had just emerged.[42]

On Nick Austin's website, *Secretes of the Norman Invasion*, now also published as an ebook, he refers to a section from the *Carmen de Hastingae Proelio*, quoted earlier in this book, relating to the exchange of messages between William and Harold on the evening before the battle. William asked the returning Norman envoy, "'Where is the King?' 'Not far off' answered the monk. He said to him in his ear: 'You can see the standards'"[43]

This has led Austin to conclude that the English and Norman camps were within sight of each other. Austin makes no mention of an assembly point on

Caldbec Hill, saying that the traditional view is that Harold was camped on the ground upon which he fought and he therefore points out that Battle Hill is so low that it is impossible to see the coast from that hill. He also states that the only place nearby from which the coast can be seen is Telham Hill. He also places the Norman camp at Wilting.

On this basis the two camps would indeed have been well within sight as Telham and Wilting are less than three miles apart. If so, why was William unable to see the English army until indicated to him by the monk?

There is a possible explanation of this provided by M.K. Lawson. This is that, gleaned from the account by William of Jumièges, it seems likely that the Normans were in the vicinity of Battle the previous evening.[44] Catherine Morton and Hope Muntz add weight to this theory. They believe that William, experienced soldier that he was, would have ensured that the isthmus leading out of Hastings was in his hands. "We think," they write, "that an advance camp did exist, and that it was this camp which was alerted against surprise."[45] There is a view, put forward at least as early as 1966, that the Normans bivouacked overnight on 13 October on Baldslow ridge, which is some three miles out of Hastings.[46] Paul Hill also believes that the Normans had a "temporary encampment" on Telham Hill.[47] This, though, could only have been on the south-facing slopes of the hill, otherwise they would have been in full view of the enemy, who would have been able to observe all their movements.

If the Normans had moved up to Baldslow or Telham Hill under the cover of darkness it would explain not only why William was able to see the English camp but also why the Normans were able to surprise the English when they appeared on the summit of Telham Hill on the morning of the 14th far earlier than could have been expected if they had marched all the way from Hastings. It would also almost definitely rule out Battle Hill as the assembly point, which as we know is favoured by one or two writers, as it is far too low to be observed from a distance.

Finally, we can exclude Telham Hill and Crowhurst Park from our possible sites for the battle because no commander would arrange for his army to concentrate so close to the enemy, where they were certain to be seen and where they could have been cut up by the knights piecemeal as they arrived. No student of military history could have made such a pronouncement.

* * *

We can see, then, that Caldbec Hill contains all the features referred to in the prime sources. It has the steep, untilled ground, steep enough for the depleted English army to hold all day long; steep enough, indeed, for the English to roll rocks down upon their enemy. It has extended watercourses on its lower southern slopes that could well be the ditches into which the retreating Norman knights came to grief during the battle. It is also near Oakwood Gill, the *Malfosse*. Battle Hill cannot make such claims.

There is, fortunately, one well-known feature of the battle area of which we can be absolutely certain. This is the Watch Oak, the name of which continues in use today and is one of the local electoral wards of Battle. The oak was situated close to the London road at the lower western slopes of Caldbec Hill. From its position it would appear to be a look out point (as its name implies) along the old Lewes–London road and would have been held by a picket of men to guard against any surprise moves from this flank during the assembly of the English army.[48]

In our final observation we will turn once again to the thoughts of Jim Bradbury. In considering where the battle may have been fought, he acknowledges that "the battle accounts have always left puzzles when historians have tried to relate them to the actual ground of Battle Hill."[49] Such puzzles untangle when one places the battle on Caldbec Hill.

Chapter 10

The Archaeology

"If detailed narratives are to be fitted into their historical place, the first question that suggests itself is why battles were fought where they were."

H.B. George, *Battles of English History*

It is remarkable that there is no archaeological evidence of a battle having been fought on Battle Hill. Whilst this may seem to most as being something of considerable, if not fundamental, importance, R. Allen Brown dismisses this out of hand. Instead of attempting to unearth evidence which would support his conviction that the battle was fought on Battle Hill, he adopts a simplistic approach, i.e. the remains of an original ecclesiastical building on the site of the current abbey is all the archaeological "proof" we need.

Jim Bradbury, almost a lone voice, is not convinced with this: "It is puzzling given the enormous interest in [the Battle of] Hastings, that despite the digging of foundations for the abbey, for the old primary school, for all the houses along the main road, all the digging in gardens, the archaeological digs at various points in the abbey grounds, the road making, not a single trace of the battle has been found. There are a few tales about finds, but none which have ever been verified and which would prove that Battle Hill had been the site of a great battle. Have people simply been looking in the wrong place?"[1]

The fact that this was the largest medieval battle in Britain, with most, probably the heaviest, casualties, should mean that there would be some archaeological remains. That there is nothing must cast doubt upon the Battle Abbey ridge having been the site of such a major engagement.

David Crouch wrote that "the French who fell were all decently buried, but the remaining English bodies were left to the chances of fate." This is based on such sources as the *Carmen*, which states that after the battle William "traversed the field, and selecting the dead bodies of his friends, buried them in the bowels of the earth; but left the corpses of the English strewn upon the ground to be devoured by worms, and wolves, and birds, and dogs."[2] Orderic Vitalis interprets this slightly differently as that William gave the English permission to bury their dead. Wace tells us that the noble ladies of the land also came, some to look for their husbands and others their fathers, sons, or brothers. Theses bodies were taken to the villages, and interred at their churches.

If we therefore discount the more important English warriors and the local *fyrd*, as these, or at least some of these, must have been removed from the battlefield, we are still left with thousands of bodies left lying on the ground. William was still expecting to be attacked again, and the last thing he would have been worried about would have been the dead. Even when he decided to march upon London he still had a campaign to fight and had no time to waste cleaning up the battlefield. We can therefore believe this part of the *Carmen*'s account. We know that William returned to Hastings after the battle to regroup. So after burying their own dead, the Normans abandoned the battlefield, leaving the English to deal with their own casualties.

They would not have been buried far from where they fell, so somewhere either on or very close to the battlefield there must have been a vast grave or pit dug for the French dead. As we have said, William would not have had time for anything else and if the English dead were just left on the battlefield their remains must have been deposited somewhere by the Marmoutier monks when they cleared the ground to start their building work.

So, somewhere reasonably close to the battlefield, there will be bodies. This place, it has been suggested, may be in a mass grave on top of Battle Hill beneath the abbey. However, the abbey was largely rebuilt and extended in the thirteenth century and early fourteenth century but there are no reports of any finds.

Some indication of just how large these burial pits must have been can be gauged by the number of men killed. Any figures given by historians can only be informed estimates but it can be certain that the total must be numbered in its thousands. Peter Poyntz Wright has said that there were probably almost 2,000 Normans and at least as many Saxons. As well as the 4,000 men covering the 600 yards of the Battle Abbey ridge he believes that there must have been some 600 to 700 dead horses. This gives a minimum of six human bodies and one horse for every yard of the hill. As he also points out there was also "a mass" of broken weapons. So where are these great burial pits and where is the mass of broken weapons?

"Many would quickly perish," wrote Edwin Tetlow, "but surely some would still be there deep below the grass and topsoil. Looters would also have been at work as soon as any danger had passed … the Tapestry shows men stripping armour and vestments off fallen warriors even before the fighting was over …But they could not have taken *everything* away from the field. It seems inconceivable that no historical treasure of any kind lies deep but irretrievable."[3]

The fact that nothing has ever been found on, or around, Battle Hill has not troubled most historians, in fact they have, unwisely, dismissed this. In their efforts to make the received knowledge fit the real facts they have searched for any explanation they can use which might support the accepted version of events.

They say that because of the nature of the ground, i.e. that of limestone, the calcium bones would have dissolved over the 900-plus years since the battle. This is incorrect. The main part of Battle Hill consists of Wadhurst Clay but parts are of Tunbridge Wells Sand and another sandstone known as Ashdown Beds. Those that recognise this state that, because the ground is sandy and therefore porous, the surviving relics will have sunk many feet below the surface level.[4]

Indeed, this theory – that nothing could be expected to have survived in the corrosive or porous ground – which is almost always put forward as the reason why no archaeological remains have ever been found, has been entirely disproved because objects from the medieval period have indeed been recovered from this area. The first that we know about is an axe head which was found in a garden in Marley Lane in the 1950s. Though there has been some doubt about its military provenance and its date, it is now thought possible that it was a throwing axe. Marley Lane is not on the official battle site but is situated at the rear of Battle Hill towards Caldbec Hill. This artefact is on display in Battle Museum.

Its discovery does not prove the case for either battle site, being situated between the two, but what it does show is that items could well have survived in the ground in contradiction to the received wisdom. Items from an even earlier period, the Bronze Age, have been found in Battle. Interestingly these items could well be of a military nature as they include a sword and a "trumpet". They were found scattered along a prehistoric ridgeway.[5]

The failure to find any further evidence to support the traditional view of where the battle was fought is not from a want of trying. In 1978 extensive excavations were undertaken within the grounds of Battle Abbey. Under the auspices of the Historic Buildings and Monuments Commission for England and led by J.N. Hare, this survey continued until 1980. Its remit was to excavate the eastern part of Battle ridge, the part where the original monastery buildings were placed and where, of course, it was said that Harold was killed and where it might be supposed that the fiercest fighting took place. Hare also took the opportunity to examine material from the previous excavations conducted within the confines of the abbey grounds. His report then encapsulates all the archaeological work undertaken on the assumed battle site.

This was a highly professional and detailed investigation, the final report of which was not published until 1985. The first thing to be noted is that Hare remarks on the surprisingly limited number of excavations that have taken place around the abbey. This means that little evidence can have been removed from the site.

To cut a very long story short (his report amounts to 208 A4-size pages) we will summarise the finding and the conclusions from this extremely thorough investigation. Coins were found from as early as the reign of Edward I (1300–10 AD and not to be confused with Edward the Confessor) and such a vast quantity of metal items so extensive that the author of this particular aspect of the excavation wrote that it was "neither practical nor economical to publish an exhaustive record." Though gold and silver items were recovered amongst other precious metals and gemstones, nothing of a military nature was discovered.

The archaeologists also found glass, pottery, ceramics, animal bones and considerable architectural remains but nothing whatsoever to indicate that Battle Hill was the site of a military engagement.

Work continued after 1980 for the next four years, with trenches being cut at various points along the eastern ridge of the abbey grounds. Nothing was found that related in any way to Battle Abbey having been founded upon the site of a battlefield. The report is readily available for all to read.[6]

In addition to this, considerable work was undertaken within the grounds of Battle Abbey in 2004 and an arrowhead was uncovered. It is believed to date from some period between the eleventh and the fourteenth century and it is thought that it may have been used for hunting.

An important excavation was also undertaken at the Jenner and Simpson Mill site on Mount Street, Battle, in 1997. The excavation uncovered a considerable number of artefacts dated from around 1100 and later medieval times, but nothing from the battle. In the conclusion to the subsequent report, the author, Richard James, noted that "surprisingly little archaeological work has been undertaken in Battle outside of the Abbey Precincts."[7]

Furthermore, bones of warriors from 1066 have been uncovered nearby yet this has been overlooked, or ignored, because the place where they have been found does not fit in with their conventional view of the Battle of Hastings. These finds from the medieval period around this area of Sussex include a collection of bones and weapons discovered in 1909. In March of that year workmen who had been employed in levelling ground at Ocklynge, near Eastbourne, found a trench of skeletons two feet below the surface lying side by side. The trench ran for 100 yards before it passed under adjoining land. At the head of this row of bodies, and parallel with them, was a second row of single skeletons, about two feet apart.

It was determined that those which lay shoulder to shoulder were the common men, and those lying separately were the nobility. Iron spear heads were found embedded in some of the skulls, while short daggers were sticking in some of the ribs. The iron weapons were adjudged to be from the eleventh century, at which period of time the sea ran close to this point. Such large numbers of bodies indicates a significant encounter and though it is normally said that the Norman landings were unopposed it is thought that Ocklyne Hill might have been a position taken up by the English to try and stop the invaders.[8]

Ten years earlier just a short distance from this site at what was then Mill Field a large number of skeletons were found when the Willingdon road was being cut. The remains were buried in a pit but its position is now no longer known because the area is completely covered with housing.[9]

We also have the large collection of coins uncovered at Sedlescombe believed to have been part of Harold's military chest. Of the 1,186 coins (pennies) found, 1,136 were in very good condition and have been catalogued. These pennies bear the head of Edward the Confessor. It is known that there were originally far more coins, as the local children, believing them to be worthless hop tallies, had been playing with them until someone realised their significance. That enterprising person exchanged them with the children at their face value! The archaeologist W.A. Raper recovered the remainder. It is thought that the hoard originally amounted to between 2,000 and 3,000 coins.[10]

In discussing this subject, the archaeologist Mark Anthony Lower, M.A. F.S.A., made the following observation in 1852: "During the recent excavations for the railway from Hastings to Tunbridge Wells, which passes within a few hundred yards eastward of Battel [*sic*] Abbey, it was rather confidently expected that some traces of the battle, such as arms or human bones, would be brought to light; but this expectation was not realised." It may be worth adding the rest of Lower's words on this topic: "and this proves, I think, the correctness of my opinion, *that the battle and the retreat took place in the opposite, or westerly and north-westerly direction.*"[11]

Edwin Tetlow in considering the archaeology of the battle observed that "abundant evidence of savage hand-to-hand fighting existed, presumably, for a considerable but unknown period after it ended, but everything had gone by the time, some decades later, that the paramount historical meaning of the battle had become clear and skilled investigators started poking around the battlefield for anything they could find to fill in the picture. We may presume that clerks and others fitted by birth and brains to be classed above the unsparked peasantry would be looking for such evidence by 1100, when there could be no doubt that ... King William had successfully imposed a new ruling house upon England and consequently that the battle of Hastings had inaugurated a new epoch. But the early searchings and all the others that have followed yielded nothing."[12]

It is utterly inconceivable that there could be *no* archaeological remains from the largest medieval battle in Britain. It is inconceivable because there are abundant remains from that period of history. For example, it was announced on 1 December 2009 that over a thousand pieces of iron, including arrowheads and axe heads, were found in the vicinity of the Battle of Gate Fulford. A number of skeletons bearing the mark of weapons injuries were found during excavations at the church of St Andrew, Fishergate, in York and these may be some of those that died at that battle. Also in the 1950s a mass burial was uncovered at Ricall Landing where Tostig and Hardrada landed in 1066.[13]

Also, just twenty miles away from Battle, at Lewes, was fought the other great medieval battle in Sussex. The Battle of Lewes was fought less than 200 years after the Battle of Hastings and resulted in fewer casualties. Yet bodies were found in considerable quantities during the digging of the old Lewes to Brighton road in 1810, and had to be taken away by the cart load. When the railway line was laid across the grounds of St Pancras Priory a pit, sixty feet-deep, was found full of bones. So many bones were uncovered that they were used as ballast for the new railway track that runs between Lewes and Newhaven! Yet at Battle nothing has been found.

This "truly astonishing lack of mementoes of William's invasion" was remarked on by Tetlow. "Does any such evidence exist today? If so will it ever be located? One can only hope. It is not really such a slender hope. After all, one of the finest examples of the work of Saxon goldsmiths and metal workers – Alfred's Jewel – was not found until about 800 years after it had been created." (This beautiful object, just two and a half inches long, was unearthed by chance in a field behind the rectory at North Newton, Somerset, in 1693. It was found underneath a house which was being demolished at that time on the lands of Sir Thomas Wrothe.) "Who can say that, somewhere, does not lie some equally small and enlightening relic of William's invasion and the Enigma of Hastings?"[14]

This lack of archaeological evidence really is one of the most puzzling of the enigmas of the Battle of Hastings. If there really was something to be found in the abbey grounds it would surely have emerged by now. The only conclusion that can be drawn is that archaeologists must look elsewhere for the relics of the battle and that place, we suggest, is at the site of the *Malfosse*.

We know that it is possible that the *Malfosse* was both the site of very heavy Norman losses and possibly a mass Norman burial pit. This place, Oakwood Gill, must surely be a place worthy of investigation? It is interesting to note that the field given the name *Malfosse* was one of the earliest to have been settled by Norman knights and we know that by the middle of the twelfth century it was "partly tilled". It may well be that during this period, as the ground was brought into productive use, the bones which must have been uncovered were removed.[15] Equally, it could be that some remains are still there to be found.

If the battle was fought on Caldbec Hill and if there were already many corpses lying in Oakwood Gill, it would make sense to roll or drag the other French dead down the hill to Oakwood Gill, which was a ready-made ditch. It would be far easier to do that than carry the bodies from the *Malfosse* all the way back up the hill and dig a large pit, especially for tired troops. As William returned to Hastings on the 16th, the surviving Normans would only have one full day to bury their dead. They simply would not have had time to carry around hundreds, or possibly thousands, of bodies. Their only choice was to push them down into the *Malfosse*.

Chapter 11

Rewriting History

"History is always an unfinished project"
Stephen Morillo, *The Battle of Hastings Sources and Interpretations*

What we hope we have demonstrated is that there is little certainty about the events of Saturday, 14 October 1066, and almost every key moment leading up to and including the battle has been, or is still, disputed. How then are historians to put together an intelligible story?

As long ago as 1908 Frank Stenton faced this problem and acknowledged that "if full discussion were given to all matters which have been the subjects of controversy it would far exceed the possible limits of a [single] volume." Historians have been forced to filter out the subjects that impede their narratives and retain those that fit the widely accepted version of the Battle of Hastings. Though minor points will continue to be debated, the main story has coalesced into a generally agreed upon consensus.[1]

Many historians have been acutely aware of this slow slide into conformity. M.K. Lawson described this as a "narrowing of the range of possible interpretations" which has resulted in "little real debate about it" since the early days when the first modern historians laid out their theories. He questions the validity of this "cosy" consensus "which was established in the years around 1900 and has acted as a straightjacket upon interpretations ever since."[2]

Matthew Bennett was also aware of what he called "a great deal of apparent certitude from historians of the last three centuries".[3] Edwin Tetlow agreed that most histories "confirm broadly to a kind of approved version of the battle which has built up."[4] To reinforce this consensus, an impregnable fortress of scholarly works has built up, surrounded by a moat of vested interest. So formidable are these walls of knowledge, few dare assail them. When this refers to the most significant battle in a nation's history it is only the most reckless that dare assault the fortifications of learned conventionality.

Thus, when Jim Bradbury had the temerity to suggest that maybe everyone had got it all wrong and the Battle of Hastings was most likely fought on Caldbec Hill at the Battle Conference of 1983 he expected "howls of outrage" from certain quarters. As it happened no one seemed to notice (or maybe chose not to notice). Hoping to have opened a serious debate on the subject, he was dismayed to find that subsequent studies of the Battle of Hastings made little or no mention of Bradbury's novel idea.[5]

The problem is that if indeed the battle was fought on Caldbec Hill then all those masterly works which follow the battle in great detail are rendered, at least in part, invalid. This of course would be a travesty, as over the decades historians have produced many extremely important books which have helped the current generation of writers to understand the events of 1066 with much greater clarity.

None of them should be considered any less important just because they accepted the consensus over the site of the battle. Indeed this book could not have been written with any degree of accuracy without those works that came before. We cannot condemn them for not having considered the possibility that the battle may have been fought on Caldbec. But the facts cannot be ignored:

1. The only physical evidence to indicate that the battle was fought on Battle Hill is that the abbey was subsequently built there. Work on this building did not begin until more than four years after the battle by people that had not been present in 1066. Those people, the monks of Marmoutier abbey, started work at another site before they built the abbey (originally a monastery) on the present site, which they regarded as being "insignificant". Even if, as some historians claim, the ground around Battle must have changed over the centuries, it was evidently just as insignificant in the twelfth century as it is today.

2. It is alleged that the High Altar of the Battle monastery was erected on the very spot where Harold was killed, yet there is no certainty concerning the king's death, as the sources cannot agree on either the nature of Harold's death or whether or not he was killed in the first Norman attack or the last attack. There was also difficulty in locating his body after the battle.

3. Despite extensive excavations around Battle Abbey there is no evidence of it being the site of a major battle. A great many items from that period have been recovered yet none are of a military nature.

4. *The Chronicle of Battle Abbey*, the only document that identifies the battle site as being on Battle Hill, is known to be false. Even in the years following the foundation of the monastery no one really believed in its authenticity.

5. It is also said in *The Chronicle of Battle Abbey* that William vowed to build a monastery on the battlefield if he was victorious. No other source mentions this and the monastery was only started after a papal delegation had visited

England and had ordered William and those knights that had fought in the battle to give penance. Many modern authors now believe that Pope Alexander did not sanction the Norman invasion and that William never intended to erect any building on the battlefield until compelled to do so in order to receive absolution for the bloodshed he had caused.

6. However, it seems more than likely that there was a far more pragmatic reason for the construction of the abbey than any religious commemoration of William's victory. This was to block the invasion route from the coast and encourage settlement on an under-developed region. Its position on Battle Hill astride the Hastings to London road made its location ideal for defence and the low-lying land around it was more suitable for economic development than Caldbec Hill.

7. The monks entrusted with the building of the abbey selected the most appropriate site they could within the area of the battlefield. Caldbec Hill was entirely unsuitable for such a building. The monks would need to be able to support themselves from the surrounding countryside but the steep and broken slopes of Caldbec Hill would have made agriculture extremely problematic. So they chose a spot nearby, a hill with gentle slopes which in part were already under cultivation. That place was Battle Hill.

8. The only information we have from the primary sources with regards to the terrain upon which the battle was fought is that that the position occupied by the English was steep and "untilled" because of its "roughness". It is known that large parts of Battle Hill were in fact cultivated in 1066 whereas the nature of the ground leading up Caldbec Hill did not permit cultivation. Furthermore, the slopes of Caldbec Hill can justifiably be considered steep, whereas the southern-facing slopes of Battle Hill are comparatively gentle.

9. William of Poitiers wrote that the English "camped on higher ground, a hill close to the forest through which they had come." It is impossible to describe Battle Hill in this way as it is far lower than the Andresweald through which they had travelled. Such a description, nevertheless, would fit Caldbec Hill perfectly as it was indeed both close to the forest and higher.

10. One of the most detailed of the English sources, that of John of Worcester, states that the battle was fought at a place nine miles from Hastings. Caldbec Hill is nine miles from Hastings, whilst Battle Hill is only eight miles. It is reasonable to assume that an Englishman would have a better understanding of the geography of the area than a chronicler across the Channel in Normandy.

11. The position taken up by the English was so constricted that some men drifted away before the start of the battle as there was no room for them, and the soldiers were so tightly packed together on the hill, when they were killed their bodies did not drop to the ground. Such a description would suit steep-sided Caldbec Hill more accurately than Battle Hill.

12. Most writers agree that the assembly point of the English army was on Caldbec Hill. This is because it was a well-known place being at the meeting point of the boundaries of three Hundreds. It was also a convenient assembly point for the *fyrd as* it was at the junction of roads running east and west across the road from Hastings to London.

13. Harold is supposed to have abandoned his assembly point on Caldbec Hill to take up a position on the lower ridge of Battle Hill even though many of his men had still not arrived or were in the act of arriving. This means that even though he could see the Normans approaching he moved *further away* from his incoming reinforcements. This makes no sense at all. None of the primary sources state that the English moved from the assembly point; it has only been interpreted this way because otherwise it would mean that the battle had been fought on Caldbec Hill. In support of this is the fact that throughout history military commanders have sought to occupy the high ground, not to abandon it in the face of the enemy.

14. We know that Anglo-Saxon commanders were acutely aware of exposing their flanks to the enemy. The western side of Battle ridge was not only the lowest part of the traditional site of the battle but it also had an open flank. Caldbec Hill does not suffer from this defect. This makes Harold's supposed abandonment of Caldbec Hill even more unlikely. The unparalleled duration of the battle further indicates that the English flanks were securely held.

15. The Norman army was allowed to deploy from its line of march into battle array without being attacked by the English. If this took place at the foot of Battle Hill the Normans troops, in such close proximity to the English, would have been in extreme danger and it hardly seems likely that such a move would have been possible. By contrast, if the English troops were stationed on Caldbec Hill it is they who would have been at risk if they had left their lofty position and charged all the way down the hill to oppose the Normans as they assembled on the lower slopes.

16. The *Anglo-Saxon Chronicle*, the only absolutely undisputed contemporaneous document, recorded that the battle was fought at the "hoar apple tree" which is universally accepted as being on Caldbec Hill.

17. The primary sources state that Harold was taken by surprise. This means that he could not have been advancing to meet the Normans as his troops would have been in some kind of formation, and it implies that Harold was not taking up a pre-arranged position as both of these actions must have commenced before the Normans were seen cresting Telham Hill. The only possible interpretation of this can be that Harold was not expecting to fight at that time and was taken unawares at the concentration point with his army unformed. This must mean that the battle was fought at the English army's assembly point, which we know was Caldbec Hill.

18. The first mention of the name given to the hill on which the battle was fought as Senlac Hill was first recorded by Orderic Vitalis in the early twelfth century. Senlac means literally "sand-lake", and there was no lake close by Battle Hill at that date. However, there was a lake, or at least a pool, close by Caldbec Hill, near Oakwood Gill. Thus the assumption that Senlac Hill is Battle Hill is entirely unproven and could quite realistically refer to Caldbec Hill.

19. We have learnt that the first, almost disastrous, retreat of the Normans at the battle led to considerable numbers of the knights crashing into a ditch which ran across the rear of the battlefield. Whereas only a small ditch can be found on one side of the bottom of Battle Hill and could easily have been avoided as there is a large expanse of flat terrain next to it, there are three extensive watercourses between Caldbec Hill and Battle Hill.

20. Almost all historians now agree that the site of the *Malfosse* is at the present day Oakwood Gill to the north of Caldbec Hill. If the battle was fought on Battle Hill this would have meant that the retreating English infantry, engaged in close combat with the mounted knights, would have been able to stop fighting and outrun the Norman horses for over a mile to reach Oakwood Gill from the battlefield!

21. It is believed by the classical historian Eleanor Searle that the *Malfosse* was in fact where the Normans buried their dead. As indicated above, this is a long way from Battle Hill and there is not the least likelihood that the Normans would have dragged their dead that far just to bury them. On the other hand, to roll the bodies down the hill into Oakwood Gill, which we know at the time formed a considerable ravine, would have been easier than digging a vast grave.

22. *The Chronicle of Battle Abbey* was the first document to record the name of the *Malfosse*. Though much of what is written in the chronicle has been proven false, it is thought that the area of the "bad ditch" would have been well known locally and the chronicler described it as being "just where the fighting was going on." If Oakwood Gill is the *Malfosse* then the battle must have taken place on Caldbec Hill as just where the fighting was going on cannot possibly refer to Battle Hill.

23. The summit of Caldbec Hill is known as Mountjoy as it was there that the Normans erected a victory cairn after the battle, not on Battle Hill. It seems likely that they also lit a beacon announcing their victory on Caldbec Hill.

* * *

The consensus history of the Battle of Hastings has developed due to entirely understandable attempts at making sense out of the mass of contradictory information. This, though, has led to contorted efforts to make what is assumed to be correct fit into what we know is proven fact. Take, for instance, Amanda Clarke's explanation of the hillock shown on the Tapestry. Even though she accepts that it does not appear chronologically "in the correct place" she still believes, as so many do, that what the Tapestry shows is the *Malfosse* incident.[6] What we have in this case is an historian 900 years after the battle saying that the compilers of the Tapestry – probably the most authentic source of them all – had put the scene in the wrong place – simply because it did not fit into the accepted, consensus, version of events! All Ms Clarke is trying to do is reconcile seemingly conflicting evidence and it would be wrong to single her out for any special criticism.

Even the renowned historian Sir Frank Stenton, for example, made the same kind of statement. In referring to the first retreat of William's army he wrote: "a number of English and Normans perished together in the course of the flight, by falling into a deep depression in the ground situated *somewhere* between the base of the hill and the duke's post." He clearly could not find any such feature on the ground but rather than deviate from the norm he made a comment that he was unable to substantiate.[7]

Again, we have the distinguished historian Frank McLynn, who comments on the death of Harold. It may be recalled that William of Jumièges states that Harold was killed early in the battle. Though this is not said by the other sources, it could well be true as it would explain the ill-discipline of elements of the English army and the lack of enterprise shown by them. Professor McLynn, rather than give consideration to William of Jumièges' account, actually says that the chronicler made an error because this does not conform with the generally accepted consensus. "He was clearly confused and meant Harold's brother." Simply because this particular part of William of Jumièges' account does not comply with McLynn's perceived view of the battle the monk must be "confused" at the death of the last Anglo-Saxon king of England. At the time this was possibly the most significant event in English history that William of Jumièges was recording, yet the poor monk was so confused he mixed up Leofwine with Harold.[8]

Edwin Tetlow is scathing in his condemnation of the consensus history of the battle which, he says, "should by no means be taken to prove that the accepted version is the correct one. On the contrary, it is almost certain that this version strays quite a long way from the truth … Consequently, the more enthusiastically a modern writer goes into detail about the battle the more likely he is to be wrong."[9]

M.K. Lawson is one of those modern writers but he is sensibly circumspect in his pronouncements: "If the idea that it [the battle] was contested by about 7,000 men on each side simply around the crest of Battle Abbey ridge cannot be proved to be wrong, nor can it be proved to be right, and indeed no very convincing evidence was ever produced in its favour."[10]

Doctor Stephen Morillo is equally cautious. As he says, there is no "one correct history". History is a process, he wrote in 1996, "and debates, reinterpretations, and the search for new evidence are all part of that process."[11]

Jim Bradbury, whose daring suggestion that the battle may not have been fought on Battle Hill was the inspiration for this current book, wrote that: "One historian will disagree with another, but there is no absolute right or wrong. However much we take care, we can get it wrong. Indeed we do not truly know if we get it right or wrong, we can only do our best. It is necessary to make a careful evaluation of sources but, in the end, interpretation of them is subjective rather than objective, since none of us knows the absolute truth of what happened in the past."[12]

This was acknowledged by M.K. Lawson, who concluded that we can only be guided by the sources: "The study of Hastings must ultimately be a study of the characteristics and strength and weaknesses of those sources ... Moreover, this source criticism must necessarily be an elaborate process, and is not one ever to yield definite conclusions."[13]

* * *

It is true that we may never know for certain where the great battle was fought and no amount of academic argument is ever likely to provide conclusive proof. The fact that Battle Abbey was built on what is now called Battle Hill does not indicate that it was the site of the battle because the most likely reason for its construction was as a vital component in the defence of the road to London from the low-lying beaches of Sussex. Its construction had nothing whatsoever to do with either a commemorative or penitential act by William, other than possibly retrospectively to satisfy the envoys of Pope Alexander.

Yet we do actually possess some genuine evidence and it is the best evidence of all, the ground itself. Before the reader makes up his or her own mind on the subject a walk around the environs of the pleasant little town of Battle is essential. Stroll across the grounds of Battle Abbey, it is not a taxing exercise despite what the chroniclers may tell us. View the little hillock where supposedly vast numbers of Norman knights came spectacularly to grief and the English rolled stones down upon their enemies. Judge this for yourself.

Purchase a copy of the *Malfosse Walk* from the Battle Abbey bookshop. Follow the route over Freeman's *Malfosse* and up the difficult slopes of Caldbec Hill. Draw your conclusions, and your breath, when the summit, the place of the Mountjoy, is reached.

Continue down the steep northern slope of Caldbec Hill to Oakwood Gill. It was here that the final act in the Battle of Hastings was played out. Make your final assessment here. Could the English have ever escaped ahead of the Norman knights all the way from Battle Hill to reach this point?

Yet, in the great scheme of things, exactly where the battle was fought is of little real consequence. Placing the battle at a point less than a mile away does not amount to re-writing history. What we hope to have demonstrated, though, is that there were many good reasons why the battle might, and probably should, have been fought on Caldbec Hill and that the unqualified assumptions of generations of writers on the subject are no longer valid.

Further studies of the Battle of Hastings must take this into consideration. Even if future historians choose to deny it, they cannot ignore it. It may be the case that every schoolchild knows when the Battle of Hastings was fought – but does anyone really know *where?*

Well in answer to this final question, we will leave the last words to Jim Bradbury, who first cast doubt about the site of the battle: "On the evidence quoted so far, one might be inclined to locate the battle on Caldbec Hill."[14]

Notes

1. The Contradictory Evidence

1. Mark Anthony Lower, "On the Battle of Hastings", *Sussex Archaeological Collections*, vol.8.
2. C.N. Barclay, *Battle 1066*, p.116.
3. E. Tetlow, *The Enigma of Hastings*, Introduction.
4. D. Howarth, *1066: The Year of the Conquest*, p.8.
5. See S. Morillo, *The Battle of Hastings, Sources and Interpretations*, p.96.
6. H. Wood, *The Battle of Hastings: The Fall of Anglo-Saxon England*, p.4.
7. S. Morillo, *Sources and Interpretations*, Preface and Introduction.
8. See E. Mason, *The House of Godwine*, p.168.
9. D. Greenway, *Henry of Huntingdon: The History of the English People 1000–1154*, Introduction, xxiv.
10. C.N. Barclay, *Battle 1066*, xii and p.118.
11. Benton Rain Patterson, *Harold & William: The Battle for England 1066*, p.12.
12. D. Howarth, *1066*, p.8.
13. E.A. Freeman, *History of the Norman Conquest*, vol.3, p.757.
14. M.K. Lawson, *The Battle of Hastings 1066*, pp.14–15.
15. R. Huscroft, *The Norman Conquest: A New Introduction*, pp.3–4.
16. F. Stenton, *Anglo-Saxon England*, p.594.
17. George Duckett, "Hastings v. Senlac", *Sussex Archaeological Collections*, vol. 39, 1892, pp.28–30; M.K. Lawson, *The Battle of Hastings*, pp.57–9.
18. J. Bradbury, *The Battle of Hastings*, pp.133–4. It seems possible that the original Saxon name was Santlache (sandy area) and that this was changed by the Normans, probably by an accident of pronunciation or a misunderstanding of the word, to Senlac, T. Wise, *1066 Year of Destiny*, p.188. The French historians T Leprévost & G. Bernage, *Hastings 1066: Norman Cavalry and Saxon Infantry*, p.46, state categorically that the name was given to the hill subsequent to the battle, not before.
19. Peter Marren, *1066: The Battles of York, Stamford Bridge & Hastings*, pp.8–9.
20. E. Tetlow, *The Enigma of Hastings*, p.21.
21. W. Seymour, *Battles in Britain 1066–1746*, p.7.
22. J. Bradbury, "Battles in England and Normandy, 1066–1154", in M. Strickland, *Anglo-Norman Warfare*, p.185; J. Bradbury, *The Battle of Hastings*, pp.134–5.
23. S. Morillo, *Sources and Interpretations*, p.95.
24. Lawson, *The Battle of Hastings*, p.183.
25. J.J. Badgley, *Historical Interpretation*, vol. I, p.12.

26. J. Bradbury, *The Battle of Hastings.*, p.110.
27. E. Mason, *op. cit.* Prologue.

2. A Family Affair

1. D. Crouch, *The Normans*, pp.1–24.
2. D. Greenaway, *Henry of Huntingdon*, Introduction.
3. D. Crouch, *The Normans*, p.29.
4. Frank McLynn, *1066 The Year of the Three Battles*, p.2, says that the Danes asked for £36,000 in 1007 and £48,000 in 1012 but that these figures are disputed.
5. N.J. Higham, *The Norman Conquest*, pp.16–17.
6. N.J. Higham, *The Norman Conquest*, p.17; it seems that Robert of Normandy backed this expedition which took place in 1033, which indicates that he had come to recognise Edward's right to the English throne, Lawson, *The Battle of Hastings*, p.18.
7. W. Seymour, *Battles in Britain*, p.9.
8. A. Bridgeford, *1066: The Hidden History of the Bayeux Tapestry* pp.54–5; Earl Godwin had married Gytha Thorkelsdóttir, whose brother Ulf Jarl was the son-in-law of Sweyn I and the father of Sweyn II of Denmark.
9. *Anglo-Saxon Chronicle, English Historical Documents*, vol.2, p.106. Peter Poyntz Wright, *Hastings*, p.7, says that Edward married Edith because he was worried about the rise in the power of the House of Godwin.
10. Anne Savage, *The Anglo-Saxon Chronicles*, pp.177–8. Lawson, *The Battle of Hastings*, pp.21–2, has put forward the supposition that the reason for Eustace's visit was "a desire to press his own claim to the throne as the second husband of Edward's dead sister, Godgifu. Rupert Furneaux, *Conquest 1066*, p.15, believes that the incident at Dover was all part of a plot intended to create problems for Earl Godwin. He says that a few miles short of Dover, Eustace's knights donned their armour and that they rode into the town demanding free accommodation for the night and "spoiling for a fight".
11. Godwin was actually given five days' safe conduct to leave the country, *Anglo-Saxon Chronicle, English Historical Documents*, vol.2, p.122.
12. Apparently Edward had second thoughts about allowing Harold to go free and he sent Bishop Aldred of Worcester with a body of horsemen to Bristol where Harold and Leofwine were preparing to sail. Aldred was not happy about detaining these two Englishmen and he let them continue with their voyage to Ireland, where they sought refuge with King Dermot, Poyntz Wright, *Hastings*, p.14; *Anglo-Saxon Chronicle* D and E texts, pp.171–7.
13. D.C. Douglas, *English Historical Review*, vol. LXVIII, pp.528 & 545 referred to in Poyntz Wright, *Hastings* p.15. According to F. Barlow, *The Life of Edward the Confessor*, p.26, in describing Godwin's force, "The sea was covered with ships. The sky glittered with the press of weapons."
14. A. Thierry, *History of the Conquest of England*, p.142.
15. *Anglo-Saxon Chronicle, English Historical Documents*, vol.2, p.130.
16. Higham, *Death of Anglo-Saxon England*, p.147.
17. As William Seymour observes, Edward had no right to promise the throne to anyone. He could recommend a successor to the *Witan* but that was all, *Battles in Britain*, p.10.
18. Edward had other male relatives through his sister who married Dreux of the Vexin (a region of France). Of these nephews, one, Ralph the Timid, had followed Edward to England and had married into a prominent East Midland family. He was granted an earldom only to die in 1057 but he had a son, Walter. However, there was little precedent for succession through female descent and none were considered by Edward as potential heirs, see Higham, *The Norman Conquest*, pp.36–7.

19. Higham, *The Norman Conquest*, pp.46–7.
20. Freeman, *History of the Norman Conquest of England*, vol. II, pp.429–30.
21. Frank Stenton, *Anglo-Saxon England*, p.577, believed that Harold had reached an unrivalled position at Edward's court.
22. In a winter campaign, Harold destroyed Gruffudd's fleet base and halls at Rhuddlan and then in May 1063 led a fleet along the Welsh coast from Bristol, while Tostig launched a invasion from the landward side. This unprecedented, co-ordinated attack was too much for the Welsh, see Higham, *Death of Anglo-Saxon England*, p.147.
23. Higham, *The Norman Conquest*, p.40, wrote that even though Harold was not related by blood to Edward this was not necessarily a bar to his succession as there were similar precedents in the previous century.
24. P. Hill, *The Road to Hastings*, pp.131–2.
25. Higham, *Death of Anglo-Saxon England*, p.164; Benton Rain Patterson, *Harold & William*, p.40.
26. F. Barlow, *The Life of Edward the Confessor*, p.50–4.
27. The Count of Flanders gave Tostig a house and estate at St Omer, E. Mason, *House of Godwine*, p.132.
28. R.R. Darlington, P. McGurk and J. Bray, *The Chronicle of John of Worcester*, vol.II, p.601. It is thought that Duke William may have known about and encouraged Tostig's expedition, Frank Stenton, *Anglo-Saxon England*, p.587. See also Anne Savage, *Anglo-Saxon Chronicles*, p.194.
29. Higham, *The Norman Conquest*, p.37.
30. L. Watkiss and M. Chibnall, *The Waltham Chronicle*, p.45.
31. Thierry, *History of the Conquest of England*, p.143.
32. According to the *Vita Ædwardi Regis*, p.123, Edward's dying words to Harold were, "I commend this woman [Queen Edith] and all the kingdom to your protection." F. McLynn, *1066*, p.177, and E. Mason, *The House of Godwine*, pp.127–8 & p.139, give opposing accounts of this marriage which the latter calculates probably took place in the spring when the Easter court was convened.

3. Swords Around the Throne

1. Ponynz Wright, *Hastings*, p.14.
2. D. Matthew, *The Norman Conquest 1066*, p.74.
3. D. Bates, *William the Conqueror*, p.34, thinks the visit was "intrinsically unlikely".
4. Wood, *The Battle of Hastings*, p.38.
5. D.C. Douglas, *William the Conqueror*, pp. 59–60.
6. Wood, *The Battle of Hastings*, p.42.
7. It is said that from 1052 King Henry I of France showed support for Earl Godwin because he had learnt of Edward's offer of the English throne to William of Normandy, as he was worried about the latter's growing power, see Higham, *The Norman Conquest*, pp.27–8.
8. The pallium was a narrow band of white wool bestowed by the Holy See as a symbol of power delegated to individuals by the Pope.
9. Lawson, *The Battle of Hastings*, pp.20–1, believes that if William of Jumièges did indeed pass on such a message to William then all that followed makes sense and that most modern scholars have been convinced for the most part that Edward did give somw kind of undertaking to the duke at this time.
10. Benton Rain Patterson, *Harold & William*, pp.15–17.
11. Higham, *The Norman Conquest*, p.41; Higham, *The Death of Anglo-Saxon England*, p.154, says that the campaign against Conan confirms a date of 1064–5 for Harold's journey to the Continent; Bridgeford, pp.83–4.

12. Poyntz Wright, *Hastings*, pp.8–9.
13. E. Mason, *The House of Godwine*, p.121.
14. Higham, *Death of Anglo-Saxon England*, p.54; Wace says that these were the bones of two British saints, Ravennus and Rasyphus, and that Harold was staggered when he discovered that he had been tricked into making such an oath, Thierry, *History of the Conquest of England*, p.140; Frank Stenton, *The Bayeux Tapestry*, p.167. Tetlow, *The Enigma of Hastings*, spells out the details of the arrangement – which included the promise that Harold would place a garrison of Norman knights in Dover Castle and other key places around England as well as using all his influence and wealth to ensure that after the death of King Edward the kingdom of England should be confirmed in the possession of the Duke – and says that Harold would have been "out of his mind" to have made such commitments.
15. Higham, in *Death of Anglo-Saxon England*, p.160.
16. Little is known of Hakon, and Harriet Wood, *The Battle of Hastings*, p.48, states that even his very existence is highly suspect.
17. The fact that Harold and Tostig were no longer on good terms would mitigate such a trip as Tostig was the Count's son-in-law. Yet, as with all things connected with the Battle of Hastings, nothing is really certain and it could well be that Harold was going to Flanders to try to make amends with his brother.
18. Poyntz Wright, *The Battle of Hastings*, pp.12–13 and his *Hastings*, p.23.
19. Bridgeford, *Hidden History of the Bayeux Tapestry*, p.337; D. Greenaway, *Henry of Huntingdon*, p. 381. Poyntz Wright ibid.
20. H. Wood, *The Battle of Hastings*, pp.50–1.
21. H. Wood, *The Battle of Hastings*, pp.51–4.
22. Higham, in *Death of Anglo-Saxon England*, pp.157–8, offers yet another possibility for Harold's journey. In the bottom margin of the Tapestry at this point there are two naked male figures. Higham says that Harold may have gone to Normandy to protest at the sexual molestation of some highborn English lady.
23. F. Barlow, *The Life of Edward the Confessor*, pp.33–6.
24. Tetlow, *The Enigma of Hastings*, p.17.
25. Higham, *The Battle of Hastngs*, p.152.
26. Morillo, *Sources and Interpretations*, xiv; Howarth, *1066*, pp.161–4, 164–5 & 177.
27. Douglas & Greenaway, "William of Poitiers", *English Historical Documents*, vol.2, p.218.
28. We know none of the details of these two messages, Lemmon, "The Campaign of 1066", in Whitelock *et al.*, *The Norman Conquest, Its Setting & Impact*, p.79.
29. Douglas & Greenaway, "William of Poitiers", *English Historical Documents*, p.219; *William of Malmesbury's Chronicle of the Kings of England* ed. J.A. Giles, p.273. It is also given in length in *Master Wace, His Chronicle of the Norman Conquest from the Roman de Rou*, translated by Edgar Taylor , pp.115–7.
30. Bridgeford, *Hidden History of the Bayeux Tapestry*, p.120. Paul Hill wrote with regard to William coming to England with a papal banner, "It would seem that in actual fact he did not," *The Road to Hastings*, p.159.
31. D. Bates, *William the Conqueror*, pp.101–2.
32. Ian W. Walker, *Harold, the Last Anglo-Saxon King*, pp.228–30.
33. Freeman, *History of the Norman Conquest*, vol. III, p.182.
34. *Cambridge Mediaeval History*, vol. 5, 1926, p.497; J.F.C. Fuller, *Decisive Battles of the Western World*, vol.1, p.368; William of Malmesbury, *De Getis Regum Anglorum*, ed. W. Stubbs, vol. 2, p.299.
35. *Taylor (trans.) Master Wace, Roman de Rou*, pp.103–8.
36. Howarth, *1066*, p.102.

37. Poyntz Wright, *Hastings*, p.46. Charles Lemmon, "The Campaign of 1066", in Whitelock *et al.*, *The Norman Conquest*, p.83, says that William personally met with King Philip of France and Baldwin of Flanders, who, as rulers, were unable to provide official help, but who did not stop volunteers from their countries joining the expedition.
38. *Anglo-Saxon Chronicle, English Historical Documents*, vol.2, p.144.
39. The date usually stated for the disbanding of the *fyrd* is the Nativity of St Mary, the 8th of September, *Anglo-Saxon Chronicle, English Historical Documents*, vol.2, p.146.
40. Douglas, *William the Conqueror*, p.396.
41. Poyntz Wright, *Hastings*, p.50.
42. Leprévost and Bernage, *Hastings 1066*, p.4.
43. Douglas & Greenaway, "William of Poitiers", *English Historical Documents*, p.218.
44. In modern Norwegian it would be spelt Hardrade. Hard means hard and rade means council, therefore hard council or hard bargainer, see Howarth, *1066*, p.107.
45. Hardrada's claim was based on an alleged agreement in 1038 between his predecessor Magnus and Harthacnut, see Lemmon, "The Campaign of 1066" in Whitelock *et al.*, *The Norman Conquest*, p.87.
46. Bridgeford, *Hidden History of the Bayeux Tapestry*, p.125.
47. F.W. Brooks, *The Battle of Stamford Bridge*, East Yorks Historical Society, 1956, p.11.
48. R. Allen Brown, *The Normans and the Norman Conquest*, pp.135–6, stresses that we really have no information about the numbers or composition of Harold's army.
49. Though this is a little over-simplistic, R. Allen Brown, "The Battle of Hastings", in Morillo, *Sources and Interpretations*, p.203, says that there is "more than sufficient contemporary evidence to show that Old English armies habitually fought on foot."
50. McLynn, *1066*, p.201.
51. T. Wise, *1066 Year of Destiny*, pp.157–9.
52. P. Hill, *The Road to Hastings*, p.150.
53. *Anglo-Saxon Chronicle, English Historical Documents*, vol.2, p.146.
54. F. W. Brooks, *op cit.*, p.16.
55. Douglas, *William the Conqueror*, p.399.

4. The Opening Moves

1. Stenton, *Anglo-Saxon England*, p.591. It has been calculated that high tide at St Valéry would have been at 15.14 hours, "The Pevensey Campaign: brilliantly executed plan or near disaster?" in Morillo, *Sources and Interpretations*, p.139. These days access for yachts is at high tide plus or minus two hours but that is no indication of tidal conditions in 1066.
2. William's ship *Mora* had at the prow a boy wrought in gold, pointing to England with his right hand and holding to his lips an ivory horn in his left, R. Allen Brown, *Normans and the Norman Conquest*, p.129. It is said that William anchored in mid-Channel to await the rest of the fleet, in which case the *Mora* must have had a very long anchor line indeed!
3. McLynn, *1066*, p.210.
4. Fuller, *Decisive Battles of the Western World*, vol. 1, p.372; Poyntz Wright, *Hastings*, p.47; Lemmon, "The Campaign of 1066" in Whitelock *et al.*, *The Norman Conquest*, p.90.
5. Freeman, *History of the Norman Conquest*, vol. II, p.410. William later made the people of Romney pay blood money for killing his men, Leprévost and Bernage, *Hastings 1066*, p.9.
6. E. Searle (trans.), *Chronicle of Battle Abbey*, p.18.
7. R. Furneaux, *Conquest 1066*, p.103; McLynn, *1066*, p.211; Leprévost and Bernage, *Hastings 1066*, p.9.
8. *Master Wace, Roman de Rou*, (trans.), ed. Taylor, pp.127–8.

9. As it is likely that the poorer *fyrdsmen* did not travel north, the lack of opposition to the Norman landing can be explained by the fact that all the leading warriors were absent.

10. Leprévost and Bernage, *Hastings 1066*, p.4. Orderic Vitalis states that Tostig visited Normandy during his period of exile, so some collusion is possible, see Marjorie Chibnall, *Orderic Vitalis, Historia Ecclesiastica*, vol.ii, p.143.

11. Douglas & Greenaway, "William of Poitiers", *English Historical Documents*, vol.2, p.220; Leprévost and Bernage, *Hastings 1066*; Lawson, *The Battle of Hastings*, pp.172–3. Brigadier Barclay, *Battle 1066*, pp.66–70, who consulted a meteorologist, has no doubt that the weather alone was not the reason why William waited so long before setting off across the Channel.

12. Lemmon, "The Campaign of 1066", Whitelock *et al.*, *The Norman Conquest*, p.89.

13. Brian Smailes, *The 1066 Country Walk*; McLynn, *1066*, p.211.

14. Poyntz Wright, *Hastings*, p.49.

15. Leprévost and Bernage, *Hastings 1066*, p.15.

16. Richard Glover, "English Warfare in 1066", in Morillo, *Sources and Interpretations*, p.175.

17. D. Bates, *William the Conqueror*, p.103.

18. McLynn, *1066*, p.212.

19. J.A. Williamson, *The English Channel*, p.80.

20. Frank Stenton, *William the Conqueror*, pp.190–1.

21. Fuller, *Decisive Battles of the Western World*, vol.1, p.373.

22. Douglas, *William the Conqueror*, p.399.

23. Tetlow, *The Enigma of Hastings*, p.142.

24. Poyntz Wright, *Hastings*, p.74.

25. Tetlow, *The Enigma of Hastings*, pp.142–3.

26. Morillo, *Sources and Interpretations*, p.181. Surprisingly the march on foot from York to Battle was attempted by Huron Mallalieu in 2006 and he did manage to cover the entire distance of around 260 miles in thirteen days, see Huron Mallalieu, *1066 And Rather More*.

27. Douglas & Greenaway, "William of Poitiers", *English Historical Documents*, vol.2, pp.223–4; Thierry, *History of the Conquest of England*, p.161. Freeman, *History of the Norman Conquest*, vol. III, pp.432–3 says that it was most likely William who sent the first messenger as it was perfectly in character that an invader who assumed the character of a legal claimant should play his part by "offering the perjurer one last chance of repentance." See also Peter Rex, *1066: A New History of the Norman Conquest*, p.59.

28. Tetlow, *The Enigma of Hastings*, p.153.

29. C. Morton and H. Muntz eds, *Carmen de Hastingae Proelio*, p.19.

30. McLynn, *1066*, p.212; J.F.A Mason, "The Rapes of Sussex and the Norman Conquest", *Sussex Archaeological Collections* (vol.102, 1964), pp.75–7.

31. Tetlow, *The Enigma of Hastings*, pp.143–4.

32. Mallalieu, *1066 And Rather More*, p.204.

33. Bridgeford, *Hidden History of the Bayeux Tapestry*, p.132; McLynn, *1066*, p.213.

34. McLynn, *1066*, p.213.

35. Freeman, *History of the Norman Conquest*, vol. III, p.435.

36. Howarth, *1066*, p.163; Freeman, *History of the Norman Conquest*, vol. III, p.437.

37. McLynn, *1066*, p.214.

38. Stenton, *William the Conqueror*, p.198 and Mason, *The House of Godwine*, p.157. This is, however, disputed as even though Edwin and Morcar may not have sent any troops south, the presence of their cousin the Abbot of Peterborough with Harold's army would

appear to demonstrate their support for the king, Higham, *The Death of Anglo-Saxon England*, p.212.

39. Mason, *The House of Godwine*, p.162. "He gave over to bishop Ealdred the much booty and harness which he had gained from the Norsemen", Thomas Hardy and Charles Martin, *Lestorie des Engles solum La Translacion Maistre Geffreu Gaimar*, lines 5250–5255.

40. When Edmumd Ironside had raised an army on behalf of his father, Æthelred, in 1016 to oppose Canute, the men had refused to fight – quite legitimately it appears – because Æthelred was not present and it was the King's duty to lead his people, H. Wood, *The Battle of Hastings*, p.169.

41. R. Allen Brown, *Normans and the Norman Conquest*, pp.139–40.

42. Stenton, *Anglo-Saxon England*, p.592.

43. D. Howarth, *1066*, p.165.

44. Furneaux, *Conquest 1066*, p.121; Benton Rain Patterson, *William and Harold: The Battle for England 1064–1066*, p.158.

45. Lemmon, *The Field of Hastings*, pp.39–40; W.A. Raper, "On the silver pennies of Edward the Confessor found at Sedlescombe", *Sussex Archaeological Collections*, vol. 33. It might well be that this is some of the loot taken from the Vikings at Stamford Bridge.

46. P. Marren, *1066*, p.94.

47. N.P. Brooks, and H.E. Walker, *Proceedings of the Battle Conference*, p.32.

48. Poyntz Wright, *Hastings*, p.48; Howarth, *1066*, p.165; Lemmon, *The Field of Hastings*, pp.18–19.

49. Mason, *The House of Godwine*, p.165.

50. Rex, *1066 A New History of the Norman Conquest*, p.67.

51. M.A. Lower, *Contributions to Literature*, p.38.

52. Bradbury, *The Battle of Hastings*, p.136.

53. Barclay, *Battle 1066*, pp.44–5.

54. Douglas, *William the Conqueror*, p.217; Fuller, *Decisive Battles of the Western World*, vol.1, p.374; Poyntz Wright, *Hastings*, p.81.

55. Douglas, *William the Conqueror*, pp.197–8.

56. Barclay, *Battle 1066*, p.71.

57. Bradbury, *The Battle of Hastings*, p.38.

58. McLynn, *1066*, p.215, believes that the main element of Harold's army may not have reached Caldbec Hill until 0200 hours on Saturday morning.

59. Freeman, *History of the Norman Conquest*, vol. III, pp.441–2.

60. R. Allen Brown, *Normans and the Norman Conquest*, p.141.

61. E.A. Freeman, *A Short History of the Norman Conquest*, p.75.

62. Wace, *Le Roman de Rou*, ed. Holden, vol. ii, pp.156–7. See also *William of Malmesbury*, ed. Giles, p.276; *Master Wace, Le Roman de Rou*, Taylor, pp.155–6; *William of Malmesbury*, ed. Stubbs, ii, p.302. See also Bradbury, *The Battle of Hastings*, p.150.

63. D. Howarth, *1066*, pp.171–2.

64. Furneaux, *Conquest 1066*, pp.122–3.

65. Tetlow, *The Enigma of Hastings*, p.152. Bradbury, *op. cit.*, p.128.

66. McLynn, *1066*, p.216.

67. Morton and Muntz, *Carmen de Hastingae Proelio*, pp.74 & 77, are quite emphatic about this statement by William of Poitiers being on the morning of the 14th, not the day before. However, they also say that Duke William may have had an advanced camp further inland from Hastings.

68. Tetlow, *The Enigma of Hastings*, p.163.

69. Freeman, *History of the Norman Conquest*, vol. III, p.457; Bridgeford, *Hidden History of the Bayeux Tapestry*, p.137. It is Charles Lemmon, amongst others, who has given us

heathland for Hecheland, "The Campaign of 1066" in Whitelock *et al.*, *The Norman Conquest*, p.103.

70. D. Howarth, *1066*, p.169.

71. R. Allen Brown, *Normans and the Norman Conquest*, p.144, thinks that the *housecarls* would have stood with their respective lords, thus Harold's would have gathered around him, Gyrth's around him and the same with Leofwine. Benton Rain Patterson, *William and Harold*, p.164, has groups of *housecarls* interspersed in groups among the *fyrd*.

72. Morton and Muntz, *The Carmen de Hastingae Proelio*, p.25.

73. Edward Creasy, *The Fifteen Decisive Battles of the World*, p.280, copying E. Taylor, *Wace, Roman de Rou*, p.177.

74. P. Rex, *1066*, pp.64 & 67 cites Marianus Scotus, who said that the English were in seven divisions, suggesting a seven-wedge formation closely ranked together. Freeman, *History of the Norman Conquest*, vol 3, p.759, suggests that these "Danes" may in fact have been Northumbrians as that land had long been settled by the Danes.

75. Tetlow, *The Enigma of Hastings*, p.165.

5. Men at Arms

1. C. Warren Hollister, *Anglo-Saxon Military Institutions*, pp.127–132.

2. F. Stenton, *Anglo-Saxon England*, p.582.

3. Nickolas Hooper, "The Housecarls in England in the Eleventh Century", in M. Strickland, *Anglo-Norman Warfare*, p.10, does not consider that these forty ships had anything to do with the *housecarls*.

4. Nicholas Hooper, "Anglo-Saxon Warfare on the Eve of the Conquest: A Brief Survey", in R. Allen Brown, *Proceedings of the Battle Conference 1978*, pp.84–5.

5. Nickolas Hooper, in M. Strickland, *Anglo-Norman Warfare*, p.15.

6. R. Abels, "Bookland and Fyrd Service in Late Saxon England", in Morillo, *Sources and Interpretations*, pp.58–60. Bookland was land held by book from ecclesiastical entities which had been granted privileged lands by the king for the remission of his sins. Unlike other methods of holding land, these grants were transferred by a written book (boc), diploma, or *privilegium*. Land held by book, or bookland, sanctioned by both church and state held greater rights in heritability and mobility than other lands not held by book, e.g. folkland and *laenland*. Generally, holding land required complying with the customs which burdened the land. Occupants of the land might owe rents, royal fines, building services, military service, and agricultural service. From these praedial burdens, the king granted immunities. Holders of privileged bookland were often immune from all earthly service except the commonly reserved three burdens of military service, *burhbot* and *brycegeweorc*.

7. J.H. Round, *Feudal England*, pp.44–69.

8. Quoted in R. Abels, *op. cit.*, p.64. A simpler reading of this obligation is revealed in the Berkshire entry of the Domesday Book: "If the king took an army anywhere, only one soldier went from five hides, and four shillings were given to him from each hide as subsistence and wages for two months. This money, indeed, was not sent to the king but was given to the soldiers", see N. Hooper, *op. cit.*, p.88.

9. T. Wise, *1066 Year of Destiny*, p.41.

10. A. Clarke, *The Battle of Hastings*, p.49.

11. C. Gravett, *Hastings 1066*, p.29; *Master Wace, Roman de Rou*, Taylor, p.173; N. Hooper, *op. cit.*, p.87.

12. Lemmon, *The Field of Hastings*, p.36.

13. Tetlow, *The Enigma of Hastings*, p.159.

14. Lemmon, "The Campaign of 1066", in Whitelock *et al.*, *The Norman Conquest*, p.87.

15. McLynn, *1066*, p.215.
16. This has really emanated from *Master Wace, Roman de Rou*, ed. Taylor, p.173, though has been followed by others such as Edward Freeman, *History of the Norman Conquest*,vol.3, pp.472–3 and Denis Butler, *1066 The Story of a Year*, p.234.
17. Wise, *1066 Year of Destiny*, pp.184–5.
18. The subject of the English navy is examined in detail in T. Wise, *1066 Year of Destiny*, pp.63–6.
19. *Master Wace, Roman de Rou*, E. Taylor, p.106.
20. Leprévost and Bernage, *Hastings 1066*, p.39.
21. Wise, *1066 Year of Destiny*, pp.61–2.
22. Leprévost and Bernage, *Hastings 1066*, p.26.
23. C. Gravett, *Hastings 1066*, pp.24–5.
24. M.A. Lower, "On the Battle of Hastings", *Sussex Archaeological Collections*, vol.8, 1856; Gravett, *Hastings 1066*, p.32.
25. Lemmon, *The Field of Hastings*, p.15.
26. Freeman, *History of the Norman Conquest*, vol.3, p.444.
27. Oman, *History of the Art of War in the Middle Ages*, vol.1, p.165.
28. Darlington and McGurk, *The Chronicle of John of Worcester*, p.601.
29. Rex, *1066*, p.69.
30. Erling Monsen (ed.) & A.H. Smith (trans.), *Snorri Sturluson, Heiskringla or the Lives of the Norse Kings*, pp.566–68; *Snorri Sturluson, King Harald's Saga*, M. Magnusson and H. Pálsson, p.151.
31. C. Warren Hollister, *Anglo-Saxon Military Institutions*, p.133.
32. E. Mason, *The House of Godwine*, p.164; J. Bradbury, "Battles in England and Normandy, 1066–1154", in A. Brown, *Anglo-Norman Studies*, vi., pp.11–12.
33. Douglas & Greenaway, "William of Poitiers", *English Historical Documents*, p.227.
34. C. Lemmon, "The Campaign of 1066", in Whitelock *et al.*, *The Norman Conquest*, p.101.
35. F. McLynn, *1066*, p.203.
36. Mathew Bennett and Ken Guest, "Exploding the Myths of Hastings", *Skirmish* magazine, September 1996, pp.25–7.
37. A. Clarke, *A Day That Made History*, p.17.
38. Wise, *1066 Year of Destiny*, pp.60–1.
39. Lemmon, *The Field of Hastings*, p.24
40. Wise, *1066 Year of Destiny*, p.190.
41. R. Barlow, *William I and the Norman Conquest*, p.33.
42. See John Gillingham, "William the Bastard at War", in Morillo, *Sources and Interpretations*, pp.98–100.
43. Gillingham, *op. cit.*, p.103.
44. Gillingham, *op. cit.*, p.102.
45. Gillingham, *op. cit.*, p.103.
46. Gillingham, *op. cit.*, p.109–10.
47. F. Stenton, *William the Conqueror and the Rule of the Normans*, p.198.
48. Barclay, *Battle 1066*, p.71.
49. Richard Glover, "English Warfare in 1066", in Morillo, *Sources and Interpretations*, pp.181–2.
50. *Master Wace, Roman de Rou*, (trans.) E. Taylor, p.120.
51. James's figures cited in Lemmon, "The Campaign of 1066", in Whitelock *et al.*, *The Norman Conquest*; Furneaux, *Conquest 1066*, pp.107–8
52. Fuller, *Decisive Battles of the Western World*, vol.1, p.371–2.
53. Poyntz Wright, *Hastings*, pp.56–7.

54. Wise, *1066 Year of Destiny*, p.63.
55. Fuller, *Decisive Battles of the Western World*, vol.1, p.371–2.
56. Lawson, pp.149 & 217.
57. Oman, throughout his *History of The Art of War in the Middle Ages*, tended to over-magnify the forces involved.
58. W. Spatz, *Der Schlacht von Hastings*, pp.33–4; F. Stenton, *Anglo-Saxon England*, p.593; J.F.C. Fuller, *A Military History of the Western World*, vol. I, pp.374–7; Rex, *1066 A New History of the Norman Conquest*, p.63.
59. Freeman, *History of the Norman Conquest*, vol. III, p.440.
60. Darlington and McGurk (eds), *The Chronicle of John of Worcester*, vol. II p.605.
61. *Master Wace, Roman de Rou*, (trans) E. Taylor, p.174.
62. M. Rud, *The Bayeux Tapestry*, p.78; Lemmon, "The Campaign of 1066", in Whitelock, *et al.*, *The Norman Conquest*, p.84.
63. M. Rud, *The Bayeux Tapestry*, p.81.

6. The Battle of the Hoar Apple Tree

1. Douglas & Greenaway, "William of Poitiers", *English Historical Documents*, vol. 2, p.225.
2. Lawson, *The Battle of Hastings*, p.184. Charles Lemmon, *The Field of Hastings*, pp.43–4, cites information received from the Royal Observatory, Herstmonceux, "On the day of the Battle of Hastings (1066 October 12 O.S.) sunset at Battle was approximately at 04.59 local time, and the Moon was 22 days old, that is just after last quarter." From this it follows that dawn broke about 0530 hours assisted by a less than half-sized waning moon in the southern sky.
3. F. Stenton, *William the Conqueror*, p.199.
4. Barclay, *Battle 1066*, p.55; Whitelock, *et al.*, *The Norman Conquest*, p.105.
5. McLynn, *1066*, p.217.
6. Lawson, *The Battle of Hastings*, *op. cit.*, p.190.
7. Rex, *1066*, p.64.
8. Morton & Muntz, *The Carmen de Hastingae Proelio*, p.27.
9. McLynn, *1066*, p.217.
10. Whitelock *et al.*, *The Norman Conquest*, p.105; A. Clarke, *A Day that Made History*, p.19. Rex, *1066*, p.68, says that the infantry were committed ahead of the cavalry "since the knights feared to attack the English line immediately."
11. Douglas, *William the Conqueror*, p.199. Because the Normans must have quickly run out of arrows, this first engagement cannot have lasted very long, Tetlow, *op. cit.*, p.174.
12. *Master Wace, Roman de Rou*, (trans) E. Taylor , p.186.
13. N.P. Brooks and H.E. Walker, *Proceedings of the Battle Conference*, p.4.
14. Young and Adair, *From Hastings to Culloden*, p. 16. Tetlow, *The Enigma of Hastings*, p.174, called the heavy stones tied to wooden shafts which the English threw "the forerunners of the hand grenade".
15. Furneaux, *Conquest 1066*, p.156; Douglas & Greenaway, "William of Poitiers", *English Historical Documents*, vol. 2, p.226.
16. Rex, *1066*, pp.68–9.
17. Douglas & Greenaway, "William of Poitiers", *English Historical Documents*, vol. 2, p.226.
18. Rex, *1066*, p.70.
19. It has to be said that this seems quite remarkable. The Normans were from Scandinavia and the Saxon axe was known as the Danish axe. Had they really never encountered the Danish axe before?
20. Douglas & Greenaway, "William of Poitiers", *English Historical Documents*, vol. 2, p.226.
21. S. Morillo, "Hastings: An Unusual Battle", in *Sources and Interpretations*, p.224. See also Peter Marren, *1066*, pp.124–6.

22. Douglas & Greenaway, "William of Poitiers", *English Historical Documents*, vol. 2, p.226.
23. Morton & Muntz, *The Carmen de Hastingae Proelio*, p.29. Tetlow, *The Enigma of Hastings*, p.176, states that it was only the Bretons on the left who fell back and that the still-effective Norman division wheeled westwards across the field and cut down the pursuing *fyrdmen*.
24. Douglas & Greenaway, "William of Poitiers", *English Historical Documents*, p.226.
25. Douglas, *William the Conqueror*, p.200.
26. Douglas & Greenaway, "William of Poitiers", *English Historical Documents*, vol. 2, p.226.
27. Morillo, *op. cit.*, p.224; McLynn, *1066*, p.221.
28. Morton & Muntz, *The Carmen de Hastingae Proelio*, p.31; Rex, *1066*, pp.72–3, also says that Harold sent his brother Gyrth to recall as many men as he could to try and salvage the situation.
29. Lemmon, *The Field of Hastings*, pp.46–7. In his contribution to Whitelock, *et al.*, *The Norman Conquest*, p.107, Lemmon says that "the moment for delivering a counter-attack is when the enemy has spent the main force of his attack."
30. Rex, *1066*, pp.71–2.
31. Douglas & Greenaway, "William of Poitiers", *English Historical Documents*, vol. 2, p.228; *Master Wace, Roman de Rou*, ed. E. Taylor, pp.249–50.
32. See Poyntz Wright, *Hastings*, p.87, and Douglas, *William the Conqueror*, p.200.
33. Lemmon, *The Field of Hastings*, pp.46–7.
34. Leprévost and Bernage, *Hastings 1066*, p.66.
35. *Master Wace, Roman de Rou*, (trans.) E. Taylor, p.193.
36. Poyntz Wright, *Hastings*, p.90.
37. Philip Mainwaring Johnston, "Earl Roger de Montgomery and the Battle of Hastings", *Sussex Archaeological Collections*, vol.47; Master Wace, *Roman de Ron*, (trans.) E.Taylor p.201.
38. Douglas & Greenaway, "William of Poitiers", *English Historical Documents*, vol. 2, p.227.
39. Lemmon, *The Field of Hastings*, pp.47–8.
40. Furneaux, *Conquest 1066*, p.161.
41. M.A. Lower (trans.), *Chronicle of Battle Abbey*, p.6; M.A. Lower "On the Battle of Hastings", *Sussex Archaeological Collections*, vol.8.
42. Furneaux, *Conquest 1066*, p.161.
43. Rex, *1066.*, pp.68–9.
44. E. Mason, *The House of Godwine*, p.169.
45. Wise, *1066 Year of Destiny*, p.195.
46. Rex, *1066*, p.70.
47. For a detailed discussion of this see Furneaux, *Conquest 1066*, pp.161–5.
48. Douglas & Greenaway, "William of Poitiers", *English Historical Documents*, p.228.
49. *Ibid*, p.227.
50. E. Mason, *The House of Godwine*, p.170.
51. Whitelock *et al.*, *The Norman Conquest*, p.110.
52. Furneaux, *Conquest 1066*, p.167–8.
53. Leprévost and Bernage, *Hastings 1066*, pp.69–70.
54. Morton & Muntz, *The Carmen de Hastingae Proelio*, p.31; Furneaux, *Conquest 1066*, pp.167–8.
55. R. Allen Brown, in Morillo, *Sources and Interpretations*, p.206; Douglas & Greenaway, "William of Poitiers", *English Historical Documents*, vol. 2, p.229, says that the bodies of all three Godwinson brothers were found lying together at the end of the battle; Rex, *1066*, p.65.
56. Walter de Grey Birch, *Vita Haroldi*, p.158.
57. R. Allen Brown, *The Normans and the Norman Conquest*, p.149.

58. Lemmon, *The Field of Hastings*, p.32.
59. Poyntz Wright, *Hastings*, p.80.
60. Morton & Muntz, *The Carmen de Hastingae Proelio*, p.37.
61. This discussion is held in McLynn, *1066*, pp.234–41.
62. See A. Bridgeford, *Hidden History of the Bayeux Tapestry*, p.147.
63. Douglas & Greenaway, "William of Poitiers", *English Historical Documents*, p.228.
64. McLynn, *1066*, p.217, says that the fighting on the hill must have been over by 1730 hours; R. Allen Brown, *The Normans and the Norman Conquest*, pp.150–1, sensibly is not drawn into the decades-long debate over the site of the *Malfosse*, simply saying that there are plenty of possible sites in the countryside near Battle.
65. P. Hill, *The Road to Hastings*, pp.184–8.; Douglas & Greenaway, "William of Poitiers", *English Historical Documents*, vol. 2, p.228.
66. McLynn, *1066*, p.227. P. Hill, *Ibid*, considers the possibility that the stand by the English was well organised and was therefore most likely conducted by reinforcements rather than warriors fleeing in panic. Based on the writing of Snorri Sturluson, he offers us Earl Waltheof of Northumberland as being the man who was arriving with his men to help Harold and who organised the last stand of the English at the *Malfosse*.
67. Lower, *Chronicle of Battle Abbey*, p.6.
68. Morton & Muntz, *The Carmen de Hastingae Proelio*, p.37.
69. Douglas & Greenaway, "William of Poitiers", *English Historical Documents*, vol. 2, p.229.
70. Lemmon, "The Campaign of 1066", in Whitelock *et al.*, *The Norman Conquest*, p.115, draws comparisons between the Battle of Hastings and the siege of Badajoz in the Peninsular War and the charge of the Heavy Brigade at Balaklava.
71. Furneaux, *Conquest 1066*, p.160; Douglas & Greenaway, "William of Poitiers", *English Historical Documents*, vol. 2, p.228.
72. Lemmon, *The Field of Hastings*, p.119.
73. D. Greenaway, *Henry of Huntingdon*, p.24.

7. The Sources

1. Morton and Muntz, *The Carmen de Hastingae Proelio*, p.91.
2. Bridgeford, *Hidden History of the Bayeux Tapestry*, p.19; Morrillo, *op.cit.* Introduction, xx, and Alllen Brown, *Sources and Interpretations*, p.200; D. Bates, *William the Conqueror*, p.99; Lawson, *The Battle of Hastings*, p.224; R. Huscroft, *The Norman Conquest*, p.126; Lemmon, Preface to *The Field of Hastings*; D. Bates, *William the Conqueror*, p.15; H. Wood, *The Battle of Hastings*, p.217.
3. This is a somewhat simplistic explanation of the compilation of the *Gesta Normannorum Ducum*. For more details see E.M.C. van Houts, *Gesta Normannorum Ducum*, vol.I, Introduction.
4. Douglas and Greenaway, "William of Poitiers", *English Historical Documents*, pp.217–28; H. Wood, *The Battle of Hastings*, p.224.
5. Van Houts, *op.cit.*, vol.II, pp.167–9;
6. It is thought that the Peterborough version was, during the time in question, was written at Canterbury, H. Wood, *The Battle of Hastings*, p.219.
7. *Anglo-Saxon Chronicle*, D, p.143; Anne Savage, *Anglo-Saxon Chronicles*, p.195.
8. H. Wood, *The Battle of Hastings*, p.226.
9. Darlington, McGurk & Bray, *The Chronicle of John of Worcester*, p.604
10. See R.H.C. Davis, "The Carmen de Hastingae Proelio", in R. Allen Brown [ed.] *Proceedings of the Battle Conference, 1979*, p.1; Bridgeford, *Hidden History of the Bayeux Tapestry*, p.23.
11. H. Wood, *The Battle of Hastings*, p.159.

12. Bradbury, *The Battle of Hastings*, p.133.
13. Morton and Muntz, *The Carmen de Hastingae Proelio*, pp. 21–76.
14. H.W.C. Davis, "The Chronicles of Battle Abbey", *English Historical Review*, 1914, p.427.
15. R. James, "Excavations at the Jenner and Simpson Mill site, Mount Street, Battle, East Sussex" *Sussex Archaeological Collections*, vol.146.
16. Searle, *Chronicle of Battle Abbey*, 1980, p.2; N. Austin, *Secrets of the Norman Invasion*, p.153.
17. Searle, *Chronicle of Battle Abbey*, pp.2–6.
18. Lower, *Chronicle of Battle Abbey*, pp.3–4.
19. Freeman, *History of the Norman Conquest*, vol.3, p.763.
20. What are we to make of the place called "Herste"? It has been suggested by Nick Austin (*Secrets of the Norman Invasion*, pp.155–6) that this refers to Crowhurst, which was often known by the locals within living memory as "Hurst". An ancient low wall has been identified at Crowhurst. Though a school of thought has developed which places the site of the battle at Crowhurst, there are a number of reasons why this can be dismissed. This will be discussed later.
21. Bradbury, *The Battle of Hastings*, p.131.
22. E. Searle, *Chronicle of Battle Abbey*, pp.15–16.
23. M. Chibnall, 'Charter and Chronicle: The Use of Archive Sources by Norman Historians', in C.N.L. Brooke, D.E. Luscombe, G.H. Martin, & D. Owen, *Church and Government in the Middle Ages: Essays Presented to C. R. Cheney on his 70th Birthday*, pp.12–13.
24. Marjorie Chibnall, *Orderic Vitalis, Historia Ecclesiastica*, vol.ii, pp.190–2.
25. Marjorie Chibnall, *Orderic Vitalis, Historia Ecclesiastica*, vol.ii, pp.190–2.
26. Lemmon, *The Field of Hastings*, p.66.
27. H. Wood, *The Battle of Hastings*, pp.230–1.
28. Bridgeford, *Hidden History of the Bayeux Tapestry*, p.5.
29. Wolfgang Grape, *The Bayeux Tapestry*, pp.57–8.
30. Wolfgang Grape, *The Bayeux Tapestry*, p.23.
31. McLynn, *1066*, p.239.
32. McLynn, *1066*, p.239.
33. Wolfgang Grape, *The Bayeux Tapestry*, p.24.
34. Bridgeford, *Hidden History of the Bayeux Tapestry*, p.135.
35. J. Bradbury, *The Battle of Hastings*, p.143.
36. A. Clarke, *A Day That Made History*, p.18.
37. *Master Wace, Roman de Rou*, (trans.) E. Taylor, pp.155–6.
38. *Master Wace, Roman de Rou*, (trans.) E. Taylor, pp.17–5.
39. *Master Wace, Roman de Rou*, (trans.) E. Taylor, pp.159–68.
40. Furneaux, *Conquest 1066*, p.154.
41. *William of Malmesbury's Chronicles*, ed Giles, p.277.
42. D. Greenaway, *Henry of Huntingdon*, pp.24–8.

8. The Interpretations

1. Lawson, *The Battle of Hastings*, p.224.
2. J.J. Badgley, *Historical Interpretation*, vol.I, p.12.
3. D Hume, *The History of England from the Invasion of Julius Caesar to the Revolution in 1688*, vol.I, pp.192–5.
4. Lawson, *The Battle of Hastings*, pp.129–30.

5. Henry James had pioneered the reproduction of maps by a method known as photozincography which provided an almost three-dimensional view of the ground. It became a popular way of presenting the contours of the ground to the reader.

6. Freeman, *History of the Norman Conquest*, vol.3, pp.440 & 447.

7. Freeman, *History of the Norman Conquest*, p.448.

8. Freeman, *History of the Norman Conquest*, p.468.

9. Freeman, *History of the Norman Conquest*, p.446.

10. J. Duncan, *The Dukes of Normandy*, p.110.

11. Stenton, *William the Conqueror*, p.194.

12. Fuller, *A Military History of the Western World*, vol.1, pp.374–82.

13. Lemmon, *The Field of Hastings*, pp.20 & 38.

14. Lemmon, "The Campaign of 1066", in Whitelock *et al.*, *The Norman Conquest*, p.97–8.

15. Furneaux, *Conquest 1066*, pp.125–6.

16. Denny and Filmer-Sankey, *The Bayeux Tapestry*, p.59.

17. Morton and Muntz, *The Carmen de Hastingae Proelio*, p.73.

18. Tetlow, *The Enigma of Hastings*, pp.12–14.

19. Tetlow, *The Enigma of Hastings*, pp.16–17.

20. Seymour, *Battles in Britain*, pp.27–8.

21. Seymour, *Battles in Britain*, pp.29–30.

22. Young and Adair, *From Hastings to Culloden*, p.12.

23. Wise, *1066 Year of Destiny*, pp.184–6.

24. Wise, *1066 Year of Destiny*, p.191.

25. "The Abbey of the Conquerors: Defensive Enfeoffment and Economic Development in Anglo-Norman England", in Allen Brown, *Proceedings of the Battle Conference on Anglo-Norman Studies*, 1979, pp.154–64.

26. Lower, *Chronicle of Battle Abbey*, pp.27 & 36.

27. Lower, *Chronicle of Battle Abbey*, p.28.

28. R. Allen Brown (ed.), *Proceedings of the Battle Conference*, 1979.

29. A. Clarke, *Day That Made History*, pp.13–14.

30. R. Allen Brown, *The Normans and the Norman Conquest*, pp.139 & 151.

31. J. Bradbury, *The Battle of Hastings*, pp.129–134.

32. J. Bradbury, "Let Battle Begin", *Heritage* magazine, December 2010, pp.45–8.

33. Lawson, *The Battle of Hastings*, pp.192 & 227.

34. McLynn, *1066*, p.216.

35. E. Mason, *The House of Godwine*, pp.164, 162 & 166; Darlington and McGurk (eds), *The Chronicle of John of Worcester*, ii, pp.4–5.

36. B.R. Patterson, *William & Harold: The Battle for England 1064–1066*, pp.125 & 168.

37. P. Hill, *The Road to Hastings*, pp.158–9, 173, 175 and 177.

38. A year's penance was due for the death of a man killed whilst resisting the seizure of food and three years for the death of a man resisting wanton plunder, see Furneaux, *Conquest 1066*, p.191.

39. Lower, *Chronicle of Battle Abbey*, p.14.

40. N. Austin, *Secrets of the Norman Invasion*, p.168.

41. Quoted in *The Mail on Sunday*, October 9, 2011, p.33.

9. The Battlefield

1. Tetlow, *The Enigma of Hastings*, p.151.

2. M.A. Lower, "On the Battle of Hastings", *Sussex Archaeological Collections*, vol.8.

3. Freeman, *History of the Norman Conquest*, vol.3, pp.757–8.

4. D. Wilson, *The Bayeux Tapestry*, pp.192–3.

5. R. Allen Brown, "The Battle of Hastings", in Morillo, *Sources and Interpretations*, note 120.
6. Bridgeford, *Hidden History of the Bayeux Tapestry*, p.138.
7. M. Rudd, *The Bayeux Tapestry*, p.84; P. Hill, *The Road to Hastings*, p.180.
8. A. Clarke, *A Day That Made History*, p.18.
9. Morrillo, *Sources and Interpretations*, p.xxii.
10. R. Huscroft, *The Norman Conquest*, p.126.
11. Wise, *1066 Year of Destiny*, pp.188–9.
12. R. Allen Brown, *The Normans and the Norman Conquest*, p.137.
13. Alfred Bourne devised the concept of the Inherent Military Probability, which states that in battles and campaigns where there is some doubt over what action was taken he believed that the action taken would be one which a trained staff officer of the twentieth century would take.
14. Freeman, *History of the Norman Conquest*, vol.3, pp.441–2.
15. Freeman, *History of the Norman Conquest*, p.443.
16. Lemmon, *The Field of Hastings*, p.38.
17. Rex, *1066*, p.60.
18. Seymour, *Battles in Britain*, p.27.
19. Lemmon, "The Campaign of 1066", in Whitelocke *et al.*, *The Norman Conquest*, p.99.
20. Bridgeford, *Hidden History of the Bayeux Tapestry*, p.135.
21. Poyntz Wright, *Hastings*, p.80.
22. Stenton, *Anglo-Saxon England*, pp.594–5.
23. Stenton, *William the Conqueror*, p.195.
24. R. Allen Brown, *The Normans and the Norman Conquest*, p.149.
25. Seymour, *Battles in Britain*, p.27.
26. Douglas & Greenaway, "William of Poitiers", *English Historical Documents*, p.225.
27. Freeman, *History of the Norman Conquest*, vol.3, p.458.
28. Lower, "On the Battle of Hastings", *Sussex Archaeological Collections*, vol.8, p.38.
29. Lemmon, *The Field of Hastings*, pp.34 &56.
30. Lower, *Chronicle of Battle Abbey*, p.7.
31. Furneaux, *Conquest 1066*, p.177.
32. E.M.C. van Houts, *Gesta Normannorum Ducum*, vol.II, p.169.
33. N. Clephane-Cameron and J. Lawrence, *The 1066 Malfosse Walk*.
34. See Lemmon, *The Field of Hastings*, pp.50–1.
35. Lawson, *The Battle of Hastings*, p.214: Stenton, *William the Conqueror*, p.198.
36. Lower, *Chronicle of Battle Abbey*, p.6; Master Wace, *Roman de Rou*, ed. E. Taylor, p.193. both quoted in Lower, "On the Battle of Hastings", *Sussex Archaeological Collections*, vol.8.
37. Furneaux, *Conquest 1066*, pp.154–5.
38. J. Bradbury, *The Battle of Hastings*, p.134.
39. J. Bradbury, *The Battle of Hastings*, p.199.
40. These reasons given by Lemmon, *The Field of Hastings*, pp.52–4, and Celphane-Cameron and Lawrence, *The 1066 Malfosse Walk*, include the information that medieval deeds and old maps suggest that a track crossed Oakwood Gill about the same place as the present-day track and bridge and this would explain William of Jumièges calling the site an "ancient causeway", and that deeds of Battle Abbey investigated by C.T. Chevallier which dated from as early as 1240 describe land identified as being at Oakwood Gill as being in *Malnfosse*.
41. C.T. Chevallier, "Where was Malfosse? The End of the Battle of Hastings", "On the Battle of Hastings", *Sussex Archaeological Collections*, vol. 101, 1963. Interestingly,

Brigadier Barclay, *Battle 1066*, thinks that we have made too much of the *Malfosse* incident: "I think it likely," he wrote in 1966, "that no more than a dozen, perhaps half-a-dozen, knights were involved in the affair, probably in the half-light when dealing with the English stragglers after the battle ... The survivors would tell the tale far and wide and it would not lose in the telling."

42. Douglas & Greenaway, "William of Poitiers", *English Historical Documents*, pp.217–28.
43. Morton and Muntz, *op.cit.* p.21.
44. Lawson, *op.cit.* p.187.
45. Morton and Muntz, *The Carmen de Hastingae Proelio*, Appendix B, pp.76–7.
46. Lemmon, "The Campaign of 1066" in Whitelock *et al.*, *The Norman Conquest*, p.103.
47. Hill, *The Road to Hastings*, p.178.
48. There is a tradition that Harold's lover, Edith Swan Neck, watched the battle from this point.
49. J. Bradbury, *The Battle of Hastings*, p.134

10. The Archaeology

 1. Bradbury, *The Battle of Hastings*, p.176.
 2. Morton & Muntz, *The Carmen de Hastingae Proelio*, p.37.
 3. Tetlow, *The Enigma of Hastings*, p.22.
 4. Tetlow, *The Enigma of Hastings*, p.22.
 5. Richard James, "Excavations at the Jenner and Simpson Mill site, Mount Street, Battle, East Sussex", *Sussex Archaeological Collections* (vol.146, 2008).
 6. J.N. Hare, *Battle Abbey, The Eastern Range and the Excavations of 1978–80*.
 7. Richard James, *op. cit.*
 8. W. Strickland, "A Supposed Battlefield near Eastbourne", *Sussex Archaeological Collections*, vol.58.
 9. H.M. Whitley, "Recent Archaeological Discoveries in the Eastbourne District", *Sussex Archaeological Collections*, vol.37, 1890, pp.11–15.
10. W.A. Raper, "On the silver pennies of Edward the Confessor found at Sedlescombe", *SAC*, vol. 33. Raper made another report in the *SAC* (vol. 42, 1898) in which he concluded that apart from the coins "no relic of the battle; no skeletons, no arms or armour of the slain have been found."
11. Lower, "On the Battle of Hastings", *Sussex Archaeological Collections*, vol.8, p.35.
12. Tetlow, *The Enigma of Hastings*, p.21.
13. Lawson, *The Battle of Hastings*, p.228; K.J. Allison [ed.] *Victoria Country History, A History of the County of York*, vol.3, pp.82–9.
14. Tetlow, *The Enigma of Hastings*, pp.189–190. This object is currently housed in the Ashmolean Museum, Oxford.
15. E. Searle, *Chronicle of Battle Abbey*, p.16.

11. Rewriting History

 1. Stenton, *William the Conqueror*, Preface.
 2. Lawson, *The Battle of Hastings*, pp.15–16, 150 & 224.
 3. Morillo, *Sources and Interpretations*, Preface.
 4. Tetlow, *The Enigma of Hastings*, p.186.
 5. J. Bradbury, "Battles in England and Normandy, 1066–1154", in A. Brown, Anglo-Norman Studies, vi., pp.1–12; J. Bradbury, *The Battle of Hastings*, p. 129. Lawson, *The Battle of Hastings*, p.149, mentioned Jim Bradbury's suggestion that the battle may have been fought on Caldbec Hill, and Michael Rayner, *English Battlefields*, p.168, wrote that "the location of the battlefield is disputed."

6. A. Clarke, *A Day That Made History*, p.27.
7. Stenton, *William the Conqueror*, p.198.
8. McLynn, *1066*, pp.221–2.
9. Tetlow, *The Enigma of Hastings*, pp.186–7.
10. Lawson, *The Battle of Hastings*, pp.225–6.
11. Morillo, *Sources and Interpretations*, xxi.
12. Bradbury, *The Battle of Hastings*, p.110.
13. Lawson, *The Battle of Hastings*, p.224.
14. J. Bradbury, "Battles in England and Normandy, 1066–1154", in M. Strickland, *Anglo-Norman Warfare*, p.185.

Bibliography

Primary Sources

Anglo-Saxon Chronicle, The, edited by Dorothy Whitelock, David C. Douglas and Susie I. Tucker (Eyre and Spottiswoode, London, 1961).

Anglo-Saxon Chronicles, The, The Authentic Voices of England, From the Time of Julius Caesar to the Coronation of Henry II, translated and collated by Anne Savage (Greenwich Editions, London, 2002).

Chronicle of Battle Abbey, from 1066 to 1176, translated by Mark Anthony Lower (John Russel Smith, London, 1851).

Chronicle of Battle Abbey, translated by Eleanor Searle (Oxford University Press, Oxford, 1980).

Chronicle of John of Worcester, The, edited by R.R. Darlington & P. McGurk, translated by Jennifer Bray & P. McGurk (Clarendon Press, Oxford, 1995).

Domesday Book, Sussex, edited by John Morris (Phillimore, Chichester, 1976).

English Historical Documents, vol.2, 1042–1189, edited by David C. Douglas and George W. Greenaway (Methuen, London, 1981).

Gesta Guillelmi of William of Poitiers, The, R.H.C. Davis & Marjorie Chibnall (eds) (Oxford University Press, Oxford, 1998).

Guy, Bishop of Amiens, Carmen de Hastingae Proelio, edited by Catherine Morton and Hope Muntz (Clarendon Press, Oxford, 1972).

Henry of Huntingdon: The History of the English People, 1000–1154, edited and translated by Diana Greenaway (Oxford University Press, Oxford, 1996).

Lestorie des Engles solum La Translacion Maistre Geffreu Gaimar, edited and translated by Thomas D. Hardy and Charles T. Martin (HMSO with Eyre and Spottiswoode, London, 1889).

Master Wace, His Chronicle of the Norman Conquest from the Roman de Rou, edited and translated by Edgar Taylor (William Pickering, London, 1937).

Orderic Vitalis, The Ecclesiastical History of England and Normandy, translated by Thomas Forrester, vol.2 (Henry G. Bohn, London, 1853).

Orderic Vitalis, Historia Ecclesiastica, six vols., edited and translated by Marjorie Chibnall (Clarendon Press, Oxford, 1969–80).

Snorre Sturluson, Heiskringla or the Lives of the Norse Kings edited by Erling Monsen and translated by A. H. Smith (W. Heffer & Sons, Cambridge, 1932).

Snorri Sturluson: King Harald's Saga, Harald Hardradi of Norway, translated by Magnus Magnusson and Hermann Pálsson (Penguin Books, London, 1966).

The Life of King Edward Who Rests at Westminster, translated and edited by Frank Barlow (Clarendon Press, Oxford, 1992).

Vita Ædwardi Regis qui apud Westmonasterium requiescit, The Life of King Edward the Confessor who rests at Westminster, edited and translated by Frank Barlow (Nelson's Medieval Texts, London, 1962).

Vita Haroldi: The Romance of the Life of Harold, King of England, edited by Walter de Grey Birch (Elliot Stock, London, 1885).

Wace, Le Roman de Rou, edited by A.J. Holden, three vols. (Societe des anciens textes francais, Paris, 1970–73).

Waltham Chronicle, The, edited and translated by Leslie Watkiss and Majorie Chibnall (Oxford University Press, Oxford, 2002).

William of Jumièges, Orderic Vitalis, and Robert of Torigni, Gesta Normannorum Ducum, edited and translated by Elisabeth M. C. Van Houts (Oxford University Press, Oxford, 1992 and 1995).

William of Malmesbury's Chronicle of the Kings of England by J.A. Giles (Bell and Daldy, London, 1866).

William of Malmesbury, De Getis Regum Anglorum, ed by W. Stubbs, vol. 2 (Eyre & Spottiswoode, London, 1889).

Secondary Sources

Austin, Nick, *Secrets of The Norman Invasion* (Ogmium Press, Crowhurst, 2010).

Barclay, Cyril Nelson, *Battle 1066* (Dent, London, 1966).

Barlow, Frank, *William I and the Norman Conquest* (English Universities Press, London, 1965).

Barlow, F., Lyyn, H.R., Mason, J.F.A., J. Le Patourel & A. Briggs, *1066 Commemorative Lectures* (The Historical Association, London, 1976).

Barlow, Frank, *The Norman Conquest and Beyond* (Hambeldon, London, 1983).

Barlow, Frank, *The Godwins: The Rise and Fall of a Noble Dynasty* (Longman, Harlow, 2002).

Bates, David, *Normandy before 1066* (Longman, London, 1982).

Bates, David, *William the Conqueror* (Tempus, Stroud, 2001).

Beeler, John, *Warfare in England 1066–1189* (Cornell University Press, New York, 1966).

Bennett, Matthew, *Campaigns of the Norman Conquest* (Osprey, Oxford, 2001).

Bennett, Matthew, and Guest, Ken, 'Exploding the Myths of Hastings', *Skirmish* magazine, No.100, September 1996.

Bernstein, David J., *The Mystery of the Bayeux Tapestry* (Weidenfeld and Nicholson, London, 1986).

Bradbury, Jim, *The Battle of Hastings* (Sutton Publishing, Stroud, 1998).

Bradbury, Jim, 'Let Battle Begin', *Heritage magazine* (December 2010).

Brandon, Peter, *The Sussex Landscape* (Hodder & Stoughton, London, 1974).

Bridgeford, Andrew, *1066: The Hidden History of the Bayeux Tapestry* (Harper Perennial, London, 2004).

Brooke, C.N.L, Luscombe, D.E., Martin, G.H, and Owen, D., *Church and Government in the Middle Ages: Essays Presented to C. R. Cheney on his 70th Birthday* (Cambridge University Press, Cambridge 1976).

Brooks, Frederick William, *The Battle of Stamford Bridge* (East Yorkshire Local History Society, York, 1956).

Brown, R. Allen (ed.), *Proceedings of the Battle Conference on Anglo-Norman Studies* (Boydell Press, Woodbridge 1978–1983).

Brown, R. Allen, *The Normans and the Norman Conquest* (Boydell Press, Woodbridge, 1985).

Brown, Shirley Ann, *The Bayeux Tapestry: History and Bibliography* (Boydell, Woodbridge, 1989).

Burne, Alfred H., *The Battlefields of England* (Methuen, London, 1950).

Butler, Denis, *1066, The Story of a Year* (Anthony Blond, London, 1966).

Campbell, James, *The Anglo-Saxon State* (Hambledon and London, London, 2000).

Chevallier, C.T., 'Where was Malfosse? The End of the Battle of Hastings', *Sussex Archaeological Collections* (vol.101, 1963).

Clarke, Amanda, *A Day that Made History: The Battle of Hastings* (Dryad Press, London, 1988).

Clephane-Cameron, Neil, and Lawrence, Joanne, *The 1066 Malfosse Walk* (Battle and District Historical Society, Battle 2000).

Cole, Thomas Holwell, *The Antiquities of Hastings and the Battlefield* (Hastings & St Leonards Philosophical Society, 1884).

Creasy, Edward S., *The Fifteen Decisive Battles of the World: From Marathon to Waterloo* (Richard Bently, London, 1852).

Crouch, David, *The Normans: The History of a Dynasty* (Hambledon and London, London, 2002).

Davis, H.W.C., 'The Chronicles of Battle Abbey', *English Historical Review*, No. 29, 1914.

Denny, Norman, and Filmer-Sankey, Josephine, *The Bayeux Tapestry* (Atheneum, London, 1966).

Douglas, David C., *William the Conqueror* (Eyre & Spottiswoode, London 1963).

Duncan, Jonathon, *The Dukes of Normandy from the Time of Rollo* (Joseph Rickerby, London, 1939).

Duckett, Sir George, 'The Battle of Hastings', *Sussex Archaeological Collections* (vol.42, 1894).

Duckett, Sir George, 'Hastings V. Senlac', *Sussex Archaeological Collections*, (vol.39, 1892).

Freeman, Edward A., *The History of the Norman Conquest of England, Its Causes and Its Results* (five volumes, Clarendon Press, London, 1867–1876).

Freeman, Edward A., *A Short History of the Norman Conquest of England* (Clarendon Press, Oxford, 1880).

Fuller, J.F.C., *The Decisive Battles of the Western World* (Eyre & Spottiswoode, London 1954).

Furneaux, Rupert, *Conquest 1066* (Martin Secker and Warburg, London, 1966).

Gibbs-Smith, C.H., *The Bayeux Tapestry* (Phaidon, London, 1973).

Grape, Wolfgang translated by David Britt, *The Bayeux Tapestry: Monument to a Norman Triumph* (Prestel, Munich, 1994).

Gravett, Christopher, *Hastings 1066* (Osprey, Botley, 2000).

Grehan, John, and Mace, Martin, *Battleground Sussex: A Military History of Sussex to the Present Day* (Pen & Sword, Barnsley, 2011).

Hare, J.N., *Battle Abbey, The Eastern Range and the Excavations of 1978–80* (Historic Buildings and Monuments Commission for England, London, 1985).

Higham, N.J., *The Death of Anglo-Saxon England* (Sutton Publishing, Stroud, 1997).

Higham, N.J., *The Norman Conquest* (Sutton Publishing, Stroud, 1998).

Hill, Paul, *The Road to Hastings: The Politics of Power in Anglo-Saxon England* (Tempus, Stroud, 2005).

Hollister, Charles Warren, *Anglo-Saxon Military Institutions on the Eve of the Norman Conquest* (Clarendon Press, Oxford, 1962).

Howarth, David, *1066: The Year of the Conquest* (Penguin Classics, London, 2002).

Hume, David, *The History of England from the Invasion of Julius Caesar to the Revolution in 1688* (T. Cadell, London, 1767).

Huscroft, Richard, *The Norman Conquest: A New Introduction* (Pearson Longman, Harlow, 2009).

James, Richard, 'Excavations at the Jenner and Simpson Mill site, Mount Street, Battle, East Sussex', *Sussex Archaeological Society Collections* (vol.146, 2008).

Johnston, Philip Mainwaring, 'Earl Roger de Montgomery and the Battle of Hastings', *Sussex Archaeological Collections* (vol. 47, 1904).

Körner, Sten, *The Battle of Hastings, England and Europe 1035–1066* (Gleerups, Lund, 1964).

Lawson, M. K., *The Battle of Hastings 1066* (Tempus, Stroud, 2002).

Lemmon, Charles H., *The Field of Hastings* (Budd & Gillatt, St Leonards-on-Sea, 1964).

Leprévost, Thierry, and Bernage, Georges, *Hastings 1066: Norman Cavalry and Saxon Infantry* (Heimdal, Bayeux, 2002).

Lloyd, Alan, *The Year of the Conqueror* (Longmans, London, 1966).

Lower, Mark Anthony, *Contributions to Literature: Historical, Antiquarian and Metrical*, (Books for Libraries Press, 1854).

Lower, Mark Anthony, 'On the Battle of Hastings', *Sussex Archaeological Collections* (vol.8, 1852).

Loyn, Henry Royston, *Anglo-Saxon England and the Norman Conquest* (Longmans, London, 1962).

Mallalieu, Huon, *1066 And Rather More: A Walk Through History* (Frances Lincoln, London, 2009).

Marren, Peter, *1066: The Battles of York, Stamford Bridge & Hastings* (Leo Cooper, Barnsley, 2004).

Mason, Emma, *The House of Godwine; The History of a Dynasty* (Hambledon and London, London, 2004).

Mason, J.F.A., 'The Rapes of Sussex and the Norman Conquest', *Sussex Archaeological Collections* (vol.102, 1964).

Matthew, D.J.A., *The Norman Conquest* (Batsford, London, 1966).

Morillo, Stephen (ed.), *The Battle of Hastings, Sources and Interpretations* (Boydell Press, Rochester, 1996).

Oman, Charles, *The Art of War in the Middle Ages: A.D. 378–1515* (Blackwell, Oxford, 1885).

Oman, Charles, *A History of the Art of Warfare in the Middle Ages*, 2 vols. (Methuen, London, 1978).

Patterson, Benton Rain, *Harold & William: The Battle for England 1064–1066* (Tempus, Stroud, 2001).

Phillips, Michael, and McBride, Angus, *1066: Origin of a Nation* (privately published, Bexhill, 1981).

Raper, W.A., 'On the Silver Pennies of Edward the Confessor Found at Sedlescombe', *Sussex Archaeological Collections* (vol.33, 1883).

Raper, W.A., 'The Battle of Hastings', *Sussex Archaeological Collections* (vol.42, 1898).

Rayner, Michael, *English Battlefields: An Illustrated Encyclopaedia* (Tempus, Stroud, 2004).

Rex, Peter, *1066 A New History of the Norman Conquest* (Amberley, Stroud, 2009).

Round, John Horace, *Feudal England* (Sonnenschein, London, 1895).

Round, John Horace, 'The Battle of Hastings', *Sussex Archaeological Collections* (vol.42, 1899).

Rud, Mogens, *The Bayeux Tapestry and the Battle of Hastings 1066* (Christian Eilers, Copenhagen, 1992).

Searle, Elenor, *Lordship & Community: Battle Abbey and its Banlieu 1066–1538* (Pontifical Institute of Mediaeval Studies, Toronto, 1974).

Seymour, William, *Battles in Britain 1066–1746* (Wordsworth, Ware, 1997).

Shuter, Jane, *How Do We Know About The Battle of Hastings* (Heinemann, Oxford, 2003).

Spatz, Wilhelm, *Der Schlacht von Hastings* (Ebering, Berlin, 1896).

Stenton, Frank Merry, *William the Conqueror and the Rule of the Normans* (Putman, London, 1907).

Stenton, Frank Merry, *Anglo-Saxon England* (Clarendon, Oxford, 1947).

Strickland, M., (ed.), *Anglo-Norman Warfare* (Boydell Press, Woodbridge, 1992).

Strickland, W., 'A Supposed Battlefield near Eastbourne', *Sussex Archaeological Collections* (vol. 58, 1909).

Tetlow, Edwin, *The Enigma of Hastings* (Peter Owen, London, 1974).

Thierry, Augustine, *History of the Conquest of England by the Normans* (Everyman, Dent, London, 1901).

Thornhill, Patrick, *The Battle of Hastings* (Methuen & Co, London, 1966).

Walker, Ian W., *Harold, the Last Anglo-Saxon King* (Sutton Publishing, Stroud, 2004).

Whitelock, D., Douglas, D. C., Lemmon, C. H., and Barlow, F., *The Norman Conquest: It's Setting and Impact* (Eyre and Spottiswoode, London, 1966).

Williams, Ann, *The English and the Norman Conquest* (Boydell, Woodbridge, 1995).

Williamson, James A., *The English Channel* (Collins, London, 1959).

Wilson, David M., *The Bayeux Tapestry* (Thames and Hudson, London, 1985).

Wise, Terence, *1066 Year of Destiny* (Osprey Publishing, London, 1979).

Wood, Harriet, *The Battle of Hastings: The Fall of Anglo-Saxon England* (Atlantic Books, London, 2008).

Wright, Peter Poyntz, *The Battle of Hastings* (Michael Russell, Wilton, 1986).

Wright, Peter Poyntz, *Hastings* (Windrush Press, Moreton-in-Marsh, 1996).

Young, Peter, and Adair, John, *From Hastings to Culloden* (Roundwood Press, Kineton, 1979).

Index